NEW ORIENTATIONS SERIES NO. 2

EUROPEAN IMPERIALISM
AND THE
PARTITION OF AFRICA

The *New Orientations* Series

Editors:

E. F. Penrose
Peter Lyon
Edith Penrose

New Orientations is a series devoted to critical essays on international relations, written for the educated public as well as for specialised students of international affairs and international history.

No. 1
NEW ORIENTATIONS: ESSAYS IN INTERNATIONAL RELATIONS
Edited by E. F. Penrose, Peter Lyon and Edith Penrose

The first volume in the series contains a global overview by Peter Lyon and studies of Britain's place in international relations by E. F. Penrose, of Vietnam by Jacques Decornoy and of international economic relations by Edith Penrose.

European Imperialism and the Partition of Africa

Edited by

E. F. Penrose

FRANK CASS : LONDON

First published 1975 in Great Britain by
FRANK CASS AND COMPANY LIMITED
2 Park Square, Milton Park, Abingdon, Oxon, OX14 4RN

and in the United States of America by
FRANK CASS AND COMPANY LIMITED
270 Madison Ave,
New York NY 10016

Transferred to Digital Printing 2006

ISBN 0 7146 3058 6

Publisher's Note
The publisher has gone to great lengths to ensure
the quality of this reprint but points out that some
imperfections in the original may be apparent

Contents

Preface

This collection of essays on, or related to, the European Partition of Africa, has been previously published in the *Journal of Imperial and Commonwealth History*, Vol. III, No. 1 (October 1974). The essays were originally commissioned from their authors by Professor E. F. Penrose.

The authors, and the Editor of the *Journal of Imperial and Commonwealth History*, wish to record their thanks to Professor Penrose, not only for his kindness in permitting the publication of this material both in the *Journal* and in its present form, but also for his original initiative and continuing interest, without which some at least of these essays would probably never have seen the light.

G.N.S.

The European Partition of Africa:
Coincidence or Conjuncture?

by

G. N. Sanderson*

1: The Problem

The sudden, rapid and almost complete European partition of Africa in the last two decades of the nineteenth century is interesting not only as a spectacular episode in European history and, more importantly, as a major event in African history; but also because it seems to present a crucial test of the historian's ability to explain and interpret the events that he traces.

The partition takes place over a period so brief that the links between the detailed monograph and the synoptic survey are considerably closer and more substantial than in some comparable fields of investigation, and so recent that the documentary record has survived almost intact. The official record, in particular, is especially complete and revealing, coming as it does from a period when departmental papers were carefully and systematically preserved but just before the widespread use of the telephone began to discourage the art of thinking and communicating on paper. Virtually the whole of this material has for some time been accessible to scholars. So have the private papers of most of the European policy-makers; and the records of many, though not all, of the unofficial organisations—commercial, religious, philanthropic—which were interested in Africa before and during the partition. Moreover, much of this material had already been studied and analysed in published monographs and doctoral dissertations.

In short, the conditions for a 'general explanation' of the partition of Africa are just about as favourable as they could possibly be. A variety—indeed, an embarrassing variety—of such interpretations has in fact been put forward. The most stimulating of these have emerged from the detailed study of some important episode in the partition, or of the origins and development of partition in some comparatively restricted area. But to promote conclusions derived from the study of a limited field to the status of general explanations of the partition is obviously a very risky undertaking. Not surprisingly, general theories derived from special studies differ from one another not merely in nuance and emphasis, but on fundamentals.[1] Moreover, no general theory has successfully accounted for all the observed phenomena; and

* Professor of Modern History, Royal Holloway College, University of London.

many of them have failed to grapple with certain problems whose solution is an essential part of any satisfactory general explanation.

Faced with this situation, some historians have abandoned the quest for a general theory, and have asserted that one cannot go beyond studying 'each particular case of annexation as a special problem'. If this procedure fails (as it does fail) to explain why 'cases of annexation' suddenly and unexpectedly became epidemic in the 1880s, there is simply nothing we can do about it.[2]

This is a discouraging conclusion; but any serious acquaintance with the facts does suggest very strongly that the plurality of the 'causes' of partition is indeed irreducible. It is however possible to ask questions about the partition which, in principle at least, do not rule out the possibility of general answers in spite of the existence of special reasons for 'each particular case of annexation':

(i) Why did the partition begin when it did (c. 1879–80), after a long period when the European Powers had normally taken only the most languid interest in Africa?

(ii) Why, when the partition had once begun, did its pace accelerate so rapidly that within two decades it had engulfed almost the whole continent—i.e., why did the partition develop into a 'scramble'?

Quite apart from the 'operational' value of these questions, any general theory worthy of the name ought to include precise and empirically verifiable answers to them. By no means all of the general theories even attempt to do this.

II: General Theories of the Partition of Africa

These are usually divided into the two categories of 'Eurocentric' and 'Afrocentric' theories; but it is also useful to distinguish between theories based more or less directly on detailed African case-studies, and the more general 'background' theories—some of which are indeed theories of imperialism rather than specifically of the partition of Africa.

A. Background Theories

A satisfactory general theory (whether 'background' or other) must be able to demonstrate that between about 1875 and 1900 circumstances in Europe, or in Africa, or in both continents, differed from those of the pre-1875 period in ways which can be directly linked with specific 'annexationist' decisions by the European policy-makers. General theories which rely upon broad, macroscopic, developments—socio-political, economic, ideological, technological—in the European and African 'backgrounds', find it especially difficult to establish this close connection. In particular, their answers to the question 'why did the partition begin when it did?' are usually very unsatisfactory. For instance, had the 'technological gap' between European and African societies been non-existent or negligible, no partition—and certainly no scramble—would have taken place. At the time of the partition this gap was doubtless wider than ever before; but it had already been very wide for at least a century. The technological gap may help to explain the pace of partition; it does not explain why the policy-makers of half a dozen different European states should suddenly and almost simultaneously have decided to profit by it, after having ignored it for so long.[3]

It is equally difficult to link with specific policy decisions, and in any precise way with the onset of partition, such ideological phenomena as the rise of 'Social Darwinism' and the aggressive racialism and nationalism which this creed tended to encourage—especially, according to some historians, among the industrial 'masses'.[4]

Another background theory points to alleged changes in the political balance of European societies, bringing to power new ruling élites which are supposed to have been especially interested in overseas expansion. There is indeed a good correlation in time between the onset of large-scale African expansion and the success of militantly 'bourgeois' French politicians in overthrowing, between 1877 and 1879, the *République des Ducs* and replacing it by the *République des Républicains*.[5] But if some *Républicains* were expansionists, many others were not, as Jules Ferry learned to his cost in 1885. All that can be said is that those *Républicains* who did support colonial expansion would have had other and more urgent preoccupations had French domestic politics taken a different course.

Nor can this theory be easily generalised. In England, the link between socio-political changes and specific annexationist decisions is tenuous until the emergence of Joseph Chamberlain as a key policy-maker in 1895; but in 1895 the scramble was entering its final phase. In Bismarckian and post-Bismarckian Germany it seems even more tenuous until, at the earliest, the opening of the Bülow–Tirpitz era in 1897. In Portugal, and probably in Italy, the theory fails because its premise of significant political change is not satisfied. And Leopold II puts this theory completely to rout. Leopold's imperialism was, both constitutionally and in every other way, his own private and personal policy; while the dominant bourgeoisie of his model bourgeois kingdom greeted it with indifference and even hostility.

Outside the ranks of non-Marxist professional scholars, the most popular background theories are perhaps still those derived from the theses put forward by Hobson and Lenin, which attribute the partition (and *fin-de-siècle* imperialism in general) to the alleged economic necessities generated by the development of capitalism. For Hobson, under-consumption due to the maldistribution of purchasing power in a capitalist society led to 'over-saving' by the rich, and to the search by this politically powerful group for profitable investments and speculations overseas. When in due course the rich demanded the protection of the flag for these investments, their voice rarely went unheeded by the policy-makers. For Lenin, the formal political institutions of capitalist states were mere façades behind which the real holders of power—bankers in control of monopolistic cartels—engrossed the raw materials of the world and, by the export of capital, promoted and controlled the exploitation of its inhabitants.[6]

During the last twenty years non-Marxist historians have demolished these models almost to the point of 'overkill'. It has been repeatedly demonstrated that 'investors' and 'bankers' were far less influential in policy-making than Lenin or even Hobson supposed; that in the relevant period capital exports to tropical Africa were insignificant; that some very active imperialist Powers (Italy, Portugal) had no surplus capital to export but on the contrary suffered from a chronic shortage; and that throughout the later nineteenth and early twentieth centuries the markets and the raw materials of tropical Africa were alike of almost negligible importance to the European economy.[7] It has indeed been suggested that the whole concept of economic imperialism is baseless—a 'mythological beast'.[8] But the Hobson-Lenin theories of capitalist imperialism do not exhaust the category of economic theories possibly relevant to the partition. Other such theories should not be relegated, unexamined, to the mythical bestiary merely because of guilt by association. They may turn out on investigation to be real live animals. Indeed, in a story where Cecil Rhodes and Leopold II—to name only two—loom so large, the attempt to exclude or trivialise the economic factor must seem a little perverse. *Tamen usque recurret.*

B. Eurocentric Theories

Economic theories of the partition have however attracted very few academic supporters of late, though there are recent signs that they are now beginning to make a come-back. By far the strongest Eurocentric contender has been:

1. The Strategic Theory: This forms one leg (the other is the Afrocentric 'local crisis theory') of the powerful and attractive thesis developed by R. Robinson and J. Gallagher.[9] In this model, the process of partition begins when a European Power (Britain) reluctantly saddles itself with new territorial responsibilities in Africa in order to defend the strategic security of older imperial possessions. But this move injures the interests of another Power (France) which retorts by counter-annexations, some of them merely as 'compensation', but others intended also as a strategic threat to Britain's new African acquisitions. Britain then seeks security for these new acquisitions by yet further strategic annexations. Meanwhile, other Powers exploit the rivalry of France and Britain to make annexations of their own, some of which are also strategically dangerous to Britain.

This model seems at first sight to work admirably in the Nile Valley, where in 1882 the British occupied Egypt primarily to safeguard the Suez route to India, thereby provoking (but surely rather belatedly?) a French strategic challenge to the security of the waters of the Upper Nile and so to the security of Egypt itself. To this challenge, in both its potential and its actual phases, the British responded by a variety of diplomatic and military expedients designed to halt the French at Egypt's 'new frontiers of insecurity' in the remote fastnesses of East and Central Africa. Meanwhile, in the early stages of the Anglo-French dispute, Leopold II and Bismarck had seized the opportunity to stake their claims. It will be seen that the model is not that of a static situation; it incorporates a very plausible dynamic factor to cover the 'scramble' element in the partition.

The model can also be made to work, up to a point, in South Africa. Here the strategic threat—to the security of imperial maritime communications at the Cape, 'the true centre of the Empire'—came from the 'Revolt of the Afrikaner', itself a reaction to the 'confederation' policy of the Earl of Carnarvon (Colonial Secretary 1874–8).[10] It was indeed largely strategy that kept the 'imperial factor' in play in South Africa after the fall of Carnarvon. But until the final act under Chamberlain and Milner, imperial strategy as a factor in the Southern African scramble played second fiddle to the local rivalries which long pre-dated the European partition. Indeed, the 'imperial factor' sometimes (as in 1881) sought security by reducing rather than by extending its territorial commitments, and from 1880 to 1895 it was always a 'reluctant imperialist'. When under Chamberlain and Milner it at last ceased to be reluctant, it was playing for far higher stakes than mere maritime security at the Cape.[11]

In West Africa, however, British policy can only be fitted to the model on the assumption that Britain was willing to make territorial sacrifices here in order to buy security in the Nile Valley. But this assumption seems very doubtful. Britain's major concession to France in West Africa was the 'light land' conceded in the Agreement of 5 August 1890.[12] But Salisbury then sacrificed little or nothing that he could reasonably have hoped to acquire; nor were the French in 1890 even believed to be threatening the Upper Nile. In 1894, when they *were* believed to be threatening it, the Foreign Office flatly refused to make the concessions in West Africa which might well have bought them off.[13]

Applied to other Powers, the 'strategy' model provides them with an opportunity, but leaves their motive a mystery. What strategic imperative drove Leopold II into the Congo, Bismarck into East, West and South Africa, Italy into Ethiopia—or even France into the Senegal hinterland, a region quite irrelevant to 'Nile-Valley' strategy? Indeed, the model is by its very nature not generalisable. It is essentially an analysis of British defensive reactions to a series of challenges to an 'unofficial empire' which had previously existed to a greater or lesser extent all round the ocean coasts of Africa outside a few small and unimportant French enclaves. Down to about 1880, Britain enjoyed an almost complete monopoly of influence on these coasts and often in their immediate hinterlands. Her situation was, quite literally, unique. It is impossible to use this unique case as the basis of a general theory of 'strategic imperialism'.

The strategic theory also encounters difficulties in the overwhelming importance which it attributes to the Egyptian situation both as initiator of the partition and as the main drive behind its explosive extension. 'When the British entered Egypt on their own, the scramble began.[14] But did it? Whenever the partition of tropical Africa began, it was not in 1882 or 1883. By 1882–3 it was already well under way, with the French conquest of the Senegal hinterland already fully launched, the British and French actively competing for territory on the West Coast, and the French confronting King Leopold on the Congo. Moreover, in West Africa proper, the crucial French decisions to go forward had been taken as early as 1879–80, when the amicable Anglo-French condominium of influence in Egypt was still alive and well.[15]

In the Congo, too, both France and King Leopold had begun to move forward in 1879. But it has been argued that the crucial event here was not de Brazza's treaties of 1880 with the Congo chief Makoko (which he had not been authorised to make), but their ratification by the French Chamber in November 1882. The British, who had commercial interests of their own to defend in the Congo, had already made pointed enquiries about these treaties. But, we are told, 'after the Egyptian affair had reached its climax, Paris did not feel the old need to pay deference to British susceptibilities', and on 10 October the Foreign Minister Duclerc decided to ratify.[16] This assumes that there was already in October 1882 an active dispute over Egypt. Nothing could be further from the truth. At that time there was no dispute and Duclerc was doing his best to avoid one. Convinced that Britain could not manage an insolvent Egypt without French co-operation, and that the British refusal to restore the Anglo-French dual control of Egyptian finances was due simply to muddle-headedness and divided counsels, he prescribed a strictly non-provocative policy as an aid to clarity of thought at London. Even when in January 1883 France 'resumed her freedom of action' in Egypt, she did so 'avec regret, mais sans manifestation d'aigreur': this was still to be a difference between friends. As late as January 1884 the French Consul in Egypt was still under strict instructions to co-operate actively with his British colleague; and Sir Evelyn Baring himself testifies that these instructions were obeyed.[17]

Duclerc's successor Jules Ferry was no less anxious for a friendly settlement, in spite of the disquieting evolution of a 'veiled British protectorate' in Egypt during 1883–4.[18] Only after his humiliating failure, in June 1884, to settle Egyptian finances à deux with London, did Ferry write off the British as hopeless and begin cautiously to respond to the German proposals for 'common action' against Britain in Africa.[19]

When Duclerc ratified de Brazza's treaties in November 1882, the focus of French popular agitation was not Egypt but the Congo. Hero-worship of de Brazza (who well knew how to evoke it), detestation of Stanley, Leopold's ill-concealed attempts to prevent ratification—these factors had excited French opinion to a point where it would have been very unpopular not to ratify. Moreover, there seemed to be no good reason for abstention. The British would be content, or so the French believed, with assurances of complete free trade; the immediate adversary, King Leopold's 'International Association of the Congo', was a non-state, a purely private organisation. As the Government spokesman told the Chamber, 'aucune complication [internationale] n'est donc à prévoir'; and Duclerc seized the opportunity to score a diplomatically harmless popular success by ratifying de Brazza's treaties not with the usual mere *décret*, but with all the publicity and solemnity of a *loi*.[20]

'From start to finish the partition of tropical Africa was driven by the persistent crisis in Egypt.'[21] But was it? The Egyptian crisis did not initiate the partition; nor, down to mid-1884, did it have much discernible effect in driving on a partition that had aready begun.[22] French expansion in West Africa, in particular, had a dynamic that was quite independent of the Egyptian situation. From 1879 to about the end of 1883, when there was no Anglo-French quarrel in Egypt, or none that the Quai d'Orsay would recognise, it had gone ahead very rapidly. In 1884–5, just when the Egyptian quarrel became open and embittered, it slowed down almost to a standstill. Enormous expenditure, and military setbacks both in the Niger Sudan and elsewhere, created a mood of disillusionment with overseas expansion; the 'official mind' even began to wonder whether some of the recent acquisitions were really worth the expense of obtaining them. There was some recovery in 1886; but French expansion did not fully regain its momentum until 1889–90, with the revival of aggressive military imperialism in West Africa and the emergence in France itself of a powerful and well-organised imperialist movement. But this movement was not primarily interested in Egypt or the Upper Nile; down to 1893 it concentrated almost entirely on the creation of a great continental empire centred on Lake Chad.[23]

In 1894 and after, British and French strategies and counter-strategies on the Upper Nile were certainly the strongest drive in the scramble, though even now the Chad Plan sometimes ran them a very close second. But so far as the Upper Nile is concerned, the Egyptian crisis, and the Sudan crisis which accompanied and followed it, had a very slow fuse. For several years after 1882, the British were blissfully unconscious of the very existence of Egypt's 'new frontiers of insecurity'. Obsessed with the problem of Egyptian finance, they helped to create a vacuum of power on the Upper Nile by insisting on the withdrawal of Egyptian troops even from regions where they were not threatened by, or had successfully resisted, the Mahdists. At Massawa, a strategic gateway to the middle Nile, they evicted in 1885 their own Egyptian puppets in favour of the Italians—who at least did not burden the Egyptian budget. It was not until 1888 that the British began to feel uneasy about the Nile waters, and not until 1892 that they began to fear a challenge from the French. In fact, although the possibility of penetration towards the Upper Nile had since 1887 occasionally been discussed by French officials and politicians, down to the beginning of 1893 the French policy-makers still hoped to settle the Egyptian question by friendly negotiation, and rejected the aggressive Upper Nile strategy.[24] In 1893 Delcassé at last made an abortive attempt to launch a mission under P.-L. Monteil. In October 1894 Victor Liotard, the administrator of the Upper Ubangi, was ordered to advance to the Nile. But he made little progress; and it was not until Marchand got under way in 1896 that French action became effective.

2. *Diplomatic Theories:* It is not difficult to demonstrate that, once the partition had begun, territorial concessions might be made in Africa in order to gain diplomatic advantages in Europe.[25] Sometimes, indeed, territorial advances might be undertaken with a similar object: the clearest and best-attested case is the 'Anglo-Egyptian' advance in the northern Sudan in March 1896.[26] Bismarck's fit of colonial acquisition in 1884-5 was once regarded as the most spectacular example of this technique. Bismarck, it was said, sought colonies not because he wanted them, but so as to pick a quarrel with Britain in order thereby to make his desire for a rapprochement with France more credible to the Quai d'Orsay. The whole operation was, purely and simply, 'a move in Bismarck's European policy'.[27] It was never very clear why Bismarck should have preferred a rapprochement with France to the maintenance of her isolation, unless—as he himself told the French—he needed her naval collaboration to support his own bid for colonies: a motive that would flatly contradict the 'European-policy' thesis. Nor was it clear why, if he did desire such a rapprochement, he should have needed to quarrel with England in order to get it; nor, if he did need such a quarrel, why he chose to foment it by colonial competition rather than by exploiting England's very vulnerable diplomatic position in Egypt. Recent work has pressed home these objections; and has demonstrated, using previously unexploited sources, that Bismarck 'simply changed his mind and decided that there must be German overseas possessions'. To obtain these with the least possible risk, he needed France in order to create an 'equilibrium on the seas' against Britain.[28] Moreover, even if the 'European policy' thesis were valid for Germany, it could not be generalised to include all the partitioners—the most obvious exceptions being Portugal and Leopold II. Nor could it do anything to explain the onset of partition.

Another type of diplomatic theory explains the partition (and *fin-de-siècle* imperialism in general) as 'an extension into the periphery of the [international] political struggle in Europe'.[29] This looks plausible enough at first sight; one might indeed regard the 'steeple-chases' and 'incidents' that punctuate the scramble as a cheap and comparatively bloodless substitute for European war. But it does not explain why the Powers suddenly decided to extend their struggle to Africa; and it fails to resolve certain contradictions. Powers that were allies in Europe became rivals in Africa, and *vice versa:* thus England became embroiled with her 'oldest ally' Portugal and, rather less obviously, with her 'newest ally' Italy;[30] while France and Germany, whose unresolved conflict was at the very core of 'the political struggle in Europe', were during the period of actual partition normally on quite friendly terms in Africa. Moreover, if the partition of Africa was in essence an extension of the European power-struggle, it seems paradoxical that the non-Power Leopold II should have been allowed to get away with so enormous and so rich an African prize.

3. *The Imperialism of Prestige:* 'Prestige' is a disconcertingly nebulous concept with which to operate; but it is sometimes possible to demonstrate that a sense of injured national self-esteem was a major, or even *the* major, motive for annexation in Africa. For instance, both during the partition and long before it, influential sections of the French official mind—above all the *ministère de la Marine*—deeply resented the British monopoly of 'la police des mers' in African waters—and for that matter elsewhere, e.g. in the South Pacific. In these circles coastal and insular annexations were often proposed (and sometimes effected even before the onset of partition) both as a demonstration that this monopoly was incomplete and as a means of making it less complete by the acquisition of potential naval bases.[31]

Again, when the French decided to occupy Tunisia in 1881, the crucial factor was not the material interests that were at stake there (though these were considerable); but the belief that failure to take action would entail the intolerable humiliation of seeing a long-standing unofficial preponderance overthrown by the despised Italians. 'Europe is watching us, is making up its mind whether we amount to anything or not; a single act of firmness, of will and determination . . ., and we shall regain our rightful place in the eyes of other nations; but one more proof of our weakness, and we shall end up by letting ourselves sink to the level of Spain.' It was with arguments like this that the diplomatists overcame the initial reluctance of Ferry and Gambetta.[32]

Above all, it was injured self-esteem, the conviction that France was being denied her rightful influence in the world that, far more than considerations of the 'Mediterranean balance', moved those French policy-makers who sought to force Britain to abandon her unilateral occupation of Egypt by a threat of interference with the Nile waters—the grandiose strategy which reached its climax with the confrontation of Marchand and Kitchener at Fashoda on 19 September 1898.[33]

The French were not of course the only practitioners of the imperialism of prestige. Bismarck's determination to acquire African territories was certainly hardened by his resentment, as an affront to Germany, of the British pretension to exclude other Powers from African territories that they did not themselves possess or even occupy —their 'Monroe doctrine for Africa', as he called it.[34] Italian imperialism in Ethiopia and the Nile Valley seems to have stemmed mainly from the conviction (particularly strong with Francesco Crispi) that because other Powers were acquiring African colonies, Italy would look more like a Great Power if she imitated them.[35] And what motive other than prestige can be seriously adduced for the sudden determination of Portugal to revive an apparently moribund empire in reaction to British encroachments upon it?

There is in fact more solidity in the imperialism of prestige than might appear at first sight. But it does little to explain why the quest for prestige through annexations in Africa suddenly became the fashion. And if French jealousy of the British *police des mers* had existed long before the partition, why did it produce so little disturbance of the *status quo* until after 1880?

4. Economic Theories: (a) The Search for New Markets and the Fear of the 'Closing Door' in Africa. The demonstration that African territories were not economically important, and that the political policy-makers were rarely if ever the puppets of 'finance capital' disposes of the 'classical' theory of capitalist imperialism, but it does not thereby exclude the possibility of economic motives for annexation. 'If we want to explain the motives for . . . expansion, what matters is not whether African territories were economically important . . ., but whether policy-makers thought they might become important and formulated policies designed to achieve economic objectives.'[36]

There is in fact clear evidence that many policy-makers of the 1880s, concerned at the stagnation of the European economy which had set in during the early 1870s, did believe—or at least hope—that Africa offered potentially rich markets which might help to solve the problem of 'over-production'. This belief was certainly held by Jules Ferry and Leopold II (though Leopold's even stronger belief in the value of colonies as directly exploitable estates long pre-dated the 'Great Depression'); and Bismarck seems to have been converted to it, at least for a time.[37] That African markets might contribute to economic recovery seems indeed to have been part of the conventional wisdom of the 'educated classes' in the 1880s. Alphonse de Courcel was a diplomatist, not an economist—least of all a Marxist economist; nor was he an ardent expansionist. But in September 1884 he accepts it as axiomatic that because German notoriously suffers from a crisis of over-production, her need for African colonies must be genuine.[38]

But the search for new markets did not, in principle, imply the need or the wish to annex territory; and the case of Great Britain is often adduced to demonstrate that it did not do so in practice. In the 1870s Britain, still the most economically advanced of the Powers, was no less afflicted than others by crises of over-production. Yet in the 1880s she was a notoriously reluctant imperialist—'trade, not territory' was the almost universal slogan. But Britain's economic preponderance, combined with her unique position as a near-monopolist of unofficial empire on the ocean coasts of Africa, meant that even a partition in which she gained the lion's share would be disadvantageous to her. Even her own acquisitions, with their inevitable consequence of administrative expenditure, would represent, in the short run at least, a reduction in her margin of profit. It was, as Salisbury pointed out in July 1890, far more advantageous to be 'masters of Africa, or the greater part of it, without being put to the inconvenience of protectorates'. But as soon as British opinion began, rather belatedly, to recognise that unofficial empire had indeed ceased to exist, the clamour for annexations at once made itself heard.[39]

Leopold II and Bismarck, too, were well aware that trade did not necessarily imply annexation. Their original plans provided, not for annexation with its attendant burdens, but rather for the reservation of fields of economic activity in Africa. They were in fact attempting to take a leaf out of Britain's book of informal empire. But this phase was very brief; in Bismarck's case almost vanishingly brief. Bismarck was quickly forced into outright annexation by a British response which, albeit in a belated, confused and half-hearted fashion, attempted to forestall him by asserting the political control of London or Cape Town in those regions which interested Germany. And for Leopold, once France had in November 1882 ratified de Brazza's treaties, it had to be full political control or nothing in the Congo basin.[40]

When Bismarck entered the arena towards the end of 1883, the day of informal empire was in fact rapidly drawing to its close. The partition of Africa had already begun, not only in the Congo basin but by 1883 all along the West African coast from Sierra Leone to the Cameroons. West of Lagos and in the Niger Delta the British were already, however reluctantly, planning counter-annexations to stem the tide of French expansion which had been rising ever since 1880. In June 1883 Sir Percy Anderson, the head of the Foreign Office African Department, minuted: 'Action seems to be forced on us ... Protectorates are unwelcome burdens, but in this case it is ... a question between British protectorates, which would be unwelcome, and French protectorates, which would be fatal.'[41] Action was delayed for almost a year by those who saw less clearly than Anderson that the halcyon days of unofficial empire were no more; but it was finally taken with Consul Hewett's famous treaty-making mission to West Africa in 1884.

French protectorates would have been 'fatal' because of their increasingly restrictive trade and tariff policies, especially from 1877 when Governor Brière de l'Isle began to introduce throughout the French possessions the high Senegal duties on foreign cloth. But British 'free trade' was in practice almost as discriminatory as French protection. Textiles and hardwear, in which the British could undersell all comers, were lightly taxed; but there were heavy duties on leaf tobacco, mainly a French export; and even heavier duties upon cheap spirits, which came mainly from Germany and were indeed by far the most important item in German exports to West Africa.[42] Bismarck's experiment, first in informal then in formal imperialism, was certainly influenced by the fear that all the coastal regions of Western Africa would soon be snapped up, and all the doors to a possibly rich interior permanently closed, by the competitive annexations and restrictive customs policies of the British and the French; this point was already being made, with increasing emphasis, by the Chambers of Commerce of the Hanse towns. Bismarck's fears can only have been increased when in April 1883 one of his officials misinterpreted an Anglo-French boundary agreement of June 1882 as implying a fiscal partition of the *whole* West African coast.[43]

There is evidently a rough correlation between economic depres-

sion and the onset and early development of the partition. But there are
a number of loose ends. Leopold's appearance on the African scene is
one of them. Economic depression can hardly have been a crucial factor
here, for Leopold had been on the hunt for colonies (though not in
Africa) in the heyday of Europe's, and Belgium's, industrial expansion.
Nor would Bismarck have been spurred to action by the fear of 'closing
doors', and the possible loss of economic opportunities for Germany,
unless Britain and France had already been closing some of the doors,
and apparently preparing to close more. Britain, it seems, was reacting
to a sudden burst of French annexation. But why had France embarked
on this policy? Granted that the domestic events of 1877–9 had brought
to power men interested in overseas expansion, why did they abandon,
both on the Coast and in the Senegal hinterland, the 'peaceful penetration' which was the French version of unofficial empire; and why, on
the Coast, did they not merely abandon the time-honoured practice of
settling local disputes by friendly negotiation in Europe, but choose to
stake their political claims in regions where the British were especially
sensitive? Whatever the reasons, they are certainly not self-evidently
economic. Moreover, however severe the depression, and however strong
the belief in African markets as a solution, no partition could have taken
place had Britain been able and willing to defend her unofficial empire
against annexationist interlopers. In the early 1840s she had successfully
warned off the French; later in the century (a simple task indeed), the
Portuguese.[44] Yet between 1880 and 1885 she permitted her hegemony
to collapse so completely that not only France and Germany but even
Leopold II were able to make enormous gains at her expense. Economic
factors seem very unlikely to explain this remarkable revolution.

(b) *The 'Mythical' Theory*: This theory, developed by A. S. Kanya-
Forstner and C. W. Newbury, attributes French expansion, in particular, to the domination of the official mind by myths or delusions. These
delusions were of two main kinds: fantastically exaggerated views of
the wealth and economic potential of certain African territories, notably
the Niger Sudan; and an almost mystical faith in the efficacy of certain
strategies (above all, the Upper Nile strategy) which had never been
critically examined.[45]

The first type of delusion—we are not here concerned with the
second—is clearly an economic drive, though a less sophisticated one
than the more sober 'new markets' motivation. But perhaps the assimilation should be the other way round, for the 'new markets' themselves
were hardly less mythical than the Sudanese El Dorado. This branch of
the 'mythical' theory, extended to include less extravagant but hardly
less illusory hopes of economic gain, evidently has considerable
explanatory power, and by no means only for French imperialism.

The effect of the El Dorado myth upon French policy in the
Senegal hinterland between 1879 and 1883 has been worked out in
some detail. Fantastic official estimates of the resources and population
of the Niger Sudan—an annual trade of 100 million francs, a potential
market of 200 million people—prompted in 1879–80 the deliberate
decision to turn it into a 'second India' for France. Abandoning 'old

notions of informal empire' that had prevailed in Senegal since the departure of Governor Faidherbe in 1865, the policy-makers 'set France on a recognisably imperialist course . . . , basing their concept of Empire on political control and military domination'; and so took the first effective step towards the partition of Africa. The policy-makers responsible for this decision were the close political and personal friends Charles de Freycinet (Prime Minister and Foreign Minister) and Admiral Jean Jauréguiberry (Minister of Marine and the Colonies, and a former governor of Senegal). In supporting roles were the Marseilles businessman and financier Maurice Rouvier, and Louis-Alexandre Brière de l'Isle, Governor of Senegal from 1876 to 1881.[46]

Freycinet and Jauréguiberry, both of whom were convinced expansionists, maintained the momentum of the advance when they enjoyed a second spell in office in 1882–3; so did Rouvier, who became Minister of Commerce towards the end of 1881. Freycinet, a civil engineer and a *polytechnicien*, thought in terms of expansion through railway construction on a 'mythically' grandiose scale. In theory a form of 'peaceful penetration', this programme necessarily implied full political control; while Jauréguiberry hardly troubled to conceal his commitment not merely to political control but to military conquest. The railway made negligible progress at enormous expense. Military operations were very expensive too; but down to 1883 they were at least successful, and they had been continued by Jauréguiberry's successor at the *Marine*. Thereafter, the soaring expenditure and military setbacks which disturbed Paris quite failed to discourage the French officers on the spot, whom the political policy-makers found it increasingly difficult to control, and whose attitudes and ambitions committed them to permanent aggression and unlimited conquest.[47]

The new policy of aggressive expansion was not however confined to the Senegal hinterland. It had its counterpart on the Coast. Down to 1879, Paris had kept a tight rein on the expansionist tendencies of local officials here; annexations were confined to the acquisition of one or two bargaining counters for use in an expected comprehensive exchange of territories with Britain. But in 1879 Brière de l'Isle extended French political and fiscal control into disputed areas north of Sierra Leone; and in 1880 Rouvier successfully protested against a proposal to treat as 'matière d'échange' French interests on the Slave Coast immediately to the west of Lagos. In April 1882 Jauréguiberry threw down a direct challenge to the British in this very sensitive area by establishing a protectorate over Porto Novo, a potential trading (and customs) rival to Lagos. By January 1883 he was pressing for French protectorates westward from Porto Novo to the frontier of the Gold Coast, and was already despatching a naval squadron to make treaties of protection in the Niger Delta and the Cameroons. By this time the Quai d'Orsay had concurred in the general policy of extending French influence to the Niger-Benué region.[48]

On the Coast, however, the 'mythical' theory seems rather less convincing than in the Senegal hinterland. Certainly, the French hoped for economic gain on the Coast; but these parts were far too well known for even the most credulous to regard them as an El Dorado. Here the main drive seems to have been an almost obsessive fear of being forestalled by the British—a fear to which the expansionist tendencies of Governor Rowe at Lagos gave some colour. With far less evidence, the French also believed that the British were attempting to compete with them in the Niger Sudan—in the very El Dorado itself. Indeed, Jauréguiberry seems sometimes to have regarded coastal competition as a race to obtain points of entry to the mythically rich interior. These French fears are usually dismissed (by British historians) as more or less imaginary; but their origins seem to be worth more investigation than they have hitherto received. A better use may perhaps be found for them than as mere raw material for yet another species of the mythical theory.[49]

But the El Dorado theory is deficient in another and more fundamental way. It offers no satisfactory explanation of why this myth, which had been current for decades and even for centuries, suddenly took control of French policy in 1879–80. The originators of the theory themselves explicitly reject, as sufficient causes, local African crises, changes in the French political balance and 'pressure from private commercial interests'. As the fundamental cause of French expansion they simply put forward 'a change in official thinking', in which the crucial factor was the personal policies of two or three particular individuals who happened briefly to occupy the key ministerial positions.[50] The onset of the partitition of Africa becomes a mere by-product of a Third-Republic cabinet reshuffle. Maybe; but if so we shall have to start taking Cleopatra's nose a lot more seriously.

(c) 'Manipulated Social Imperialism': Here the fundamental drive is seen as a more sophisticated variant of the 'new markets' motive—the conviction that the expansion of the economy through acquisitions overseas is the only effective long-term prophylactic against disruptive social and political conflict at home. Here lies the point of Cecil Rhodes' remark: 'If you want to avoid civil war, you must be an imperialist.'[51] The thinking of Jules Ferry and Joseph Chamberlain embodies at least strong traces of this doctrine.[52] Bismarck has also been claimed as a convert to it; if so, his conversion must have been very short-lived, for by 1888 he had lost all enthusiasm for colonies.[53]

Whether or not Bismarck was ever a convert, 'manipulated social imperialism' seems of limited value as an explanatory model. As an explanation of the timing of the partition, it is less useful than the plain 'new markets' theory. Moreover, it tends to be a rather elusive concept; it turns up in theoretical treatises or isolated *obiter dicta* rather than in connection with specific policy-decisions. It almost seems to deserve relegation to the category of 'background theories'.

Even if 'manipulated social imperialism' be admitted as a motive of some of the imperialists for some of the time, it is difficult to believe that it was normally a dominant motive. The theory implies that overseas expansion was a matter of the utmost concern—almost a matter of life and death—to the industrial Powers of Europe. But these Powers did not normally approach the partition of Africa in that spirit. The 'old imperialism'—the competition of the maritime Powers for overseas trade and territories from the sixteenth to the eighteenth century—had generated an almost uninterrupted series of global wars. But the European scramble for Africa developed not as an armed struggle, but as a strategic and diplomatic 'game'.[54] The weapons were not shot and shell, except of course against Africans. They were the steeplechases of rival 'missions' with their stock-in-trade of national flags and printed treaty forms; and unceasing attempts to adjust diplomatic relations in Europe in ways that would promote territorial strategy in Africa. Only at the very end of the story, on the Upper Nile in 1898 and in South Africa in 1899, did the partition lose this 'game' status and become a matter of grim earnest; and in neither of these cases did 'manipulated social imperialism' have much to do with the intensification of the struggle.[55]

C. Afrocentric and other 'Peripheral' Theories

1. The Theory of the Local Crisis: Here territorial annexation is prompted by a crisis of local resistance, by black, brown or even white Africans, to existing informal European control and 'unofficial empire'. This model works excellently in Egypt; and it is certainly relevant in South Africa and in some regions of British West Africa—for instance, the Gold Coast. In the French Sudan, it is very tempting to assume that France was drawn willy-nilly into increasingly far-flung campaigns of conquest by the aggressive resistance of militant Islamic states to unofficial French influence. But closer investigation reveals that these states usually attempted to avoid rather than provoke armed conflict; and that the French campaigns were not 'involuntary imbroglios', a 'response to the pressure of local African circumstance, but a determined European bid for territory'.[56]

All too often, however, the local African crisis is not even plausible. It will not work at all in the Congo (whether for Leopold or for the French), nor for Bismarck's annexations. If the 'local crisis of resistance' cannot be generalised, neither can the more sophisticated development of this model, which sees the 'normal' origin of the local crisis (and therefore of formal European empire) in the 'breakdown of collaborative mechanisms' within the African polities concerned.[57] Moreover, in either of its versions the theory leaves the question of timing in total obscurity. Why did local crises and 'breakdowns of collaborative mechanisms' suddenly begin to proliferate around 1880? The coincidence is all the more mysterious in that at that time the duration and intensity of European influence upon different African polities varied so enormously.

2. Sub-Imperialisms: (a) 'Cat's-paw' Sub-imperialisms: These were virtually a British monopoly, a technique of unofficial empire whereby non-European client states (Egypt, Zanzibar) were permitted or encouraged to acquire coastal territories which were of strategic importance to Britain.[58] Neither Egyptian nor Zanzibari imperialism played any dynamic role in the European partition. On the contrary, both these local empires collapsed during its early phases. The Egyptian empire in the interior (where the British had normally no strategic interest in it) was overthrown by the Mahdist insurrection; on the coast it was dismantled by the British themselves, in their exclusive preoccupation with Egyptian finance. The Zanzibari hegemony collapsed in 1885–6 because the British failed to defend it against German pressure; this pressure was itself generated by the politics of an on-going partition elsewhere in Africa.[59] The collapse of Zanzibar was an effect, not a cause, of the onset of partition. Certainly, the vacuum of power in the former Egyptian and Zanzibari dominions profoundly influenced the course of the scramble in these regions from 1885 onwards; but no general theory can be validly constructed out of the peculiar quirks of the situation in East Africa and the Upper Nile.

(b) *Sub-Imperialisms Proper*: In the more usual meaning of the term, the sub-imperialists are Europeans resident or working in Africa, and therefore having a very direct interest in the acquisition of territory; and their aggressive expansion drags a more or less reluctant metropolitan government along in its wake. Obvious examples are South African settlers, with their local scramble long pre-dating the European partition; and the French sugar-planters of Réunion, with their determination ultimately to control Madagascar. But the French military in the Niger Sudan were also for a time very effective sub-imperialists; and administrators both French and British on the West Coast showed some signs of emulating them in the days of Brière de l'Isle and Rowe.

But for a general theory based on the effect of aggressive European sub-imperialisms, there are simply not enough sub-imperialists of the relevant species to go round. There were none at the outset in most of the major foci of the scramble—the Congo basin, the Upper Nile, East Africa,[60] Ethiopia and the Eastern Horn. Even where they did exist, down to about 1880 sub-imperialist activity likely to cause international competition (as in West Africa or Madagascar) was normally kept well in check by the metropolitan governments.

D. Non-Theories

Any serious investigation of the chains of events that led to the onset and development of partition in particular regions of Africa reveals a number of apparently unconnected processes which seem to have no common origin and for which it is impossible to discern any general over-riding 'cause'. True, we can concoct a mixed grill of causes: strategy, prestige, and more or less delusive expectation of economic gain, seasoned where appropriate with sub-imperialism or the local crisis, make quite a nourishing dish. But it is also an indigestibly 'pluralistic' dish; nor does it even yet contain all the ingredients necessary for an unassailably complete explanation. For instance, long after the 'Sudanese El Dorado' myth had been quite exploded, and when Paris had clearly recognised that the methods of the military were reducing a poor economy to stark destitution, the total conquest of the Sudan continued to be driven by the career ambitions of individual French officers—sometimes quite junior officers—for whom *faits de guerre*, and therefore campaigns of aggression, were the fastest road to promotion. And the Union Jack followed the Bible into the awkwardly situated territory of Nyasaland mainly because good Presbyterian voters in Scotland would have made their resentment felt at the polls had London permitted a Catholic Portuguese takeover.[61]

Was the scramble, after all, no more than the consequence of a number of independent initiatives—or responses to local African situations—which happened quite fortuitously to occur at about the same time? That the situation did in fact contain an element of coincidence seems undeniable. King Leopold, who had in 1875–6 decided to look for a colony in Africa rather than America or Asia, moved effectively into the Congo basin in 1879, the very year in which the French launched their 'recognisably imperialist' advance into the Senegal hinterland. So far as is known, there is no link whatever between these two initiatives. It is again coincidental that within two or three years of these events the Egyptian, Sudanese and South African crises should have erupted almost simultaneously.

It is indeed tempting to conclude that in 'the early 1880s a convergence of many forces resulted in the rapid partition of Africa. Each of these forces had multiple causes. Each one in turn requires a pluralistic explanation.'[62] But in spite of its apparent scholarly respectability, the 'multiple causes' model is very unsatisfactory. Its explanatory power is minimal. Half-a-dozen European Powers, some of them previously totally uninterested in Africa, none of them recently interested in acquiring extensive territories in tropical Africa, suddenly fall upon that continent almost simultaneously and gobble up almost the whole of it within two decades. It is almost a non-explanation to say of a process like this: 'Well, it just happened that way—the coincidental result of several independent chains of events, each with multiple causes.' If this is the best the historian can do in a precise and short-lived situation where the evidence is quite exceptionally copious and reliable, he had better at once abandon any claim to elucidate the more imponderable 'long-term' trends in history, and indeed all those comparatively poorly-documented developments which make up the great bulk of his subject-matter.

Moreover, pluralistic explanations completely fail to solve the problem of timing. Why did the numerous forces which converged to produce the scramble all 'go critical', in the sense of causing annexations, within one particular short period of time? The more pluralistic the explanation and the more numerous and various the forces, the more inscrutably mysterious this coincidence becomes.

III: A Suggested Covering Hypothesis: The Disruption of a Previously Stable Situation by the Disappearance of its Stability Factors

Why did the partition of Africa begin when it did? Why did it not begin much earlier in the nineteenth century? (The factors inhibiting a still earlier onset are well understood, and will not be discussed here.) On

any showing, Africa (apart from its extreme north and south) is from
1815 to about 1880 a remarkably stable system so far as European
conquest and annexation are concerned. Even successful invasions, like
the British Ethiopian and Ashanti campaigns of 1868 and 1874, are not
followed by territorial annexations. In and after 1880, this stability
collapses very rapidly. A stable system can of course be disrupted by
new inputs, and of these there is all too embarrassing a wealth in
Europe's relations with Africa from 1880 onwards. But it can also be
disrupted by the disappearance or weakening of existing inputs which
happen to be crucial for its stability. Indeed, it is quite conceivable that
the new factors tending to disruption would have been ineffective, had
the older stabilising factors retained their former strength. And it is at
least possible that, in the particular case of Africa, these older stabilising
factors will turn out to be less unmanageably heterogeneous than the
'new inputs' on which attention has hitherto been rather narrowly
concentrated.

If a model on these lines can be made to work, the partition of
Africa ceases to be a mere assemblage of coincidences, no matter how
disconnected its various regional foci may be, and no matter how
numerous and miscellaneous the forces which 'converged' to produce it.
Any and every motivation can be accommodated, so long as it is armed
with proper credentials derived from empirical investigation; whatever
else it may be, this model is at least no Procrustean bed. Even the
motivations implied by the 'background theories' can be considered on
their merits. Moreover, if this approach has any explanatory power at
all, it ought to go far to explain the timing of the onset of partition—that
crucial fence which most of the 'general theories' either fail or refuse to
jump. It may even throw additional light on that rather mysterious
change of attitude 'within the [French] policy-making framework,
within the official mind',[63] which seems to have initiated the partition.

IV: The Stabilising Factors, 1815–c. 1875

A. British naval hegemony

This has only to be mentioned to be at once recognised as the indispensable foundation of the British 'unofficial empire'—itself the outward
and visible sign of the existence of the stable system. Based on the
British maritime preponderance over France established during the
Napoleonic Wars, and consolidated by the acquisition of the Cape and
Ile de France (Mauritius) as naval bases, British naval hegemony on
the ocean coasts of Africa was for long unassailable. It was continuously
demonstrated (and also kept in effective operational trim) by the pro-
longed campaign to suppress the slave trade. Oceanic hegemony was
supported by a less total, but usually effective, preponderance in the
Mediterranean, consolidated by the acquisition of Malta. Normally no
more than a potential threat to possible interlopers with their eye on
African territory, British maritime hegemony was on occasion actively
exerted, notably against Portuguese occupation at the Congo mouth and

(rather less brutally) against real or suspected French designs on Morocco and Tunisia.[64]

B. The Lack of Interest in Africa by Major Powers other than Britain and France

In 1877 the British Minister at Lisbon, Sir Robert Morier, pointed out that there were in Africa 'four great landlords'—Portugal, Egypt, Zanzibar and 'ourselves'. Significantly, he did not include the French, whose African possessions (other than Algeria) were indeed by no means extensive at that time. Two of these landlords, being not only weak but non-European, had by the 1870s fallen under the unofficial control of the one overwhelmingly strong landlord, Britain; as Morier put it, Egypt and Zanzibar 'do pretty well what we tell them to do'.[65] The fourth great landlord, Portugal, was weak enough to be bullied with impunity whenever necessary. Of the minor European landlords in Africa, the Danes and Dutch had already by 1871 sold out to Britain, and Spain as an imperial Power seemed to be in a terminal coma. The 'new' Powers which were to take part in the scramble were mostly still in the making until 1870. France, though still only a minor landlord in tropical Africa, was Britain's only serious rival; but an isolated French challenge to British hegemony and unofficial empire was very unlikely to be successful. And there was no other Power in the field with both the means and the motive to combine with France in such a challenge.

C. The Anglo-French modus vivendi in Africa from 1845 to 1875

The French had in fact made a serious attempt to assert themselves against the British in Africa in the early 1840s; but this attempt had achieved very little, and was not repeated until the onset of the partition. It was promoted by French naval officers seeking a substitute India (or at least a substitute Mauritius) in East Africa or Madagascar; by the Réunion planters who also coveted the great island; and by merchants and bureaucrats—especially the latter—who believed that territorial footholds in Guinea were essential for the safeguarding of French commerce. Guizot, for all his devotion to the Anglo-French entente cordiale, had the greatest difficulty in containing these forces and avoiding a breach with England which would have been very disadvantageous to France in Europe.[66]

Contain them he did, however, saving face in public by the proclamation in March 1843 of a politique de points d'appui which amounted in practice to a renunciation of all genuine territorial expansion. Under British pressure, Madagascar was renounced publicly and by name; the treaties establishing the three new French comptoirs in West Africa (Grand Bassam, Assinie and Gabon) were re-negotiated so as to restrict French authority to mere 'external' sovereignty and to guarantee complete free trade; and Guizot was forced to forego all territorial annexation after a successful campaign against Morocco in 1844.[67] France secured two more consolation prizes (Mayotta in the Comoros, Nossi-Bé off Madagascar); but no partition of Africa began in the early

1840s. The upshot might have been very different had there been another major Power with African aspirations, and willing to promote those aspirations by supporting France against Britain.

The French consolation prizes implied no real diminution in the British hegemony. But France was now accepted more readily by Britain as a 'junior partner' in Africa,[68] on the tacit condition that she refrain from further major advances on the African seaboard. The terms of the *modus vivendi* were well understood at Paris. In 1860 Napoleon III, who had no more wish than Guizot to quarrel with Britain in Africa, vetoed plans for large scale expansion on the Red Sea and Somali coasts for fear of a hostile British reaction; and the Anglo-French treaty of March 1862 guaranteeing the independence of Zanzibar was in fact if not in form a French undertaking not to disturb the *status quo* between Somalia and Mozambique.[69] For some years after 1870 the precarious international situation of France made the Quai d'Orsay more than usually anxious not to arouse British ill-will by inconsiderate behaviour in Africa; hence the care taken to stifle local competition on the West Coast.[70]

V: The Decline and Disappearance of the Stabilising Factors, 1875–85

All three stabilising factors had disappeared by 1885. British naval hegemony, already shaky for some years, had been exposed as a bluff; France had abandoned the *modus vivendi* and had initiated a competition for territory in West Africa; and another major Power, Bismarck's Germany, had joined France in the attack upon Britain's unofficial empire.

A. The British Doctrine of 'Paramountcy' in Theory and Practice, c. 1875–8

The British themselves were unwittingly responsible for the earliest disturbance to the stable system, when their increasing deployment of the doctrine of paramountcy began to create in the French official mind the conviction that the British were engaged in transforming their informal empire into something rather more formal, and at any rate formal enough to restrict France for all time to her existing African possessions.

In the mid-1870s the concept of paramountcy had become popular with British policy-makers as a solution to the growing problems of 'the imperial frontier in the tropics'. In small colonies, whether islands in the Pacific, or footholds in West Africa and Malaya, British interests were never confined to the very narrow boundaries of formal sovereignty. Nor could they be. The security and economic viability of the colonies themselves (and most of them were still essentially trading posts) were all too frequently jeopardised by local power-struggles on the periphery. The choice seemed to be between further annexation; or, failing that, the abandonment of existing colonies as useless and burdensome. Both courses were equally unpopular among those sections of opinion which took any interest in colonies at all. It was, as the Earl of Carnarvon lamented in April 1874, 'a very evil choice to have to make'.[71]

'Paramountcy' was an attempt to escape from this dilemma. It was an almost infinitely flexible concept which permitted, beyond the limits of formal sovereignty, just as much or as little intervention as seemed necessary; it entailed none of the expensive permanent commitments and often embarrassing legal responsibilities which were consequent upon annexation.

The word and the concept were however also used in a rather different way: to describe a situation like that which prevailed in the Niger Delta. Here Britain had no formal possessions at all; but British interests were protected, and local politics dominated, by informal consular over-rule backed by the energetic use of gunboats.[72]

In either of these situations, the claim to paramountcy was an *exclusive* claim; it contained an implicit demand that other European Powers should refrain from intervening in areas where Britain claimed to exercise this right of informal management. From 'paramountcy' as an expedient in 'native administration' to 'paramountcy' as a means of warning off European competitors, was a short and almost imperceptible step. This step had certainly been taken by 1875, when the Colonial Office was deliberately refraining from piecemeal annexations in the South Pacific lest these, by alerting other Powers, should 'defeat the object and prevent us from *quietly* acquiring paramount influence among the Islands'.[73] Sometimes, indeed, London was prepared to negotiate a recognition of its paramountcy: as in West Africa, where the 1875 territorial-exchange proposals amounted to an offer of the Gambia in return for French recognition of uninterrupted British paramountcy over some two thousand miles of coastline from the river Pongos to Gabon.[74] But more usually London simply consolidated a paramountcy 'quietly' and then when necessary presented it as a *fait accompli*. Thus by 1875 the Foreign Office 'clearly regarded Britain as the paramount Power in the Niger delta'; while British paramountcy through the South African sub-continent was treated as axiomatic.[75]

Paramountcy in yet another form was exercised through Britain's client-states Egypt and Zanzibar, which between them claimed the whole East African coastline from Suez to Mozambique. The extent of their subordination was demonstrated in 1875–6, when London uni-laterally settled an armed clash between them on the Benadir coast. By 1877 London was openly using Egypt as a cat's paw, recognising her sovereignty on the Somali coast on the express condition that this terri-tory should never be ceded to a third Power.[76] In Zanzibar, the uses of paramountcy were more openly and actively expansionist. In 1877–8 the Foreign Office was encouraging the Sultan to extend his formal authority on the mainland with the aid of a British-trained army; and at the same time permitting Consul Kirk to assist the Scottish shipowner Mackinnon to obtain from the Sultan concessions which would have given Mackinnon complete political and economic control of Zanzibar's mainland territories.[77]

By this time, however, a much more far-reaching concept of paramountcy had emerged within certain sections of the British official mind: the view that Britain should aim at becoming the 'paramount Power', not merely in this region of Africa or that, but throughout the entire continent or at least the greater part of it. In May 1877 Sir Robert Morier at Lisbon suggested that Portugal, as well as Egypt and Zanzibar, should be systematically used as a cat's-paw in Africa. If this could be done—and Morier did not think it a difficult task—Britain would 'have it in [her] power to exercise paramount influence over that continent'.[78]

More important than Morier was the Earl of Carnarvon, Colonial Secretary from February 1874 to February 1878. Now best remembered for the fiasco of his South African confederation project and the deadly nickname 'Twitters' that Disraeli pinned upon him, Carnarvon deserves to be taken seriously, if not as a successful statesman, at least as a dedicated imperialist and expansionist. His South African policy was devised not to stave off a non-existent threat from the then weak and unstable Afrikaner states, still less to enable the 'imperial factor' to withdraw. On the contrary, he hoped to consolidate and perpetuate imperial paramountcy in South Africa by imposing the constitutional checks and balances of a federal union upon Cape Colony's enormous economic and (white) demographic preponderance over the smaller states and colonies. That was the fundamental reason why the Cape Premier Molteno opposed 'confederation' so bitterly; for him the only 'natural' development was 'the gradual annexation of the several minor Colonies and States to the Cape'—'the paramount South African colony', as he very significantly called it.[79]

Carnarvon's determination to maintain effective imperial paramountcy in South Africa is reflected in his encouragement of Eastern Cape separatism as a means of weakening Cape Colony's preponderance. A similar motive inspired a Colonial Office project for setting up a vast new province embracing the whole South African hinterland from the Atlantic to Mozambique and ruled directly by London. But Carnarvon's imperial horizon lay far beyond South Africa proper. His eye was already on the fabled riches of Ophir; and he therefore persuaded the Foreign Office to oppose all Portuguese expansion in South-Central Africa.[80] Nor was British paramountcy, actual and potential, confined to southern Africa. In the North it embraced 'Egypt and the country that belongs to Egypt'—at that time the Sudan as far south as Lake Albert. This early version of the Cape-to-Cairo dream left little room for anybody else; as Carnarvon frankly admitted when in December 1876 his attention was drawn to King Leopold's ambition to reach the Congo basin from the eastern seaboard. 'We cannot', he wrote, 'admit rivals in the East or even the central parts of Africa. . . . To a considerable extent, if not entirely, we must be prepared to apply a sort of Munro [sic] doctrine to much of Africa.'[81]

Bismarck spoke even truer than he knew. But Germany was not the only, and not the first Power to react against the 'paramountcy' technique of formally excluding rivals from Britain's informal empire.

B. The French Reaction to British Policy, 1876–83

In February 1876 Benoist d'Azy, the *Directeur des Colonies*, sounded a general alarm at the trend of British policy in Africa:

> Is it not clear that British policy aims at securing control in turn over Zanzibar (where she is pushing armed reconnaissance parties into the interior)? Meanwhile at Natal and at the Cape her explorations and conquests are extending daily. If she is allowed to subjugate Dahomey, the most formidable and warlike state of central Africa, her influence will soon spread over the whole southern portion of that great continent, and we shall eventually find our role restricted to Senegal and Algeria.[82]

The British quarrel with Dahomey was in fact a petty local affair, not greatly approved of by London. And, as it happened, Carnarvon did not encourage annexations in West Africa—though during the exchange negotiations he showed a characteristic appetite for the extension of paramountcy.[83] But the French were not to know this. It was obvious to the French, even before the British occupation of the Transvaal in January 1877, that their secular rival, the greatest maritime and colonial Power on earth, was behaving in an unusually enterprising and aggressive way in both Eastern and Southern Africa. They seem to have had at least an inkling of the cloudy dreams of universal paramountcy which haunted some British policy-makers. French fears interpreted cloudy dreams as settled plans; and there seemed no reason to doubt that West Africa, too, was included in these plans.

On the contrary. The collapse of the territorial exchange negotiations early in 1876 was, as it happened, accompanied and followed by some unusually brisk local action by the British. The designs of the Lagos administration on Porto Novo in Dahomey were no secret. When in February 1876 the British imposed a blockade on Dahomey, this was regarded as the beginning of a forward policy. The blockade was lifted in May 1877; but the French relief was short-lived. In September 1879 Governor Ussher asserted British influence on the Dahomey coast with the aid of a gunboat, and hoisted the Union Jack at a point which interrupted Porto Novo's communications both with the sea and with the French. Away to the north, Governor Rowe, plagued by falling revenues, was by 1877 extending Sierra Leone's political and fiscal control northwards into territory which Brière de l'Isle considered to be French; Brière, having failed effectively to forestall Rowe, thereupon established a military post in territory which Rowe considered to be British.[84]

Rowe also attempted to revive the languishing economy of Sierra Leone by sending native agents to re-open peaceful trading links with the states of the Upper Niger. These missions were naturally very suspect to the French. By 1878 Brière was convinced that the scramble had begun, not only on the coast but in the interior. Thereafter, every British attempt—indeed, every unconfirmed rumour of an attempt—to make informal contact with the interior was interpreted as part of a settled British plan to forestall France in the upper Niger basin, which was by 1879–80 becoming the goal of Paris as well as of Senegal. As usual, the British did just enough to confirm the worst French suspicions. In 1881, in the interests of Sierra Leone trade, an official mission under Administrator Gouldsbury was sent to the interior. It achieved little and led nowhere; but it was naturally interpreted by the French as the first open move in the British 'forward policy' on the upper Niger. By the middle 1880s, with France at war in the Niger basin, these contacts, whether real or imaginary, had become doubly suspect: in 1884 Governor Bourdiaux was convinced that the British were fomenting African resistance; and in 1886 the Quai d'Orsay credited a report that a British agent was installed at Timbuktu.[85]

Until the end of 1879, however, the Quai d'Orsay handled these local quarrels with great restraint. William Waddington, Foreign Minister since 1877, was profoundly convinced that British friendship was essential to the European security of France. In February 1879 he became Prime Minister as well as Foreign Minister; but his team was joined by Jauréguiberry and Freycinet (at Public Works). The two latter ministers at once began to plan the advance into the Niger Sudan; but policy on the Coast did not change for the time being. Even when Freycinet replaced Waddington as Prime Minister and Foreign Minister in December, no sharp change is detectable in coastal diplomacy. Freycinet was not in fact particularly combative towards England in West Africa; but, unlike Waddington, he was neither a trained diplomatist nor a half-English anglophile, and he certainly did less to restrain those who were combative. Rouvier, not yet in office but already very influential, was one of these; but above all there was Jauréguiberry, who was not a French admiral for nothing. From first to last he never wavered in his almost obsessively suspicious anglophobia: 'we have rivals, implacable rivals, who constantly oppose the influence which we already exert in Senegal. They strive to frustrate us in every possible way.' By January 1882, when Freycinet and Jauréguiberry returned to office, these views had made considerable headway even at the Quai d'Orsay. Even before Jauréguiberry had launched his major coastal strategy in January 1883 (and long before there was a quarrel over Egypt), French 'pin-pricks' on the Coast were being accompanied by a much more intransigent diplomatic tone.[86]

It was not only in West Africa that French expansion was triggered off by fears of British encroachment and the extension of British paramountcy. Since the 1860s, the French had not seriously challenged the British preponderance of influence in Madagascar in spite of pressure by the Réunion planters to adopt a more active policy. In July 1881 however, a British naval visit to Madagascar aimed just a little too obviously at encouraging the dominant Hova dynasty to extend its rule throughout the island—as a means, in French eyes, of neutralising French influence with non-Hova groups in the south and west of Madagascar. The French consul, Théodore Meyer, at once warned the Hova Prime Minister not to 'become English'. But Meyer, who had originally been posted to Madagascar because of his conciliatory disposition, was considered by the Ferry government to be unequal to this situation, and in September 1881 he was replaced by the notoriously aggressive Auguste Baudais.[87]

In January 1882 Rouvier, now Minister of Commerce, pressed Gambetta for positive action in Madagascar. The terms in which he did so are significant.

> We cannot oppose too energetically that pretension to rule the waves that the British navy is all too ready to take upon itself ... I am prepared, as I told you in my letter of the 10th, to work out with you the ways and means of a more effective and more direct intervention on our part in the affairs of the great island of Madagascar.[88]

Three days after this letter was written, Gambetta was out of office. But in Madagascar, Baudais was already preparing the way for intervention by raking up old disputes with the Hova. Gambetta's successor Freycinet, far from curbing him, spurred him on, telling him in March 1882 that 'our one and only preoccupation is to guarantee the defence of our rights and interests'.[89] Thus given *carte blanche* to engineer a crisis, Baudais duly did so in May. In December a Hova embassy to Paris rejected terms which amounted to the assertion of French paramountcy in Madagascar. Naval action was initiated in February 1883: François de Mahy, the Deputy for Réunion, happened to be acting Minister of Marine in a three-week stop-gap government; and he seized this opportunity of serving his constituents.[90]

It is true that the French did not reveal their full demands to the Hovas until it became clear that England, with her troubles in Egypt, was most unlikely to intervene. But French policy had been set on a collision course in Madagascar—indeed, the collision had already occurred—while Britain and France were still co-operating closely in Egypt. France began to embark on this course immediately after the British naval visit of 1881. Once again, a British attempt to improve upon the *status quo* had provoked the French to action which led to its speedy collapse.[91]

C. The Apparent Vulnerability of Britain Overseas from c. 1879

The French were provoked to a forward policy in Africa by real or imagined extensions to British paramountcy; they may well have been encouraged in this change of course by the apparent evidence that the British had over-reached themselves and were in serious difficulties overseas. In October 1879 the Governor of Réunion suggested to Jauréguiberry that 'the time had come to re-assert our rights in Madagascar while Great Britain is engaged in so many disastrous wars all over the world'; and Jauréguiberry recommended his views to the 'plus particulière attention' of Waddington at the Quai d'Orsay.[92] This argument is not likely to have had much weight with Waddington. But it certainly impressed Jauréguiberry, one of the two main architects of French expansion and the one who was much the more combative towards England.

Britain certainly suffered spectacular setbacks in 1879. Isandhlwana in January, widely regarded on the Continent as a grave symptom of military decline, was followed in September by the massacre at Kabul. Nor did the impression greatly improve in 1880, with another setback in Afghanistan; or in 1881, with the failure to restore British rule in the Transvaal after the humiliation of Majuba. But there was sounder evidence for Britain's vulnerability than defeats —some of them soon to be redeemed—in 'little wars' overseas. By the late 1870s British naval preponderance, the very foundation of her paramountcy in all its varied forms, was becoming dangerously insecure. According to A. J. Marder, from 1878 that preponderance began to be challenged by intensive French building; and by the early 1880s it had virtually disappeared. By 1882 the British navy was already, and very ominously, outnumbered in first-class ships by the French and German navies combined. By 1884–5 France alone could equal Britain in first-class ships built and building. Worse still, many of the British ships were technologically obsolescent; and the most recent *Admiral* class battleships (building from 1880) were notoriously unsatisfactory in design. British naval officers were well aware of these deficiencies: Admiral Bacon, Admiral Colomb, Admiral Hewett with his sardonic remark at the 1887 Jubilee review—'Most of what you see is mere ullage.'[93] It is difficult to believe that this precarious situation can have passed totally undetected by an able French naval officer, Admiral Jean Jauréguiberry.

D. Salisbury's Attempt to Restore Stability in Africa, 1878–80

In so far as the French were aware of the vulnerability of Britain overseas, they were certainly not wrong. Nor were they entirely misguided, (except, ironically enough, in West Africa) when from 1876 onwards they became suspicious and apprehensive about the general course of British policy in Africa. But in one very important respect they were the victims of a delusion. In February 1878, a year before Jauréguiberry took office, Carnarvon had resigned; and with his departure dreams of universal paramountcy ceased to haunt the British official mind. In April 1878 Salisbury took over the Foreign Office from Derby,[94] who had encouraged the forward policies of Kirk and Mackinnon in East Africa, and had permitted Morier to make the opening moves in his scheme for 'managing' Portugal.[95] Salisbury's policy was sharply focused on Europe and above all on the Near Eastern crisis. He was determined not to be distracted by imperial adventures in Africa; and above all not to be frustrated by African squabbles which might jeopardise Anglo-French co-operation in Europe.[96]

In the interests of his European policy, Salisbury sternly repressed, so far as he was able, all tendencies to annexation or the unilateral extension of paramountcy in Africa. In effect, he was attempting to restore the stability which the behaviour of Carnarvon and Derby had disturbed. In East Africa, he sabotaged Mackinnon's prospective concession by secret instructions to one Dr. Badger, Mackinnon's agent and Arabic interpreter. Morier's machinations were frustrated by slow-motion correspondence and obscure instructions which had by May 1880 reduced the whole affair to 'a dreadful mess'. In West Africa, similar delaying tactics met Colonial Office proposals likely to be un-welcome to France. The Colonial Office murmured at Salisbury's con-stant pressure for conciliatory handling of disputes and for graceful concessions in territorial negotiations; while the full measure of Salisbury's wrath was poured out upon 'insupportable proconsuls' whose excess of zeal fanned the flames that he was striving to quench.[97]

But

The moving finger writes; and having writ,
Moves on ...

It surpassed even Salisbury's great political skill to set the clock back by neutralising the fear and suspicion which British behaviour during the previous years had aroused in those sections of the French official mind traditionally combative to England. Moreover, there were regions where, since no 'civilised' Power was directly involved, Salisbury's writ did not run. The forward moves of 1879 in Zululand and Afghanistan were both, as it happened, local initiatives—the former, indeed, in defiance of instructions from London. But in Paris, they can only have discouraged any disposition to recognise that the British were now reformed characters; and encouraged the tendency to read a sinister significance into the comparatively innocuous British moves in West Africa and Madagascar.

E. The Collapse of the Old System and the Transition to the Scramble, 1883–5

As late as the end of 1882, 'annexationist' instability in tropical Africa was still confined to four comparatively limited areas. These were: Madagascar, which for both geographical and diplomatic regions was an isolated side-show; the Senegal hinterland, where the French were not opposed by any European rival (although they often believed that they were); the northern approaches to the lower Congo, where they were faced only by a private 'Association' and where Jauréguiberry was opposed to territorial annexation;[98] and the West Coast, where Anglo-French competition was indeed brisk, but still a comparatively small-scale affair. However, on the West Coast the French were already planning greatly to extend the scale of their operations, and in the course of 1883–4 the British felt compelled to defend their interests by following suit.[99] But there was still no inherent reason why this instabi-lity should have spread so rapidly that by early 1885 enormous areas of Eastern, Central and Southern Africa had been drawn into the annexationist vortex. Stability collapsed completely when the interven-tion of Germany, and her rapprochement with France in the summer of 1884, ended the traditional Anglo-French *tête-à-tête* in Africa.

This collapse was however hastened by the sorry performance of British diplomacy between 1883 and 1885. In 1880 the Liberals under Gladstone had been returned on a platform of international conciliation and total opposition to imperial expansion. Less than four

years later the informal British hegemony in Africa, which had come to
be regarded almost as a law of nature and which was of course the
unexpressed assumption underlying the policy of colonial self-denial,
had quite suddenly ceased to exist. Moreover, Britain's international
position had deteriorated to a point where even a Palmerstonian government, enjoying (as Gladstone's did not) an unassailable naval preponderance, might well have shrunk from any attempt to re-assert unofficial
empire. The only action possible was to try and rescue something from
the wreckage by the proclamation of protectorates.

   Such a policy was of course most unpalatable to the Liberal
Ministers, who in any case found great difficulty in understanding a
new and totally unexpected situation which made nonsense of their
fundamental assumptions about British policy overseas; and which had
transformed Africa, almost overnight, from a British Tom Tiddler's
Ground to a dangerous and uncharted diplomatic minefield. Not surprisingly, their response was slow, fumbling and confused. As late as
November 1883, Granville at the Foreign Office and Derby at the
Colonial Office were still playing their obsolete 'paramountcy' card
against Bismarck in South Africa. Yet the Cabinet Minute of the same
month, which authorised Consul 'Too-Late' Hewett's treaty-making in
West Africa, seems at least partially to recognise the new situation. A
full year later, however, Gladstone himself flatly refused to recognise it.
He scornfully vetoed Granville's proposal to establish a protectorate on
the Zanzibari mainland of East Africa; and re-asserted an anachronistic
Liberal fundamentalism by denouncing any 'system of annexations
designed . . . to forestall other countries'.[100] No wonder the record of
British diplomacy in Africa between 1883 and 1885 is one of almost
unmitigated defeat.

1. Britain and the Congo, 1883–4: When Duclerc ratified de Brazza's
Congo treaties in November 1882, he had believed that London was
satisfied with his public and private assurances of complete free trade.
But he was mistaken. British trade on the lower Congo was comparable
in value with that on the Niger; and in view of the notorious, and
increasing, protectionism of France in her West African possessions,
Granville had little faith in Duclerc's assurances. He had even less faith
in King Leopold's 'non-descript association' as a possible counterpoise
to France. To safeguard the Congo mouth he therefore turned to
Morier's policy, rejected by Conservative and Liberal ministers alike
since 1878, of securing control through a Portuguese cat's paw.[101]

   It was already dangerously late in the day for a successful exercise
of this kind. The mere opening of the negotiation with Lisbon gave a
further jolt to stability: Duclerc promptly over-rode Jauréguiberry's
order forbidding further French annexations in the Congo region.[102]
Even so, an arrangement recognising Portugal's historical claims at the
Congo mouth, but guaranteeing *de facto* British control, might still
have been a useful diplomatic weapon if it could have been concluded
quickly. But the Foreign Office 'sat down to think of all the things we
can ever want from Portugal in Africa.'[103] The Portuguese, their pride

already hurt by the cat's-paw role assigned to them, resisted these demands. When the treaty was finally signed on 26 February 1884, it was born into a world very different from that in which the negotiations had begun. Both France and King Leopold were by now firmly established in the Congo basin; above all, Bismarck had entered the African scene. France, Germany and a number of minor powers promptly raised detailed objections to the treaty; and on 7 June Bismarck killed it stone-dead by refusing to recognise it in any form.[104] By September 1884 the French, despairing at last of any change of British policy in Egypt, were ready to assist him in bringing the Congo question—and indeed the general question of coastal annexations in Africa—before an international conference. The Berlin Conference simply ignored obsolete British notions about 'informal empire' and 'paramountcy'; and established, for the international recognition of European claims on the African coast, a new criterion of 'effective occupation' which was in itself a very powerful stimulus to further competitive annexation.[105]

2. The Intervention of Bismarck, 1883–5: Bismarck's hostility to Britain in Africa during 1884–5 was the direct result of the provocative incompetence, and worse, with which London had treated his originally modest claim to an unofficial 'sphere' in South-West Africa. As in their rapacious but leisurely negotiation with Portugal, the British at first behaved as if their old informal hegemony were still in full working order; indeed, in November 1883 they attempted to exclude Germany by an assertion of the doctrine of paramountcy. When Bismarck riposted by requesting the production of British title-deeds in South-West Africa, London remained silent for almost six months. When he began to press, the Foreign Office seemed to play hide-and-seek behind the Colonial Office and the Cape Government. Finally in June 1884, after some brutally plain speaking by Bismarck through his son Herbert, Gladstone and Granville agreed not to stand in his way; but meanwhile other Ministers—notably, Derby—were planning to reduce Germany's South-West-African territory to a derisory enclave.[106]

However, Bismarck's intervention in southern Africa posed some exceptionally difficult problems for London. The British found it hard to believe that Bismarck intended to make a major issue out of the notoriously worthless South-West Africa. But in fact he did not do so until the British had both affronted and alarmed him by flourishing their 'Monroe doctrine for Africa' at him.[107] (This doctrine was not only quite inadmissible in itself; if it were admitted in South-West Africa it might also be used to exclude Germany from other African territories of real importance to her.) Again, both in South-West Africa and elsewhere, between the end of 1883 and the middle of 1884 Bismarck moved by almost imperceptible stages from the acquisition of unofficial influence to outright territorial annexation; and, in his justified fear of being forestalled, he deliberately concealed from London the final phases in this evolution.[108] But if the British found Bismarck's intentions and motives hard to fathom, it was at least partly because they were until June 1884 far more preoccupied with Anglo-Cape relations than with Anglo-German relations. In 1883–4 London was more than usually determined not to act as the Cape's cat's-paw in the administration of turbulent and un-remunerative frontier areas. They had just agreed to take over a Basutoland that the Cape was patently unable to control; and some Cape politicians wished to burden the 'imperial factor' with two more problem areas, Bechuanaland and the Transkei. As for South-West Africa, in the 1870s the Cape itself might have been willing to annex— indeed, in 1876 Carnarvon had held out Cape annexation in this region as a reward for good political behaviour in the 'confederation' question. But by 1883, thanks to phylloxera, the Great Depression and the mili-tary expenditure consequent on a 'firm native policy', the Cape was insolvent. In these distressing circumstances the Cape Ministers thought it the plain duty of London to protect South African interests—if necessary, at British expense.[109]

As late as October 1883 the Colonial Office was inclined to treat South-West Africa as useless, especially as the Cape was now unwilling to annex. Scanlen, the Cape Premier, who was in London, was not however asking necessarily for Imperial annexation; but he did in-sistently press for 'a South African Monroe Doctrine, and all European Powers . . . given to understand that it must be "hands off" '. Unless London was prepared to meet South African wishes to at least this extent, it was most unlikely that the Cape government could be brought to take a less negative view of its responsibilities in other frontier areas, especially Bechuanaland. Moreover, the Foreign Office was uneasy at the prospect of a German presence so close to a strategic centre of empire. Hence the decision in mid-November to play the paramountcy card.[110] When on 31 December Bismarck trumped it by asking for the evidence, the Foreign Office delayed its reply not only because it had no valid reply to make, but also to give the Colonial Office time to cajole or worry the Cape into an annexation which would forestall Bismarck without burdening London.

Then, between late April and early June 1884, just when Bismarck was becoming really pressing and Granville was seeking to hide behind the Cape Government, Berlin learned not only that Cape Town had at last decided to annex South-West Africa, but that London was about to make a preclusive move in West African regions where Germany had serious commercial interests. In British eyes Consul Hewett's mission to West Africa was an anti-French rather than an anti-German move, a rather belated response to the French attempts of 1883 to acquire protectorates in the Niger delta and the Cameroons. To Bismarck it was another step in a deliberate campaign of underhand obstruction.[111] He retaliated not only by forestalling Hewett in Togo and the Cameroons but by attacking Britain at a point of obvious weakness in Africa, and a point where he could be sure of obtaining French support—the Anglo-Portuguese Congo treaty.

Bismarck was however after bigger game than a mere treaty. As he had explained to the French on 14 May, his goal was nothing less than the destruction of the British unofficial empire by international agreement. In August the sharp deterioration of Anglo-French relations in Egypt brought Bismarck the support of France for this plan.[112] But at the Berlin Conference (November 1884–February 1885) Bismarck's attack upon British unofficial empire hardly needed French support, because the British made no attempt to defend their position by contesting the principle of 'effective occupation'. Such a defence would indeed have been a difficult task. 'Unofficial empire' was a tender plant that could flourish only in the shades of legal and political ambiguity, and was likely to wither in the glare of formal international scrutiny; and the British in fact confined their resistance to a rather pettifogging attempt to whittle down the juridical and administrative implications of 'effective occupation' in protectorates. But this apparently prudent behaviour was not prompted by any real grasp of the situation. The British negotiators were exclusively pre-occupied with minimising the administrative 'burdens' entailed by a Protectorate, and seem to have been quite unaware that the Berlin provisions for formal notification and effective occupation (however attenuated) in themselves wrote the epitaph of unofficial empire. As late as 16 January 1885 the Foreign Office sought to impress Bismarck by a merely historical justification of the British hegemony in the Zanzibari dominions. And even Percy Anderson hailed it as 'a triumph' when Bismarck ultimately accepted— as well he might—the British 'minimal' position on the responsibilities imposed by 'effective occupation' on a protecting Power.[113]

In 1885, when Britain was further distracted by disaster in the Sudan and a major confrontation with Russia in Central Asia, Bismarck showed what he thought of historical arguments for paramountcy by almost effortlessly destroying, through pressure on Zanzibar, the British hegemony on the East African coast and forcing London to share the mainland on the new basis of effective occupation.[114] He thus opened up a new focus of competitive instability, which was soon to extend both northward to the Upper Nile and southward towards Cecil Rhodes' 'sphere of aspiration' between Lakes Tanganyika and Nyasa. Only in Zanzibar itself, and in southern Africa where Britain had not only a strategic position to defend, but settlers' aspirations to satisfy, did unofficial empire continue to exist. A further German offensive in South Africa, in particular, would have aroused an implacable and permanent British hostility, which Bismarck had no intention of incurring. He therefore refrained from attempting to extend South-West Africa across the Cape's northern hinterland; and, once London had yielded in the Cameroons, he not only withdrew his claim at St. Lucia Bay on the Zululand coast but in March 1885 secretly undertook to make no further claims between Natal and Delagoa Bay.[115] For all his detestation of 'preclusive imperialism', Bismarck was constrained to permit its survival in the very region where he had first attacked it.

Elsewhere in Africa, however, Bismarck's intervention had destroyed the last vestiges of informal British hegemony. The former stable system had been replaced by a very unstable system—multiple competition, sanctified and intensified by the new doctrine of effective occupation, along the whole eastern and western coastlines of tropical Africa. Coastal annexations bred hinterland disputes; and as, by convention, the 'effective occupation' criterion was soon extended from the coast to the interior, the foci of instability on the coast tended to spread inland until they coalesced. In the absence of successful African resistance, nothing short of the total partition of the Continent could now re-create a comparatively stable system in Africa.[116]

3. The Emergence of the Congo State, 1884–5: Over a broad zone of Equatorial Africa, from 10 degrees north to about 12 degrees south, this rapid extension of competitive instability to the interior was promoted by a special factor—the emergence and political behaviour of King Leopold's Independent Congo State.

Duclerc's light-hearted ratification of de Brazza's Congo treaties in November 1882 had forced Leopold at once to revise radically his plans for a purely commercial monopoly in Central Africa. Once de Brazza had, as Leopold rather quaintly put it, 'introduced politics' into the Congo basin, it was clear that anything less than an internationally recognised sovereignty would be unable to survive. Already by the end of October 1882 Leopold was instructing Stanley to obtain the full surrender of soverign rights in the local treaties he made.[117]

But it was a far cry indeed from treaties with petty African chiefs to European recognition of a 'sovereignty' derived from such instruments. Moreover, Leopold had not only France but Britain to contend with; and the British sponsorship of the Portuguese claims at the Congo mouth, their riposte to Duclerc's ratification, was even more dangerous to Leopold than the French encroachments. The King fought back by attempted sabotage of the Anglo-Portuguese negotiations, not least through its British opponents, who included men as influential as Kirk and Mackinnon; and by deceptive promises of complete free trade in his new state. He failed to prevent the signature of the Anglo-Portuguese treaty; however, a transatlantic propaganda campaign through his American associates brought him in April 1884 the useful though far from decisive gain of United States political recognition.[118]

In the same month Leopold, after disquieting the French by dropping hints of a possible cession of his rights to Britain, disarmed Jules Ferry's opposition and gained French recognition by granting to France the right of first refusal (*droit de préférence*) should the 'International Association of the Congo' dispose of its territory.[119] In June, Bismarck's outright opposition to the Anglo-Portuguese treaty relieved Leopold of the immediate threat from England. At the opening of the Berlin Conference King Leopold's 'Association', though still unrecognised by the Conference itself and represented only through agents 'planted' in the Belgian and United States delegations, was already in a very strong position: a week previously (8 November 1884), Germany had recognised its flag as that of a 'friendly state'. For Bismarck, with his very genuine anxiety for free trade in Africa, recognition of the 'Association' was an admirable way of restricting French protectionism in the Congo basin without incurring an embarrassing diplomatic conflict with France; while the French raised no objection, confident that Leopold's enterprise would soon collapse and that they would inherit it through their *droit de préférence*.[120]

The German recognition placed the British in a dilemma. Their delegates at Berlin, especially Percy Anderson, well understood that to refuse British recognition would incur Bismarck's extreme displeasure, and that to oppose Leopold would now be to play into the hand of the French. But the Foreign Office still intensely resented Leopold's having granted France the right of pre-emption—'a shabby and mischievous trick'; and was scandalised at the prospect of recognising a 'state' whose constitution and boundaries were alike unknown. It took Bismarck's threat of opposition on the Niger to extort British recognition in December 1884.[121] Leopold had not only exploited the Anglo-French rivalry with great skill; he had also convinced Bismarck (and this was crucial) that his Congo Association offered a means of frustrating the 'preclusive imperialism' of the British without admitting the hardly less unwelcome protectionism of the French.

The fantastically far-flung frontiers of the new state were then established with surprising ease. In August 1884 Leopold had submitted to Bismarck frontiers which embraced 'an immense quadrilateral including . . . all central Africa, the very core of the continent'.[122] When the French, happy with their right of pre-emption, raised no objection to these frontiers, Bismarck concurred. For precisely the same reason, in February 1885 Paris recognised frontiers which in the far interior included an enormous southward extension of the August 1884 claim. In August 1885 these new frontiers, with some further extensions in the far south-east, were communicated to the signatory Powers of the Berlin Act, including Britain. London, especially in view of the French *droit de préférence*, had every interest in restricting Congolese territorial extension; the Foreign Office nevertheless accepted these claims without argument! It was August; Percy Anderson was on holiday; by a 'stupid blunder' in the Office the proposed boundaries of the Congo Free State were confused with those (which London had already recognised) of the Congo Free Trade Area.[123]

In this way an enormous European sovereignty was created in 'the very core' of Africa, a sovereignty that approached the hinterlands of almost all the other partitioning Powers. Its mere existence meant a vast increase in the area of active competition and therefore of instability. Thanks to Leopold's policy and personality, these effects were felt powerfully and almost immediately. Leopold had long been convinced that overseas possessions—the more the better—were essential to the future prosperity, perhaps even the viability, of his small, thickly populated and highly industrialised kingdom. But his appetite for African territory, rational enough in origin, was by the later 1880s already an obsession, almost a mania. His vast territories of 1885, of which he then actually controlled only a minute proportion, seemed to him a very poor share of the African cake. As early as 1887 he was reaching out towards the Upper Nile; indeed, his ambitions knew no frontiers short of the Mediterranean and the Indian Ocean.[124] The other partitioning Powers sometimes paused in their career of annexation when faced with the daunting problems of actually administering the territories they had already acquired on paper.[125] King Leopold's more robust constitution never suffered from this 'post-annexation hangover'. Even when in the early 1890s the Congo State threatened to bankrupt him, his appetite for territory remained as ravenous as ever.[126]

VI: The Scramble for Africa, 1885–99

A. North of the Zambezi: Strategy, Diplomacy, 'Myth' and Prestige

In the middle period of the partition, from about 1886 to about 1893, King Leopold's restless expansion was certainly the main force driving the scramble in north-central Africa and the western basin of the Upper Nile; and a very important force in south-central Africa. It was certainly a far more potent force than the Egyptian question. Here the Quai d'Orsay, its rapprochement with Germany disrupted by the mood of *revanchiste* chauvinism of which General Boulanger was the inadequate symbol, was pursuing an increasingly moderate policy and rejecting the temptation to intervene on the Upper Nile; while the active French colonialists were distracted from the Nile Valley by the distant gleam of Lake Chad.[127]

Leopold's career of expansion, and his primacy in the central Africa scramble, were however abruptly terminated by successful French and German opposition to the Anglo-Congolese Upper Nile Agreement of May 1894. Leopold was forced to relinquish almost all of the Upper Nile territories which the British, hoping to use him as a buffer against France, had leased to him.[128] Leopold did not of course abandon his quest for further territory—far from it;[129] but he made no more territorial gains, and was henceforth to be little more than a perturbing influence of secondary importance to the scramble. In the summer of 1894 he was decisively outclassed by the more active commitment of the heavyweights—Britain, France and Germany—within his 'spheres of aspiration'.

The Anglo-Congolese Agreement had intensely irritated French opinion by its provocative flaunting of British 'rights' on the Upper Nile, and it led very rapidly to a reversal of French priorities as between Lake Chad and the Nile Valley. The Chad Plan, with its 'mythical' economic vision of 'a vast domain which it will be ours to colonise and make profitable',[130] was not of course abandoned; indeed, in 1897–8 some of its repercussions were to generate dangerous Anglo-French friction in West Africa. But from June 1894, when Eugène Etienne told the Chamber that in the Anglo-Congolese Agreement 'c'est la question égyptienne qui s'ouvre ... devant vous', French opinion, and the French official mind, became increasingly committed to the goal of restoring French prestige by a threat to the Nile waters which would force Britain to 're-open the Egyptian question'.[131] In August 1894 the obstructive presence of King Leopold on the south-western approaches to the Upper Nile, with which French diplomacy had been ineffectively fumbling ever since 1891, was swept away almost overnight. In November the Upper Nile strategy, which had in 1893 been the unauthorised move of a junior minister (Delcassé), became the official policy of France. And if by the spring of 1895 this strategy had already lost much of its momentum, later in that year Marchand's personal initiative sufficed to get it moving again on the long trail to Fashoda.[132]

British imperialism north of the Zambezi, from 1895 down to the fall of Salisbury in 1892, had been almost entirely an exercise in the diplomatic defence of East African areas which were sensitive either strategically or because they were already of importance to British interest-groups which it would have been politically hazardous to ignore. Strategically, the key areas were Zanzibar; and the Upper Nile, with its approach through Uganda where British missionaries and (from 1888) Mackinnon's East African Company were already active. But Salisbury did not have much to give away in the area between Lakes Nyasa and Tanganyika, where there was already a strong missionary interest, and which had by 1889 become the 'frontier' of a Cecil Rhodes whose dissatisfaction could increasingly embarrass the 'imperial factor' in South Africa.[133]

In all these areas Germany was the competitor; but from 1886 to 1889 her competition was not very active. Bismarck had become disillusioned when his colonies turned out to be more productive of expense and political embarrassment than of any tangible advantage. Moreover, the rise of *Boulangisme* in France and a new bout of instability in the Balkans had prompted an Anglo-German rapprochement which African squabbles could not be permitted to disrupt. But those very sections of German opinion which normally supported Bismarck most strongly did not share his views on Africa. By 1889 they were disquietingly loud in complaint against his refusal to compete in Uganda and his 'passivity' in the face of Rhodes' encroachments (through Johnston) in the Nyasa–Tanganyika region. When in October 1889 Bismarck declared a protectorate over the Benadir coast (worthless in itself, but with a hinterland extending to the Upper Nile) he was evidently securing *matière d'échange* to improve his chances of satisfying colonialist demands in the forthcoming hard bargaining with London.[134]

When Bismarck fell in March 1890 his immediate successors were only marginally more favourable to *Kolonialpolitik*; and, having refused to renew the 'Reinsurance Treaty' with Russia, they were even more anxious than Bismarck for a friendly African settlement with Britain. But they were far less capable than Bismarck of keeping colonialist enthusiasm in check. Salisbury faced similar difficulties. His domestic political situation was precarious; the disputed areas in Africa were either strategically vital or else the special interest of some influential pressure group. Having almost nothing to give away in Africa, in June 1890 he cut the knot by giving away Heligoland, correctly guessing that Wilhelm II's naval enthusiasm was even greater than his colonial enthusiasm.[135] A month later he bought off French opposition in East Africa by a lavish concession of West African 'light land', which

enabled the French Chad Plan to go ahead comparatively undisturbed
by diplomatic complications until 1893.[136]

In the Anglo-German negotiations, Salisbury had been compelled
by political circumstances to provide not only for strategic security at
Zanzibar and on the Upper Nile, but for the acquisitive sub-
imperialisms of Rhodes and even of the normally insignificant
Mackinnon.[137] But he himself still regarded African territory as of little
intrinsic value. During the negotiation he showed himself much more
anxious to limit German expansion than to claim an explicitly British
'sphere'; and he could not refrain from jibes both public and private at
mythical El Dorados and the absurdity of paper partitions of unexplored
wildernesses whose very lakes might turn out to be mere 'beds of
rushes'.[138]

Rosebery, his successor at the Foreign Office, was much more
positively concerned with 'pegging out claims for the future'; and by
1894 Percy Anderson of the African Department had developed an
acquisitiveness which was by no means confined to strategically essential
regions. In September 1894, with the Anglo-Congolese Agreement in
ruins behind them, the British attempted to negotiate an Upper Nile
settlement directly with the French; the attempt failed partly at least
because they refused to make the territorial sacrifices in West Africa
which even Anderson admitted might be necessary to 'keep France
entirely off the Nile'. This failure to define priorities as between acquisition in West Africa and strategy in the Nile Valley re-appeared in
1897–8 as a major personal and departmental conflict at the very heart
of British policy-making, when Salisbury, his eye already fixed on the
Upper Nile, tried in vain to prevent Chamberlain from threatening
France with war over obscure villages in West Africa.[139]

Rosebery's failure to reach agreement with France in 1894 was
the more serious because he had since 1892 allowed Anglo-German
relations to deteriorate seriously both in Europe and in Africa. In
Europe, Berlin suspected that Rosebery was planning to transfer
entirely to Germany the burden of defending Austrian interests at the
Straits. In Africa, misunderstandings and disputes on minor questions,
against the background of a growing colonial appetite in the German
official mind, provoked both Berlin and London to mutual retaliation by
increasingly vigorous African pin-pricks. By the beginning of 1894, the
Wilhelmstrasse had convinced itself that British policy in Africa was
systematically hostile; hence the bitter German opposition to the Anglo-
Congolese Agreement in the summer of 1894.[140] When Salisbury returned to office in July 1895, relations were so unfriendly that he felt
unable to resume his former policy of 'leaning towards' the Triple
Alliance. Instead, he sought to improve relations with both France and
Russia. With Russia he had little success. But by early 1896 relations
with France were for a moment better than they had ever been since
the early 1880s; so good, indeed, that Berlin was already being haunted
by the spectre of a general Anglo-French entente.[141]

This development was sharply halted by the crushing Ethiopian
victory over Italy at Adowa in March 1896. For Italy, and for Italy's

position as a worth-while partner in the Triple Alliance, this was a major crisis. As Salisbury fully recognised, for Britain 'to sit quite still while [the Italians] were being crushed' would have been interpreted in Berlin as a final and definitive desertion of the Triple Alliance, and an openly hostile gesture with implications far outside Africa. Forced to choose between a French entente which was fundamentally precarious so long as the Egyptian dispute remained unsettled, and a resumption of closer relations with the Triplice, he chose the latter. He therefore made the minimal advance into the northern Sudan for which the Italians were asking—ostensibly to distract the Mahdists from attacking the Italian outpost at Kassala, really as a simple gesture of solidarity. But this gesture contained a built-in guarantee of good faith; for, as the Germans had expected, the Anglo-French rapprochement did not survive it.[142]

The 'Anglo-Egyptian' advance into the Sudan in March 1896 was (unlike 'Germany's first bid for colonies') in origin almost entirely a move in European policy. But thanks to Kitchener's ambitions, and the stiff resistance of the Mahdists which ultimately compelled the commitment of British troops, the minimal advance of March 1896 gradually developed into a campaign for total reconquest. On 2 September 1898 Kitchener annihilated the Mahdist army and state outside Omdurman. Seventeen days later he confronted Marchand at Fashoda; and enabled Salisbury, whose diplomacy had been preparing for the crisis since the beginning of the year, to win the great Nile strategy prize-fight by a knock-out.[143]

At Fashoda, however, far more than defensive strategy was at stake. Defensive strategy did not dictate that, under implicit threat of war and as a preliminary to any negotiation, the French should agree to withdraw from the *whole* of the Upper Nile basin; still less did it dictate the enormous British territorial acquisitions made under the transparent fig-leaf of an Anglo-Egyptian 'condominium'. But France at Fashoda was attempting to thwart Britain's will in a 'sphere' where she had claimed a monopoly of influence since 1890, and where she had just victoriously concluded her most serious war since the Crimea. The French pretensions must therefore not only be crushed, but be totally and unequivocally crushed. Moreover, British opinion, especially in Salisbury's own party, was insisting that spectacular victory be crowned by equally spectacular acquisition. This was the 'New Imperialism' with a vengeance; and Salisbury, at heart still the sceptical and pragmatic strategist, had little sympathy with it. He staved off, as diplomatically undesirable, the strong demand for a formal protectorate over Egypt itself. And his personal preference would certainly have been for a mode of proceeding less humiliating to France, and the concession, as a sop, of some strategically harmless area of the Bahr al-Ghazal.[144]

Yet Salisbury recognised, no less than the most chauvinistic of his contemporaries, that Fashoda was far more than an exceptionally dramatic move in the partition-of-Africa 'game'. At Fashoda, to the discomfiture of the French, Britain in fact ceased to treat the partition as a game. Not only was the security of the Nile waters at stake but, in

British eyes, the relative rank and 'weight' of Britain and France as
Powers. Fashoda itself, squalid and pestilential, was as Queen Victoria
remarked, a 'miserable object' to bring two countries to the brink of war.
Ten years earlier it would have been a sitting target for Salisbury's
'flouts and jeers'. But in September and October 1898 Salisbury was
not joking.[145]

B. South of the Zambezi. Local Conflicts and the 'Imperial Factor'— An Old Song in a New Key

In southern Africa, a local scramble in the interior, which the 'imperial
factor' sometimes attempted to control, had been in existence long
before the collapse of general British hegemony and the onset of international competition. In spite of Bismarck's intervention in 1884–5, the
scramble in the South continued to be driven mainly by the interaction
of the local and imperial forces; and the fluctuating patterns of European
diplomacy, so inextricably bound up with the scramble north of the
Zambezi, were rarely of more than peripheral importance.

Bismarck's intervention has sometimes been credited with the
British advance into Bechuanaland in 1885. But this key area, where
the Cape's 'road to the north' was threatened by an Afrikaner advance
westward from the Transvaal, had long been an acute *local* problem—
so acute that it had already prompted a rather half-hearted political
intervention by the 'imperial factor' in support of the London Convention of February 1884. In the summer of 1884, well before the threat
of German encroachment had become apparent, London was already
making contingency plans for military intervention against the tiny
'freebooter republics' of Stellaland and Goshen, the political spearheads
of the Afrikaner advance. What the German threat did do was to hasten
a decision which could in any case hardly have been postponed indefinitely; and to ensure that the military force despatched was strong
enough to guarantee instant success.[146]

Once Bismarck had in March 1885 renounced all claim on Zululand, German intervention in southern Africa was minimal until the
mid-1890s; any prospect of German support for Portugal's 'archaeo-
logical' claims in south-central Africa receded with the improvement in
Anglo-German relations in the later 1880s and disappeared with the
Anglo-German Agreement of July 1890. In 1891 Salisbury was able
to impose his own settlement upon an isolated Portugal.[147] Between
1893 and 1896, in the 'era of bad feelings' between Britain and
Germany, Berlin sought to challenge British paramountcy by intervention in Anglo-Transvaal relations. But in the absence of support from
any other major Power, above all France, this policy tended merely to
stiffen British resistance; and after the fiasco of the 'Kruger Telegram'
it was gradually abandoned.[148] Even as a stimulus to the local power-
struggle, German intervention was largely a work of supererogation.
South African conflicts did not depend upon European incitement for
their lusty development.

The significant new forces which emerged south of the Zambesi
after 1885 were both home-grown. One was the spectacular gold-

nourished rise of Paul Kruger's South African Republic, whose development threatened the local economic and political preponderance of Cape Colony; and therefore, if local 'paramountcy' were ultimately to migrate from Cape Town to Pretoria, the continued existence of an effective 'imperial factor' in South Africa. The other was Cecil Rhodes' unlimited expansion to the north, a 'personal' sub-imperialism far transcending the traditional Cape goal of local paramountcy, but yet serving it: 'Rhodesia' was expected to develop rapidly into a strong economic and political counterpoise to Kruger's republic, and its failure to do so was partly responsible for tempting Rhodes to rasher policies.[149]

A limit was set to Rhodes' territorial expansion by the Anglo-German Agreement of 1890, by King Leopold's prior occupation of the Katanga, and by the Anglo-Portuguese settlement of 1891. Abandoning, under extreme pressure from Salisbury, the armed invasion of southern Mozambique which he had already launched,[150] Rhodes behaved from 1891 to 1894 as a fairly orthodox exponent of Cape 'paramountcy'. The Cape Dutch were willing enough to see a Cape-dominated closer union in South Africa, provided it could be achieved without open conflict with the Boer Republics. With the support of Hofmeyr and the Afrikaner Bond, Rhodes attempted to achieve it by harassing and cajoling Kruger into a rudimentary South African Common Market These tactics made no impression on the President's adamant opposition to the slightest erosion of his independence and freedom of action.[151] As an additional and possibly decisive means of pressure, Rhodes wished to acquire from Portugal the Transvaal's outlet to the sea at Lourenço Marques; but German diplomatic opposition forced London to veto this plan. Towards the end of 1894 Rhodes, already a mortally sick man, decided to hurry matters along by the active subversion of Kruger's state through its Uitlander population. From mid-1895, with Chamberlain at the Colonial Office, the 'imperial factor' connived at this policy, not least as an insurance against the much-feared domination of the Transvaal by Germany.[152]

In January 1896, Rhodes over-reached himself with the fiasco of the Jameson Raid; and having thus forfeited the confidence of the Cape Dutch and become a mere embarrassment to London, was forced temporarily to retire from the game. But the Cape, with its politics in confusion and its white inhabitants increasingly polarised into 'Boers' and 'British', was in no shape to continue the campaign against Kruger. The 'imperial factor'—Chamberlain and Milner—then took up the struggle directly, at first by diplomatic pressure, ultimately by armed force. But though the imperial factor replaced the Cape, it was no longer playing the Cape's game. With the Cape politically crippled, and the South African Republic soon (it was hoped) to be cowed or conquered, the way seemed clear for Milner to work towards a more direct form of imperial control than even Carnarvon had dreamed of.[153]

Portuguese imperialism in southern Africa is of course a different story. It was an imperialism of pure prestige—economically the Portuguese colonies were a grievous burden upon a grossly 'under-developed' home country. It was stimulated by the contempt and rapacity with

which the other partitioners, and above all the British, treated Portugal
as an imperial Power. To most politically conscious Portuguese, national
self-esteem—indeed, even national identity—seems to have been bound
up with the maintenance of the Lusitanian imperial heritage. Portugal
reacted not only by re-asserting her grip on an almost derelict empire,
but by developing a will to imperial power which outlasted that of all
her European-based competitors.[154]

C. North and South. The Scramble and the 'New Imperialism'

The wide variety of motivations for the scramble in the north and its
intimate connection with the mainstream of Great-Power diplomacy,
contrast sharply with the simpler, more provincial pattern in the south
—no more, fundamentally, than a variation on themes which had
already been announced in the 1870s.

But in spite of these contrasts, there is one feature common to both
north and south: as the scramble develops, the competitors bring to it
an ever increasing strength of political, military and even emotional
commitment, an increasing recklessness, an increasing willingness to
resort to force or threats of force. In the 1880s British policy in South
Africa sought to compose rather than to foment disputes; in the late
1890s it progressed from the clandestine encouragement of subversion
to an aggressive war which Salisbury, for one, believed to be mistaken
and unnecessary.[155] In the Nile Valley the French policy-makers moved
from straightforward diplomatic manoeuvre to a strategy of attempted
ecological blackmail which was at once a wild political gamble and a
practical impossibility. In Germany, Bismarck's coolly pragmatic
approach to colonies gave way in the 1890s to an official conviction
that Germany's future greatness depended, to some extent at least, on
further expansion overseas; and therefore to pressure for repartition.
Germany's aggressive behaviour towards Britain in Africa in the middle
1890s was a genuinely imperialist phenomenon and not merely, or even
mainly, a device to worry London into a closer relationship with the
Triple Alliance.[156]

The increase in military commitment is no less striking. Britain's
first South African war consisted of a few petty skirmishes; her second
was her greatest military effort since the Napoleonic wars. Baratieri led
four brigades to defeat at Adowa in 1896; Kitchener led six to victory
at Omdurman in 1898. A force at least as large was deployed by French
civilian policy-makers against Madagascar in 1895.[157] Smaller, but still
considerable forces were launched by the French against Dahomey in
1892-4 and against Rabih Zubair in 1901. In 1898 Chamberlain
deployed over two thousand men under Lugard to resist French encroachments in 'Nigeria'. Leopold's last great throw on the Upper Nile,
an expedition of over three thousand men under Dhanis in 1896, was at
the time incomparably the strongest European force ever despatched
to this region.[158]

Fin-de-siècle emotional commitment to African competition sometimes approached the hysterical. In the disastrous opening weeks of
the second South African war, the British reaction could hardly have

been stronger had British rather than Afrikaner independence been at stake in the struggle. During the Fashoda crisis many Frenchmen—and especially many Parisians—behaved almost as if the very national existence of France was being threatened; the tendency to link the disavowed Marchand[159] with the martyred Joan of Arc speaks for itself. But these extreme reactions were not entirely inappropriate; they reflected the fact that, in north and south alike, the partition had at last ceased to be a diplomatic and strategic game. At Fashoda, a French forcing play in this game failed to pay off when Britain refused to abide by the rules. 'Jamais on ne prévit qu'on pût être amené à quitter le terrain diplomatique'[160]—this rueful admission goes to the heart of the matter. A similar fate befell Kruger's defensive strategy of calculated delay and carefully-rationed concessions to the Uitlanders. Unlike Kruger, who had no alternative but to fight when the game ran out, Delcassé at Fashoda was from the outset determined to avoid carrying the struggle beyond the 'terrain diplomatique'. But it was by no means a foregone conclusion that French opinion would permit him to back down.[161] Fashoda suggests that had any other considerable areas of Africa still been the subject of active dispute, the great imperialist wars of early modern times might have had a bloody epilogue. As it was, in 1911 Italy went to war with Turkey for the prize of Libya; and in the same year Berlin imposed upon France a minor repartition in the Congo basin by at least appearing to threaten war over Morocco. Kiderlen, the author of the Agadir crisis, then looked forward to the ultimate acquisition of the Belgian Congo—presumably by similar tactics.[162]

In the later 1890s this growing intensity of commitment underlay the immediate 'causes' of decisions to annex or to advance, and drove on the scramble with increasing speed and mounting violence. This development was of course partly a feed-back from the actual events in Africa, the all too melodramatic 'steeplechases' and 'incidents' which periodically excited the newspaper-reading public. But there was more than this to the creation and diffusion of an aggressively imperialistic climate of opinion; and in the exploration of this phenomenon the 'background theories' at last find a useful part to play.

1. Imperialism as an Economic Imperative: As a conviction in the official mind, economic motives for imperial expansion were even more compelling in the 1890s than a decade earlier. In spite of the pother about 'new markets', annexations in the 1880s were often no more than expedients to safeguard specialised and very limited sectors of the home economy; or at most the taking up of admittedly speculative options. But to a Rosebery, a Chamberlain or an Etienne, and to some elements at least of the German official mind in the 1890s, 'pegging out claims' to African estates was an imperative necessity for a Great Power that wished to remain great: a Power unable to exploit the resources (including, according to some French imperialists, the military man-power) of overseas estates would fatally handicap itself in the inter-national struggle for existence during the twentieth century.[163] For

Chamberlain, at least, 'imperialism was . . . not only a form of survival. It was *the* sole policy for survival'.[164] True, Jules Ferry had expressed rather similar views in the 1880s,[165] and Leopold II had adapted them even earlier to the supposed necessities of a highly industrialised and thickly populated minor Power. But at that time these had been rather isolated voices. A decade later the crucial importance of 'pegging out claims' was hardly contested except by the diminishing band of those who opposed colonial expansion in all its forms.

2. *The Popularisation of Imperialism as the Creed of the 'Nationalistic Masses'*: If 'the masses' be defined as the manual workers in agriculture, industry and 'services' (who comprised, in widely varying proportions, the great majority of the population of all the imperialist Powers) it seems very doubtful whether they were enthusiastic imperialists at any time in this period. There seems to be no evidence that British farm labourers or continental peasants were enthusiasts for colonial expansion. As for the industrial masses, such evidence as there is suggests that in France, Germany and Italy they were always indifferent and sometimes hostile.[166] Only in Britain can a case be made out for the existence of an imperialist urban proletariat. But it does not seem a strong case. Music-hall songs and isolated bouts of chauvinist hysteria ('mafficking') are not very cogent evidence.[167] The mushroom growth of the halfpenny press, much of it stridently imperialist in tone, is at first sight a more convincing argument; but these newspapers, 'written for office-boys by office-boys', found their readership at least as much among the sub-professional and white-collar classes as among the 'masses' proper.

There is on the other hand very convincing evidence that between 1885 and 1900 imperialism made many converts among manufacturers and businessmen, public officials both major and minor, academics, teachers and professional men, and miscellaneous white-collar employees. In Germany this development seems to have been unusually precocious. By the middle 1880s, when in England it had hardly begun, it is already clearly discernible.[168] In France, however, the conversion of the middle classes was slower and far less complete. Convinced colonialists were never more than a small minority; but some of them were exceptionally well placed to influence the course of French policy.[169]

In England, imperialism made a much slower start than in Germany, thanks to the far greater strength of liberalism with its faith in international comity and peaceful economic competition, and its conviction that formal empire was both immoral and unprofitable. These convictions remained strong among certain elements of the liberal rank and file; but by 1898 the official attitude of the Liberal Party, which had by now dropped both Morley and Harcourt as potential leaders, was hardly less imperialistic than that of the Conservatives.[170] Moreover, during the 1890s imperialism had not only acquired a host of middle-class converts, but had made a virtually complete conquest of the central and local ruling élites, from the Court and the armed services to the

City and the Chambers of Commerce of the great provincial towns.[171] Above all it had become the unquestioned orthodoxy of the schools which catered for the 'Establishment' and its middle-class auxiliaries. Nor was imperialist indoctrination of the young confined to the hours of formal instruction. Henty, Rider Haggard and the *Boys' Own Paper* saw to that.[172]

3. Social Darwinism: This creed was being preached in the 1880s; but at that time, in France and Britain at least, it was still heresy rather than orthodoxy. In July 1885 Jules Ferry provoked uproar in the Chamber when he attempted to justify colonisation by invoking the 'rights' of 'superior' over 'inferior' races.[173] Nor does it seem likely that Benjamin Kidd's *Social Evolution* would have been a best-seller had it been published in 1884 rather than in 1894. By the 1890s, however, Social Darwinism was a strong competitor to 'liberalism' (however defined) as the conventional wisdom of the British 'educated classes'.[174] It was an important influence on certain key policy-makers: Rhodes and Milner explicitly regarded themselves as Social Darwinists, Rosebery and Chamberlain were at least fellow-travellers. Even Salisbury's coolly analytical mind did not remain unaffected by the prevailing 'climate of opinion'; from 1895 he was thinking in terms of 'living' and 'dying' nations.[175] Social Darwinism was not of course confined to Britain. It was at least equally widespread and influential in Germany, where it could graft itself easily enough on to certain established habits of thought—notably that which saw German history as the struggle of the *Volk* to extend its territory and achieve political unification in the face of alien opposition from both East and West. Its most important German exponent, the biologist Ernst Haeckel, found a large ready-made readership when in 1899 he published his major work *Die Welträtsel*.[176]

The importance of Social Darwinism lay not only in its assertion of the right, and indeed the duty, of the 'superior' white race to dominate and exploit the 'inferior' coloured races. Conflict *between* European nations, also—and very significantly—called 'races', was similarly equated with the biological struggle between species. Success in conflict, in any conflict, was therefore the only thing that really mattered; the intrinsic importance of the actual bone of contention was a secondary consideration. Seen in this light, disputes about even the most un-promising African territories were of 'world-historical' significance. Above all, Social Darwinism preached the supreme importance of the 'struggle' itself as the sole mechanism of progress and evolution, as the means by which the 'higher' races rose to yet greater heights. It was 'the fiery crucible out of which comes the finer metal'[177] To shrink or withdraw from the struggle was therefore, if possible, even more fatal to a nation than to be vanquished. It amounted to a public confession of irredeemable decadence.[178]

The earlier phases of the partition do not seem to have been generated, or even (except perhaps in Germany) accompanied, by any profound or widespread changes in 'world outlook' within the European societies concerned. By the 1890s this was no longer true. An ideology of imperialism hitherto confined to individual enthusiasts or small coteries had become widely diffused among the educated classes of Europe. The content of this 'new imperialism' was tough-minded to the point of brutality. It prescribed the seizure and exploitation of the largest possible colonial area not only for profit, but as an indispensable means of strengthening the imperial Power for the unending future struggles against its rivals.[179] On the strength of a 'scientific' interpretation of politics which was in reality a farrago of factual error and intellectual confusion, it elevated material greed, national arrogance and racial prejudice to the rank of cardinal virtues.

Logically enough, on its own premises, this ideology also advocated the ruthless use of technological superiority to crush the last remnants of African resistance. The policy-makers were willing listeners. By the 1890s the crude calculation that

> Whatever happens, we have got
> The Maxim gun and they have not[180]

was no longer an attitude peculiar to special and rather peripheral groups of Europeans: 'modern travellers' like H. M. Stanley and Carl Peters; military cliques like the *officiers soudanais*; or settler communities that employed armed force as a routine measure of 'native policy'. It had become an integral part of the mental furniture of the metropolitan official mind. In 1892–4 in Dahomey, in 1895–6 in Madagascar, the French government consciously decided to solve its political problems by military action which would enable it to exploit the 'technological gap'. The same principle inspired the British in their railway logistics and ruthless use of superior fire-power in the Sudan during 1898. The Italian invasion of Ethiopia and the South African War were planned as similar exercises; but here calculations went badly astray, for Amhara warriors and Boer commandos turned out to be more efficient military technicians than Italian conscripts or British regulars.

In the last decade of the century, imperialism in Africa was indeed (to use a cliché popular with Social Darwinists) 'red in tooth and claw'. It is not surprising that many Africans, whose immediate forbears felt the full impact of that 'tooth and claw', still see the Partition as a deliberate exercise in militaristic politics, predatory economics and racialist sociology;[181] and are apt to be impatient with academic historians whose investigations lead them to less simple theories—or to non-theories. But this African view, though far from the whole truth, is also by no means wholly false; and European scholars and publicists who neglect or deride it are doing no service either to Europe or to Africa.

NOTES

1. Contrast, e.g., R. Robinson and J. Gallagher, *Africa and the Victorians* (London, 1961) with H.-U. Wehler, *Bismarck und der Imperialismus* [hereafter: *Bismarck*] (Köln/Berlin, 1969).
2. D. K. Fieldhouse, *The Theory of Capitalist Imperialism* (London, 1967), 192–3. Cf. L. H. Gann and P. Duignan, 'Reflections on Imperialism and the Scramble for Africa', in Gann and Duignan (ed.), *Colonialism in Africa*, I (Cambridge, 1969), 127–8.
3. Cf. D. S. Landes, 'Some thoughts on the nature of economic imperialism', *Journal of Economic History* XXI (1961), pp. 496–512, ad finem, where the improvements in small arms in the third quarter of the nineteenth century are held to be crucial. Yet the French and the Turco-Egyptians in North Africa, and the Afrikaners in South Africa, had been able to conquer and dominate vast areas without the aid of *armes perfectionnées*.
4. D. K. Fieldhouse, ' "Imperialism"—an Historiographical Revision', *Economic History Review*, 2nd Series, XIV, 2 (1961–2), 187–209; C. J. H. Hayes, *A Generation of Materialism, 1871–1900* (New York, 1941), 216–29; H. Arendt, *The Origins of Totalitarianism* (3rd edn., London, 1967), 150–5. For a more cautious view, G. Shepperson, 'Africa, the Victorians and Imperialism', *Revue Belge de Philologie et d'Histoire*, XL, 4 (1962), 1228–38. Cf. infra, 42–3.
5. J. D. Hargreaves, 'Towards a History of the Partition of Africa', *J[ournal of] A[frican] H[istory]*, I, (1960), 97–109. Cf. infra, 10–14.
6. J. A. Hobson, *Imperialism: A Study* (London, 1902); V. I. Lenin, *Imperialism, the Highest Stage of Capitalism* (1916). However, Lenin evidently did not intend this analysis to apply unamended to late nineteenth-century imperialism. He explicitly states that the 'beginning of the twentieth century marks the turning-point from the old capitalism to the new'; and that 'colonial policy and imperialism existed before the highest stage of capitalism'. He is moreover at pains to point out that 'the colonial policy of capitalism in its previous stages is essentially different from the colonial policy of finance capital'. But he does not enlarge upon these 'essential differences'; he was after all not concerned to explain the partition of Africa, but to demonstrate that the war of 1914–18 was essentially a struggle to re-partition the markets and resources of the world.
7. Robinson and Gallagher, op. cit.; Fieldhouse, 1967, op. cit.
8. R. Robinson, review of H. Brunschwig, *Mythes et Réalités de l'impérialisme colonial français* [hereafter: *Mythes*] (Paris, 1960) J.A.H. II, 1 (1961), 158–60.
9. Robinson and Gallagher, op. cit.; eidem, 'The Partition of Africa', *New C[ambridge] M[odern] H[istory]*, XI (Cambridge, 1962), 593–640.
10. Robinson and Gallagher, 1961, op. cit., 53–75.
11. Infra, 29–31, 38–9. Cf. L. Thompson, 'Great Britain and the Afrikaner Republics', in M. Wilson and L. Thompson (ed.), *The Oxford History of South Africa*, II (Oxford, 1971), 289–324; J. S. Marais, *The Fall of Kruger's Republic* (Oxford, 1961), passim and esp. 323–32.
12. E. Hertslet, *The Map of Africa by Treaty* [hereafter: Hertslet] (3rd edn., London, 1909), II, No. 229.
13. G. N. Sanderson, *England, Europe and the Upper Nile, 1882–1899* [hereafter: *Upper Nile*] (Edinburgh, 1965), 192–204. Cf. infra. 35–6.
14. Robinson and Gallagher, 1961, op. cit., 465.
15. Cf. infra, 12–13.
16. Robinson and Gallagher, 1961, op. cit., 170.
17. D[ocuments] D[iplomatiques] F[rançais, Ie Série], IV (Paris, 1932), Nos. 525, 539, Tissot (London) to Duclerc, 14 Sep., 7 Oct. 1882; 551, 576, Duclerc to Tissot, 28 Oct., 13 Dec. 1882; 584, 594, 597, Duclerc to Courcel (Berlin), 27 Dec. 1882; to Tissot, 4 Jan. 1883; to Raindre (Cairo), 8 Jan. 1883.

D.D.F. V (Paris, 1833), No. 26, Raindre to Challemel-Lacour, 1 May 1883. [P.R.O.] F.O. 633/6 (Cromer Papers), No. 22, Baring to Granville, 19 Jan. 1884.

18. The crucial event was Baring's virtual *coup d'état* of January 1884, by which he forced the pliant Armenian Nubar Pasha Boghos upon the Khedive as Prime Minister. At this point, for the first time, a note of real bitterness appears in the French official papers. Cf. D.D.F., V, No. 185, Barrère (Cairo) to Ferry, 7 Jan. 1884; No. 186, Ferry to Barrère, 9 Jan. But it was not until April 1886 that France adopted a policy of deliberate obstruction in Egypt: D.D.F., VI (Paris, 1934), No. 226, Freycinet to d'Aunay (Cairo), 14 Apr. 1886. Baring noticed the difference: F.O. 633/6, No. 66, Baring to Iddesleigh, 24 Oct. 1886.

19. For these negotiations from the French point of view, see D.D.F., V, Nos. 254–350 passim. Even after this fiasco, Ferry's response to the German proposals remained very cautious: D.D.F., V, No. 376, note by Ferry, n.d. [c. 22 Aug. 1884]; No. 402, Ferry to Courcel, 19 Sept. 1884.

20. H. Brunschwig, *L'avènement de l'Afrique Noire* [hereafter: *Avènement*] (Paris, 1963), 149–63; idem, *Le Partage de l'Afrique Noire* (Paris, 1971), 48–9; J. Stengers, 'L'impérialisme colonial de la fin du XIXe siècle: Mythe ou Réalité' [hereafter: 'Impérialisme colonial'], *J.A.H.*, III, 3 (1962), 469–91; cf. D.D.F., IV, No. 540, Brin (Brussels) to Duclerc, 7 Oct. 1882.

21. Robinson and Gallagher, 1961, op. cit., 465.

22. Stengers, 'Impérialisme colonial'; C. W. Newbury, 'Victorians, Republicans and the Partition of West Africa', *J.A.H.*, III, 3 (1962), 493–501; C. W. Newbury and A. S. Kanya-Forstner, 'French Policy and the Origins of the Scramble for West Africa' [hereafter: 'French Policy'], *J.A.H.* X, 2 (1969), 253–76.

23. Newbury, *J.A.H.* 1962, ut supra; Newbury and Kanya-Forstner, 'French Policy'; Stengers, 'Impérialisme colonial'. C. W. Newbury, 'The Development of French policy on the Lower and Upper Niger, 1880–1898', *Journal of Modern History*, XXXI, 1 (1959), 18–23. A. S. Kanya-Forstner, *The Conquest of the Western Sudan* [hereafter: *Conquest*], (Cambridge, 1969), 113–37, 156–70, 266–8; idem, 'French African Policy and the Anglo-French Agreement of 5 August 1890', H[istorical] J[ournal], XII, 4 (1969), 628–50. C. M. Andrew and A. S. Kanya-Forstner, 'The French "Colonial Party"; its Composition, Aims and Influence, 1885–1914', *H.J.*, XIV, 1 (1971), 99–128; J. D. Hargreaves, 'British and French Imperialism in West Africa' [hereafter: 'British and French Imperialism'], in P. Gifford and W. R. Louis (ed.), *France and Britain in Africa* [hereafter: Gifford and Louis, *France*], (New Haven, 1971), 261–82.

24. Sanderson, *Upper Nile*, 17–19, 27, 34, 42–46, 97–8, 120–34. A. S. Kanya-Forstner, 'French Expansion in Africa—the Mythical Theory', [hereafter: 'Mythical Theory'], unpublished paper, Oxford Seminar on Theories of Imperialism, February 1970. An abridged version has been published in R. Owen and B. Sutcliffe, *Studies in the Theory of Imperialism* [hereafter: *Studies*], (London, 1972), at 277–92. References are to the original paper.

25. Salisbury's West African concessions to France in August 1890 were made at least as much for 'European' as for 'African' reasons: cf. G. N. Sanderson, 'England, Italy, the Nile Valley and the European Balance, 1890–91' *H.J.*, VII, 1 (1964), 94–119. So too were the German concessions to France on the Cameroon frontier in February-March 1894: idem, *Upper Nile*, 106–10, 165–7, 176–8.

26. Infra, 36–7.

27. A. J. P. Taylor, *Germany's First Bid for Colonies, 1884–1885. A Move in Bismarck's European Policy*, (London, 1938).

28. Wehler, *Bismarck*, H. A. Turner, 'Bismarck's Imperialist Venture: Anti-British in Origin?' [hereafter: 'Bismarck's Imperialist Venture'], in P. Gifford and W. R. Louis, *Britain and Germany in Africa* [hereafter: Gifford and Louis, *Germany*], (New Haven, 1967); 47–82. H. Pogge

von Strandmann, 'Domestic Origins of Germany's Colonial Expansion under Bismarck', *Past and Present*, 42 (1969), 140–59.

29. Fieldhouse, *Economic History Review*, 1961–2, ut supra.

30. Sanderson, *H.J.* 1964, ut supra.

31. Brunschwig, *Avènement*, 53–63. G. S. Graham, *Great Britain in the Indian Ocean, 1810–1850* (Oxford, 1967), 73–109; cf. infra, 19–20.

32. J. Ganiage, *Les Origines du Protectorat Français en Tunisie* (Paris, 1959), 550–661, citing (p. 632) St.-Vallier to Barthélémy St.-Hilaire, 26 Jan. 1881; cf. Roustan to Noailles, 23 Feb.; St.Vallier to Noailles, 21 Mar. 1881, at 634–5.

33. G. N. Sanderson, 'The Origins and Significance of the Anglo-French Confrontation at Fashoda, 1898' [hereafter: 'Fashoda'], in Gifford and Louis, *France*, 285–331.

34. [*Die*] *G[rosse] P[olitik der europäischen Kabinette]*, IV, No. 743, Bismarck to Münster (London), 1 June 1884. Bismarck complains that this 'Monroe Doctrine' is 'eine Verletzung unseres Nationalgefühls'.

35. The Italian statesman di Rudinì remarked in 1908 that Italy had sought colonies 'in a spirit of imitation . . . for pure *snobism*'. Cited W. L. Langer, *The Diplomacy of Imperialism* (2nd edn., New York, 1951), 281.

36. Kanya-Forstner, 'Mythical Theory', 3.

37. Brunschwig, *Mythes*, 73–77, citing Ferry's speech in the Chamber, 28 July 1885. J. Stengers, 'King Leopolds' Imperialism', in Owen and Sutcliffe, *Studies*, 248–75; Turner, 'Bismarck's Imperialist Venture', in Gifford and Louis, *Germany*; Wehler, *Bismarck*, 299–325, 420–50; idem, 'Bismarck's Imperialism, 1862–1890', *Past and Present*, 48 (1970), 119–55.

38. D.D.F., V, No. 410, Courcel to Ferry, private, 28 Sep. 1884. Cf. Wehler, *Bismarck*, 112–40, on 'der ideologische Konsensus'.

39. The years 1889–90 seem to mark an important stage in this evolution. Cf. Stengers, 'Impérialisme colonial'; idem, 'British and German Imperial Rivalry: A Conclusion', in Gifford and Louis, *Germany*, 337–47; Sanderson, *Upper Nile*, 52–3, 55–8.

40. J. Stengers, 'King Leopold and Anglo-French Rivalry, 1882–1884' [hereafter: 'King Leopold'], in Gifford and Louis, *France*, 121–66. idem, 'Impérialisme colonial'; Wehler, *Bismarck*, 264–82, 425 f.; Turner, 'Bismarck's Imperialist Venture'.

41. Anderson, 11 June 1883, cited Stengers, 'Impérialisme colonial', 483. C. W. Newbury, *British Policy towards West Africa*, (Oxford, 1971), prints Anderson's memorandum in full at pp. 179–81.

42. C. W. Newbury, 'The Tariff Factor in Anglo-French West African Partition', in Gifford and Louis, *France*, 221–59. Idem, 'Victorians Republicans . . .', *J.A.H.* 1962, ut supra; Wehler, *Bismarck*, 325.

43. Wehler, *Bismarck*, 437–50; idem, *Past and Present* 1970, ut supra; Turner, ut supra. The official concerned was Heinrich von Kusserow. For the Anglo-French Agreement of 28 June 1882, see Herstlet, II, No. 224. It is worth recalling that Hamburg, the main centre of German trade with West Africa, and Bremen, the home-town of Lüderitz, were not merely great and politically important cities, but constituent states of the *Reich*.

44. Infra, 18–20.

45. Kanya-Forstner, 'Mythical Theory'; Newbury and Kanya-Forstner, 'French Policy'. Some Frenchmen even saw an El Dorado in the Bahr al-Ghazal: J. Stengers, 'Une facette de la question du Haut-Nil: Le mirage soudanais', *J.A.H.*, X, 4(1969), 599–622.

46. Newbury and Kanya-Forstner, 'French Policy', esp. at 274–5. Kanya-Forstner, 'Mythical Theory', 4; idem, *Conquest*, 55–72.

47. Newbury and Kanya-Forstner, ut supra; Kanya-Forstner, 'Mythical Theory'; idem, *Conquest*, 13–15, 20–1, 57–60, 66–72, 84–120.

48 Newbury and Kanya-Forstner, ut supra. Kanya-Forstner, *Conquest*, 100–4. J. D. Hargreaves, *Prelude to the Partition of West Africa* [hereafter: *Prelude*], (London, 1963), 235–6; Stengers, 'Impérialisme colonial', citing at

477–80: Jauréguiberry to Duclerc, 19, 25 Jan. 1883; to the Commander of the West African Naval Division, 30 Jan. 1883.

49. Newbury and Kanya-Forstner, ut supra, Kanya-Forstner, *Conquest*, 59–60, 103–4; Stengers, ut supra, Hargreaves, *Prelude*, 192; cf. infra., 20–7.

50. Newbury and Kanya-Forstner, ut supra, 272–5.

51. To W. T. Stead, in 1895; cf. Langer, op. cit., 80.

52. 'La paix sociale est, dans l'âge industriel de l'humanité, une question de débouchés.'—Jules Ferry, *Le Tonkin et la Mère-Patrie* (Paris, 1890), 52; cf. Ferry's speech in the Chamber of 28 July 1885, cited Brunschwig, *Mythes*, 73–4. For Chamberlain, cf. Langer, op. cit., 77, 80.

53. The claim is made by Wehler: somewhat hesitantly in *Bismarck* (449–87; but cf. 425–40); more confidently in 'Bismarck's Imperialism', *Past and Present* 1970. But cf. Pogge von Strandmann, *Past and Present* 1969, ut supra.
    Bismarck seems even less plausible as a practitioner of that variant of 'manipulated social imperialism' which strives *à la Bülow* 'to direct the gaze from petty party disputes and subordinate internal affairs on to ... world-shaking and decisive problems' by means of an aggressively expansionist policy. P. M. Kennedy, 'German Colonial Expansion: Has the "Manipulated Social Imperialism" been ante-dated?', *Past and Present*, 54 (1972), 134–41; cf. Wehler, *Bismarck*, 469–87.

54. Cf. Sanderson, 'Fashoda', in Gifford and Louis, *France*.

55. Infra, 37–9.

56. Robinson and Gallagher, *Africa and the Victorians;* eidem, 'The Partition of Africa', *New C.M.H.*, XI, at 609, 619–20; cf. A. S. Kanya-Forstner, 'Myths and Realities of African Resistance', *The Canadian Historical Association, Historical Papers* 1969, 185–98; idem, *Conquest*, 263–72; Newbury and Kanya-Forstner, 'French Policy', at 272–3.

57. R. Robinson, 'Non-European Foundations of European Imperialism: sketch for a theory of collaboration', in Owen and Sutcliffe, *Studies*, 118–40.

58. Infra, 21.

59. Infra, 31.

60. Mackinnon's career as an effective sub-imperialist in East Africa hardly begins before 1888. Cf. Robinson and Gallagher, 1961, op. cit., 48–9, 193–202.

61. Newbury and Kanya-Forstner, 'French Policy'; Kanya-Forstner, *Conquest*, 178–208, 216–27, 266–71; R. Oliver, *The Missionary Factor in East Africa* (London, 1952), 119–28; A. J. Hanna, *The Beginnings of Nyasaland and North-Eastern Rhodesia, 1859–95* (Oxford, 1956), 123–48. For the importance of the Scottish vote to Salisbury in 1890, cf. Salisbury to the Queen, 1 June 1890, L[etters of] Q[ueen] V[ictoria], III, I, 608–9.
    These two phenomena might perhaps just be squeezed into the category of sub-imperialisms; but if so, they are very eccentric species of the genus, and are on any showing striking illustrations of the bizarre variety of 'causes' and 'motives' with which the historian has to contend. The crucial importance of missionary nationality for the annexation of Nyasaland was quite exceptional. Elsewhere, missionary nationality was at best one consideration among many; and quite often (notably in the Cameroons and 'Tanganyika'), it was completely ignored in the final territorial settlement.

62. Gann and Duignan, *Colonialism in Africa*, I, 127–8.

63. Newbury and Kanya-Forstner, 'French Policy', 274.

64. Graham, op. cit., 1–14. For Portugal, R. Anstey, *Britain and the Congo in the Nineteenth Century* (Oxford, 1962), 15–19, 43–53. For France: H. Richmond, *Statesmen and Sea-Power* (Oxford, 1962), 262–3; A. Adu Boahen, *Britain, the Sahara and the Western Sudan* (Oxford, 1964), 138–9; F. Guizot, *Mémoires*, VI (Paris, 1864), 267–9; VII (Paris, 1865), 141–82.

65. Morier to Derby, 15 May 1877, cited by Anstey, op. cit., 86.

66. Brunschwig, *Avènement*, 53–63; idem, 'Anglophobia in French African Policy' [hereafter: 'Anglophobia'], in Gifford and Louis, *France*, 3–34; R. Coupland, *East Africa and its Invaders* (Oxford, 1838), 431–51;

C. S. Nicholls, *The Swahili Coast* (London, 1971), 163–93. The later stages of the African crisis were complicated by the even more dangerous, if fundamentally less important, Anglo-French confrontation in the Pacific.

67. Brunschwig, *Avènement*, loc. cit.; idem, 'Anglophobia'. P. Renouvin, *Histoire des Relations Internationales*, V (Paris, 1954), 184; Guizot, *Mémoires* VII, loc. cit. Guizot admitted in the Chamber in January 1845 that the Moroccan campaign had been carried out 'en face des vaisseaux anglais qui suivaient les nôtres pour assister à nos opérations et à nos combats' (ibid., 177).

68. Graham, op. cit., 106. For 'partnership' on the West Coast, cf. Hargreaves, *Prelude*, 107–10.

69. Hertslet, II, No. 222. Under both the July Monarchy and the Second Empire, the Quai d'Orsay continued to discourage naval and consular initiatives on the East Coast. Cf. Coupland, op. cit., 353–6, 449–58; eundem, *The Exploitation of East Africa* [hereafter: *Exploitation*], (2nd edn, London, 1968), 21–2, 33–6; H. Deschamps, *Histoire de Madagascar* (Paris, 1961), 172; Brunschwig, 'Anglophobia', ut supra.

70. Hargreaves, *Prelude*, 181, 190–1, 198–9, 213–4, 223–5, 229–30, 234–5. For similar caution on the East Coast, cf. Coupland, *Exploitation*, 195–7.

71. W. D. McIntyre, *The Imperial Frontier in the Tropics* (London, 1967), 8–9, 278–9, 359–60; cf. ibid., 143–4, citing Kimberley to Cardwell, 26 July 1873.

72. Ibid., 359–74, 384–5. K. O. Diké, *Trade and Politics in the Niger Delta* (Oxford, 1956), 128–208; Hargreaves, *Prelude*, 312.

73. Sir Robert Herbert (P.U.S., Colonial Office), 5 May 1875, cited McIntyre, op. cit., 356, 369; cf. ibid., 369, for Kimberley's assertion of an exclusive paramountcy in Malaya as early as Sept. 1873.

74. Hargreaves, *Prelude*, 174–81. It is obvious that the British had no intention of imposing their *formal* authority over much of this enormous 'sphere'.

75. McIntyre, op. cit., 369–70. The assumption of British paramountcy in South Africa was implicit in every approach to the South African problem, whether bold or cautious, in the 1870s and early 1880s. Cf. C. F. Goodfellow, *Great Britain and South African Confederation* (Cape Town, 1966), 78–9 fn., and passim: C. W. de Kiewiet, *The Imperial Factor in South Africa* (Cambridge, 1937), 314.

76. Coupland, *Exploitation*, 271–99. Anglo-Eyptian Agreement of 7 Sept. 1877 (Hertslet, II, No. 178).

77. Coupland, *Exploitation*, 241–69, 300–14.

78. Morier to Derby, 15 May 1877, cited Anstey, loc. cit.

79. Goodfellow, op. cit., 49–150, esp. 73–8, 91–7, 107–10, 133–5; cf. 208–11.

In the mid-1870s the white population of the Cape was more than three times the combined white populations of Natal, the Transvaal and the Orange Free State; and the value of its external trade was about five times that of Natal (Goodfellow, op. cit., 1–6).

80. De Kiewiet, op. cit., 73–4, citing memorandum by Carnarvon, Jan. 1876; Goodfellow, op. cit., 67–8, 96.

81. Carnarvon to Frere, 12 Dec. 1876, cited by Goodfellow, op. cit., 117; cf. McIntyre, op. cit., 252–3. Carnarvon was also instrumental in causing the Prince of Wales to withdraw his patronage from King Leopold's 'international' and 'philanthropic' project.

82. Hargreaves, *Prelude*, 192, citing (in translation) note by d'Azy, 19 Feb. 1876.

83. Ibid., 201–3, 173–9, 185–6, 217–20.

84. Ibid., 201–23. cf. Brunschwig, *Avènement*, 122–4.

85. Hargreaves, *Prelude*, 243–7, 259, 264–8, 290; Newbury and Kanya-Forstner, 'French Policy'; Kanya-Forstner, 'French African Policy and the Anglo-French Agreement of 5 August 1890', *H.J.* 1969, ut supra; idem, *Conquest*, 58–60, 71–8, 100–4, 123–5: Brunschwig, 'Anglophobia'; and

Hargreaves, 'British and French Imperialism', in Gifford and Louis, *France*, at 26, 266–7.

86. Hargreaves, *Prelude*, 223–37, 278–82, 287–9, 293–7, 303–7; Kanya-Forstner, *Conquest*, 63–72, 91–3, 100–6; Newbury and Kanya-Forstner, 'French Policy', citing at 268 Jauréguiberry in the Senate, 17 Feb. 1881.

87. J. S. Swinburne, *The Influence of Madagascar on International Relations, 1878–1904*, unpublished M. Phil. thesis, University of London, 1969, 17–29, 92–99, 105–12, 116–9.

88. Ibid., 119, citing M[inistère des] A[ffaires] É[trangères], Madagascar 13, Rouvier to Gambetta, 22 Jan, 1882.

89. Ibid., 39–40, 118, citing M.A.E. ut supra, Freycinet to Baudais, 2 Mar. 1882.

90. Ibid., 28–9, 39–40; Deschamps, op. cit., 184–5; F. Berge, *Le Sous-secrétariat et les Sous-secrétaires d'Etat aux Colonies*, (Paris, 1962), 20–21.

91. Swinburne, op. cit., 116–21, 195.

92. Ibid., 105–6, citing M.A.E. Madagascar 11, Jauréguiberry to Waddington, 15 Nov. 1879, enclosing despatch from Cuinier (Governor, Réunion); Cassas (Consul, Madagascar) to Waddington, 2 Oct. 1879, reporting Cuinier's views.

93. A. J. Marder, *British Naval Policy, 1880–1905* (London, n.d. [1940]), 119–39; cf. Swinburne, op. cit., 171–81.

94. Edward Henry Stanley, 15th Earl of Derby. Foreign Secretary under Disraeli, 1874–78; joined the Liberal Party, 1880; Colonial Secretary under Gladstone, 1882–85—for his activities in this capacity cf. infra, 27–31.

95. Coupland, *Exploitation*, 305–13; Anstey, op. cit., 53–6, 86–8.

96. He also had the contempt of the *grand seigneur* for 'nigger wars'; cf. Hargreaves, *Prelude*, 224–5.

97. J. Flint, 'The Wider Background to Partition and Colonial Occupation' in R. Oliver and G. Mathew (ed.), *History of East Africa*, I (Oxford, 1963), 360–1; Anstey, op. cit., 90–5; Hargreaves, *Prelude*, 211–13, 224–32, 234–5, 239–40; Newbury, *British Policy towards West Africa*, II, 173, minute by Salisbury, 29 Jan. 1880.

In view of Salisbury's well documented delaying tactics on the West Coast, it seems probable that his passive obstruction of Morier's negotiation was deliberate rather than (as Anstey supposes) merely the result of pressure of other business.

98. Brunschwig, *Avènement*, 163–4, citing Jauréguiberry to Cordier, 22 Nov. 1882.

99. Hargreaves, *Prelude*, 303–15.

100. Cf. infra, 29–30 (S. Africa); supra, 11; infra, 30; Newbury, op. cit., 182–3 (Hewett and West Africa); Coupland, *Exploitation*, 382–94; Robinson and Gallagher, 1961, 189–97; A. Ramm, *The Political Correspondence of Mr. Gladstone and Lord Granville*, II (Oxford 1962), 294–5, Gladstone to Granville 12 Dec. 1884 (East Africa). *The Letters of Queen Victoria*, 2, iii (London, 1928), 593–4, Gladstone to the Queen, 23 Jan. 1885.

101. Brunschwig, *Avènement*, 159. Anstey, op. cit., 28–34, 93–106.

102. Brunschwig, *Avènement*, 164, citing Duclerc to Jauréguiberry, 3 Jan. 1883. Duclerc specifically mentions 'la reprise inopinée des pourparlers entre le Portugal et l'Angleterre'.

103. Hargreaves, *Prelude*, 301–3.

104. Anstey, op. cit., 106–12, 139–50, 161–7.

105. S. E. Crowe, *The Berlin West African Conference* (London, 1942), 62–71, 176–91; cf. D.D.F., V, No. 361, Courcel to Ferry, 14 Aug. 1884.

106. Wehler, *Bismarck*, 264–81; Turner, 'Bismarck's Imperialist Venture'; W. O. Aydelotte, 'The First German Colony and its Diplomatic Consequences', C[ambridge] H[istorical] J[ournal], V, 3 (1937), 291–313. Cf. G.P., IV, Nos. 741–52.

107. Until 1884 Bismarck had granted to Lüderitz no more than 'consular protection', and had expressly disapproved the hoisting of the German flag at Angra Pequena: Wehler, *Bismarck*, 246 f.

108. Ibid., loc. cit., and 299–325; Turner, ut supra.

109. De Kiewiet, op. cit., 289–312. J. A. I. Agar-Hamilton, *The Road to the North* (London, 1937), 365–6; Goodfellow, op. cit., 96, 107–8, 146; T. R. H. Davenport, *The Afrikaner Bond* (Cape Town, 1966), 80–98; P. Laurence, *The Life of John Xavier Merriman* (London, 1930), 71–98; D. M. Schreuder, *Gladstone and Kruger* (London, 1969), 306–435, passim.

110. De Kiewiet, op. cit., 311–17; Laurence, op. cit., 85, citing Scanlen to Merriman, 29 Nov. 1883; cf. Schreuder, op. cit., 395–6, citing same to same, 15 Nov. 1883. Aydelotte, *C.H.J.* 1937, ut supra, 295–6.

111. Aydelotte, ut supra, at 297–8, 301–10; Wehler, *Bismarck*, 264–81, 307–20.

112. D.D.F., V, Nos. 270, 372, 385, 407, Courcel to Ferry, 14 May, 17 and 30 Aug., 23 Sept. 1884. In No. 407, Courcel reports Bismarck as saying: 'Les Anglais sont portés à croire que toutes les parties du globe terrestre, qui n'ont pas été occupées déjà par une autre nation, leur appartiennent en vertu d'un droit de dévolution légale, et que c'est leur faire tort que de prendre place à côté d'eux sur les rivages des continents libres ou sur les mers. Il est d'un intérêt commun de faire cesser cette illusion . . .'.

113. W. R. Louis, 'The Berlin Congo Conference' [hereafter: 'Congo Conference'], in Gifford and Louis, *France*, at 208–14; Crowe, op. cit., 176–91.

Derby and Granville left it to the Lord Chancellor, Lord Selborne, to determine British policy on the criteria of 'effective occupation'; hence its very narrow view, legalistic rather than political.

For the 'historical defence' of Britain's unofficial empire in East Africa, see F.F. Müller, *Deutschland-Zanzibar-Ostafrika* (Berlin/D.D.R., 1959), 200. This move was evidently a substitute for Granville's plan of November 1884 (vetoed by Gladstone in December) to establish a preclusive protectorate on the Zanzibari mainland: cf. supra, 28.

114. Coupland, *Exploitation*, 395–478; Robinson and Gallagher, 1961, op. cit., 189–97.

115. Wehler, *Bismarck*, 292–8.

116. Even when, in North Africa, the Scramble encountered the major restraining force of Mediterranean strategy, it was merely retarded, not halted. Morocco and Libya had no more than a decade's reprieve. Liberia, at about the same time, became an unofficial United States protectorate. Only Ethiopia survived, thanks to its successful resistance, as a genuinely independent polity.

117. Brunschwig, *Avènement*, 159–60, citing Leopold to de Lesseps, 18 Sept. 1882. Stengers, 'King Leopold', in Gifford and Louis, *France*, at 135–143.

118. Stengers, 'King Leopold', 143–52; Anstey, op. cit., 113–38, 145–60; Crowe, op. cit., 79–81, 96–8.

119. For the terms of the *droit de préférence*, see Hertslet, II, No. 151. Curiously, Leopold seems to have originally regarded the *droit de préférence* merely as a short-term tactical weapon for use against Portugal (Stengers, 'King Leopold', 153–62). But he was quick to see and exploit its wider advantages.

120. Stengers, 'King Leopold', 162–4; Crowe, op. cit., 78–91.

121. Louis, 'Congo Conference', 198–203; Anstey, op. cit., 171–2; Stengers, 'King Leopold', 162, citing note by Lister, 20 May 1884.

122. Stengers, 'King Leopold', 163, citing Courcel to Ferry, 30 Aug. 1884.

123. Ibid., 163–4; Stengers, 'Leopold II et la fixation des frontières du Congo', *Le Flambeau*, 1963, 188 ff. The coastal delimitation with France (and with Portugal) was however a very thorny problem: cf. Louis, 'Congo Conference', 203–6.

124. Stengers, 'King Leopold's Imperialism', in Owen and Sutcliffe, *Studies*; Sanderson, *Upper Nile*, 35–6, 89–90, 306.

125. E.g., France in the middle 1880s (supra, 7); Germany in the later 1880s (infra, 35).

126. Sanderson, *Upper Nile*, 88–96, 122–30.

127. Ibid., 90–139, passim; Kanya-Forstner, 'Mythical Theory'. Andrew and Kanya-Forstner, 'The French "Colonial Party" ', *H.J.* 1971, ut supra.

128. Sanderson, *Upper Nile*, 96–100, 104–6, 110–13, 162–87; cf. Hertslet, II, No. 157, Franco-Congolese Agreement of 14 Aug. 1894; II, No. 163, Anglo-Congolese Agreement of 12 May 1894.

129. Sanderson, *Upper Nile*, 269–70, 305–7, 381; R. O. Collins, *King Leopold, England and the Upper Nile, 1899–1909* (New Haven, 1968), passim.

130. Etienne in the Chamber, 10 May 1890, cited in Kanya-Forstner, *Conquest*, 167.

131. Speech of 7 June 1894; cf. Sanderson, *Upper Nile*, 119–22, 161.

132. Ibid., 123–8, 130–61, 184–7, 206–7, 269–80; M. Michel, *La Mission Marchand, 1895–1899* (Paris, 1972), 15–59.

133. Sanderson, *Upper Nile*, 47–66; idem, 'The Anglo-German Agreement of 1890 and the Upper Nile', E[nglish] H[istorical] R[eview], LXXVIII, 306 (1963), 49–72. Robinson and Gallagher, 1961, op. cit. 214, 243–53.

134. Pogge von Strandmann, *Past and Present* 1969, ut supra. Sanderson, *Upper Nile*, 44–9, 52. Müller, op. cit., 464–70.

135. Sanderson, *Upper Nile*, 49–63; idem, 'Anglo-German Agreement', E.H.R. 1963, ut supra. For the terms of the July Agreement, see Hertslet, III, No. 270.

136. Anglo-French Agreement of 5 Aug. 1890. Cf. Kanya-Forstner, 'French African Policy...', *H.J.* 1969, ut supra.
In 1893–94, serious friction arose from the French attempt, through the Mizon Mission, to reach Lake Chad by the Niger-Benué; and (on the strength of a very idiosyncratic interpretation of the 1890 Agreement) to establish a protectorate in Adamawa: J. Flint, *Sir George Goldie* (London, 1960), 167–86, 218–19, Sanderson, *Upper Nile*, 124–5, 192–3.

137. Sanderson, *Upper Nile*, 52, 56–63. Mackinnon's exorbitant territorial demands south-west of Lake Victoria, which would almost certainly have wrecked the negotiation had they been pressed at Berlin, had strong support among Salisbury's Cabinet colleagues.

138. Ibid., 63–4. F.O. 84/2030, Salisbury to Malet (Berlin), No. 186a, 21 May 1890; Salisbury in the Lords, 10 July 1890; at the Mansion House, 6 Aug. 1890.

139. Ibid., 192–206, 224–5, 317–23; cf. Robinson and Gallagher, 1961, op. cit. 402–9; M. Perham, *Lugard, The Years of Adventure* (London, 1956), 623–713.

140. Sanderson, *Upper Nile*, 106–10, 176–8.

141. Ibid., 225–32; J. D. Hargreaves, '*Entente Manquée*: Anglo-French Relations 1895–1896', *C.H.J.*, XI, 1 (1953), 65–92.

142. Sanderson, *Upper Nile*, 232–4, 240–52.

143. Ibid., 252–4, 260–5, 322–7.

144. Sanderson, 'Fashoda', 296–302, 325–7; *Upper Nile*, 340, 346–51, 396–401.

145. Sanderson, 'Fashoda', 303–5; cf. D.D.F., XI, No. 303, d'Estournelles de Constant to Hanotaux, 3 Dec. 1894; L.Q.V., III, 3, 305, the Queen to Salisbury, 30 Oct. 1898.

146. Agar-Hamilton, op. cit., 217–401; Schreuder, op. cit., 437–64. In particular, the German irruption steeled Whitehall to brave the hostility of the Cape Dutch to imperial action against the Transvaal; cf. de Kiewiet, op. cit., 321–4.
Even the War Office memorandum of 1 Oct. 1884 (printed in Schreuder, pp. 503–11), concentrates on the local crisis and seems to regard German intervention as a remote and rather unlikely contingency.

147. Apart from German reminders that too harsh a *Diktat* would endanger the dynasty in Portugal; cf. R. J. Hammond, *Portugal and Africa* (Stanford, 1966), 144–5.

148. J. Butler, 'The German Factor in Anglo-Transvaal Relations', in Gifford and Louis, *Germany*, 192–207; cf. Sanderson, Upper Nile, 229–30, 241–4, 249–53, 324–7.

149. Robinson and Gallagher, 1961, op. cit., 221–53, 410–21.

150. Hammond, op. cit., 139–44. E. Axelson, *Portugal and the Scramble for Africa* (Johannesburg, 1967), 262–97; J. G. Lockhart and C. M. Woodhouse, *Rhodes* (London, 1963), 219–33.

151. Davenport, *The Afrikaner Bond*, 127–45. At this time, thanks to Kruger's hostile customs and railway policies, the Cape Dutch were subordinating ethnic solidarity to economic interest.

152. Robinson and Gallagher, 1961, op. cit., 410–30; Butler, 'The German Factor...', ut supra, 192–202; J. van der Poel, *The Jameson Raid* (Cape Town, 1951), 1–17, 21–34. Lockhart and Woodhouse, op. cit., 287–312; Marais, *Fall of Kruger's Republic*, 46–95.

153. Robinson and Gallagher, 1961, op. cit., 430–46; Davenport, op. cit., 163–71, 176–82, 189–209; Marais, op. cit., 171–7, 205–10, 223–8, 240, 290–99, 325–32; cf. Wilson and Thompson, *The Oxford History of South Africa*, II, 318–24.

154. Cf. Hammond, op. cit.; J. Duffy, *Portuguese Africa* (Cambridge, Mass., 1961).

155. Salisbury to Lansdowne, 30 Aug. 1899. Cited Lord Newton, *Lord Lansdowne, A Biography* (London, 1929), 157.

156. Sanderson, *Upper Nile*, 107–10, 164–7, 171–8, 225–6, 324–6. It is significant that the Germans maintained and even increased their pressure in Africa long after they had ceased to hope for any change in Rosebery's European behaviour. The question is further investigated in the author's unpublished seminar paper, 'The African Factor in Anglo-German relations, 1892–1895'.

157. It was possible to include in this force, apparently without any serious protest, a regiment of conscripts 'prélevé dans toutes les garnisons de France': J. Ganiage, *L'expansion coloniale de la France sous la Troisième Republique* (Paris, 1968), 195.

158. Dhanis' expedition was intended to forestall Marchand at Fashoda and (it was hoped) even Kitchener at Khartoum.

159. In form, of course, Marchand was never disavowed; but this was the practical effect of Delcassé's policy.

160. J. Darcy, *France et Angleterre, Cent Années de Rivalité Coloniale* (Paris, 1903), 389.

161. Sanderson, *Upper Nile*, 341–2, 349–54.

162. A.J.P. Taylor, *The Struggle for Mastery in Europe* (Oxford, 1954), 472. For the German navalists' conception of the expanded fleet as a crucial weapon in 'a new partition of the globe', see P. M. Kennedy, 'Tirpitz, England and the Second Navy Law of 1900: A Strategical Critique', *Militärgeschichtliche Mitteilungen*, 2/1970, at 38–42.

163. There is a useful discussion of the British phenomena at Langer, op. cit., 67–96. For the 'military manpower' argument (of which Gen. Mangin was later to be the most distinguished exponent), cf. Brunschwig, *Mythes*, 177–9.

164. A. P. Thornton, *Doctrines of Imperialism* (New York, 1965), 88.

165. Cf. Ferry's Chamber speech of 28 July 1885, cited in Brunschwig, op. cit., 73–7.

166. For French and Italian working-class attitudes at the time of the Fashoda and Adowa crises respectively, cf. Sanderson, *Upper Nile*, 359; Langer, op. cit., 280–1. German Social Democracy, increasingly in this period the mouthpiece of the urban working class, was outspokenly hostile to imperialism, at any rate until the turn of the century.

167. Cf. the critique of the myth of working-class jingoism during the South African War in R. Price, *An Imperial War and the British Working Class* (London, 1972).

168. J. Stengers, 'British and German Imperial Rivalry: A Conclusion', in Gifford and Louis, *Germany*, 339–41; Müller op. cit., 97–114, 134–91.

169. Andrew and Kanya-Forstner, 'The French "Colonial Party"', *H.J.* 1971, ut supra.

170. Cf. the speeches of Rosebery at Epsom (12 Oct. 1898); of Grey at

Huddersfield (26 Oct. 1898); of Asquith at Birmingham (16 Dec. 1898); and of Campbell-Bannerman at Hull (21 Mar. 1899).

171. The triumphal progress of imperialism among the British ruling élite is admirably illustrated by the increasing enthusiasm with which all sections of the 'Establishment' lionized Stanley in 1890, Lugard in 1892–3, Rhodes in 1894–5, and Kitchener in 1898–9. Cf. Sanderson, *Upper Nile*, 102, 209–11, 397–401; Stengers, 'Impérialisme colonial', *J.A.H.* 1962, 488–90.

172. The *B.O.P.* was founded in 1879, just in time to influence the first generation of new-style, 'public school' D.C.s and D.O.s.

173. Chamber speech of 28 July 1885, cited Brunschwig, *Mythes*, 75.

174. The content of British Social Darwinism is discussed in B. Semmel, *Imperialism and Social Reform* (London, 1960), esp. pp. 29–52. But the best brief discussion of its dissemination and influence is still Langer, op. cit., 67–96.

175. Cf. D.D.F., XII, No. 144, Courcel to Hanotaux, 29 Aug. 1895; Salisbury's speech at the Albert Hall, 4 May 1898.

176. M. D. Biddiss, 'Racial Ideas and the Politics of Prejudice', *H.J.*, XV, 3 (1972), 570–82.

177. Karl Pearson, *National Life from the Standpoint of Science* (London, 1900), 26–7, cited Langer, op. cit., 88.

178. '...Dans cette concurrence de tant de rivaux que nous voyons grandir autour de nous... la politique de recueillement ou d'abstention, c'est tout simplement le grand chemin de la décadence!'—Jules Ferry's Chamber speech of 28 July 1885. Cf. Stengers, Impérialisme Colonial', at 484, on the ethos of imperialism: 'Ne pas agir, ne pas s'étendre, c'est se décerner à soi-même un brevet d'incapacité, prélude à la décadence politique.'

179. Thornton, op. cit., 91, emphasises the 'fascinated pre-occupation with the future' that characterised imperialist ideology in the 1890s.

180. Hilaire Belloc, *The Modern Traveller* (London, 1898).

181. Cf. T. Hodgkin, 'Some African and third world theories of Imperialism', in Owen and Sutcliffe, *Studies*, 93–114.

Gabriel Hanotaux, The Colonial Party and the Fashoda Strategy

by

C. M. Andrew and A. S. Kanya-Forstner*

The Fashoda strategy marked the climax of the African partition. It was also the Third Republic's most ambitious colonial gamble: a grand design to force the British out of Egypt by establishing a French presence on the Upper Nile. The consequences of this gamble took the gamblers by surprise. In the short term, Fashoda merely confirmed the British occupation; in the longer term, it produced the formula which was to become the basis for the Entente Cordiale. But if the causes and consequences of the Fashoda crisis have been substantially established, the tangled sequence of events which led from the inception of the scheme to its ultimate failure has still to be unravelled.[1] The evolution of the strategy remains obscure because it has been examined within too narrow a frame of reference. In the context of international politics, it cannot be explained simply in terms of the Partition of Africa or of Anglo-French relations. The fluctuations of French policy on the Upper Nile between 1894 and 1898 were influenced by the changing pattern of relations with Russia as much as with Great Britain. In the context of domestic politics, the importance of the abdication of cabinet responsibility for foreign policy is well known if too little emphasised.[2] What has been overlooked is the power which this abdication gave to the one pressure group with a serious and continuing interest in foreign affairs: the *parti colonial*. Finally, no interpretation of the strategy has adequately explained the complex character of the man at the centre of events, Gabriel Hanotaux. Hanotaux was foreign minister for all but six months of the four years between the French government's decision to send a mission to the Upper Nile and Marchand's arrival at Fashoda. Many of the shifts in French policy during this crucial period derive from the erratic nature of Hanotaux's own personality.

I

Hanotaux's earliest ambition was to become a great historian. But history, he wrote later, 'led me to politics'. During his years as a student

* C. M. Andrew is Lecturer in History, University of Cambridge, and Fellow of Corpus Christi College; A. S. Kanya-Forstner is Associate Professor of History, York University, Toronto.

in Paris, he determined to make a name for himself both as a man of letters and as a man of action. One of his earliest heroes, and the subject of his first biography, was his distant relative Henri Martin who combined, as he hoped to do, the careers of historian and politician. Hanotaux's *Histoire du Cardinal Richelieu,* on which he worked intermittently for more than fifty years, epitomised his goals even more clearly. For he saw in Richelieu both the greatest diplomat in French history, whose model he would seek to emulate, and the founder of the *Académie Française,* the summit of his literary aspirations. His two ambitions were inseparable. Hanotaux possessed, throughout his life, 'the most profound and sincere belief that history lies at the very root of politics'. There can have been few other disciples of Gambetta who, on seeing the great man for the first time, were immediately reminded of *Henri Quatre.* Few other statesmen of his time were so convinced that, 'according to the way in which [the historian] exposes the affairs of the past, the affairs of the future will go well or ill'.[3]

Hanotaux's biography of Richelieu launched him on the road both to literary and to diplomatic success. It was as the historian of Richelieu that he was to be elected to the *Académie Française* in 1897. And it was his work on the Richelieu papers at the Foreign Ministry in 1878 which brought him to the attention of Waddington, the Foreign Minister, who offered him his first post at the Quai d'Orsay. Hanotaux rose quickly to become *chef-adjoint* in Gambetta's personal *cabinet,* and *chef de cabinet* to Ferry and Challemel-Lacour. By 1885, when he received his first overseas posting as *conseiller d'ambassade* in Constantinople, he was already established, at the age of 32, as one of the high fliers in the French foreign service. Then in 1886 he was offered the Republic an nomination at a by-election in his native department of Aisne.[4]

For the first time in a career 'till now straight as the path of a bullet', Hanotaux was forced to take a major decision about his future. The choice between a secure and successful career as a diplomat and the less certain but more brilliant prospects of politics provoked 'a crisis for which my temperament seemed not at all suited'. Hitherto, 'singularly favoured by fortune', he had swept all before him. Now, at the critical moment, he found himself 'indecisive, almost trembling ... What will become of me if I stumble like this at the first hurdle?'[5] As Foreign Minister he was several times to suffer from the same agonies of indecision and to prove unequal to the strain of the crises which he had to resolve.

Hanotaux successfully mastered his first experience of real self-doubt. He took the decision to stand for Parliament and was duly elected in April 1886. His experience in the Chamber, however, caused him to modify his earlier ambitions. Like many of his abler contemporaries, he soon became disillusioned by the triviality of parliamentary life under the Third Republic. 'In politics, one must try to think and speak like everyone else', he wrote in 1887, a year after his election. 'Just as in literature one must strive for originality, so in politics salvation lies in the pursuit of the banal'. He discovered too that parliamentary success was ephemeral. His speech on the Army Laws in July 1887 'caused a great stir, and I was very proud of it. Within three weeks it had been almost completely forgotten, and I had lost the considerable popularity which it had won me.'[6]

Life as a deputy increased Hanotaux's awareness of his own deficiencies. Although he could deliver carefully prepared set speeches effectively, he was unable to think on his feet or to intervene with any force in debate. These failings were to become increasingly obvious during his terms as Foreign Minister. 'As you know', wrote the British ambassador to Lord Salisbury in 1897, 'he cannot speak impromptu and has always to read his statements on foreign policy and trust to the Premier to undertake all the debating work.'[7] More seriously, Hanotaux found himself unable to cope with the emotional strains of public life, strains which often revealed themselves in psychosomatic illnesses. 'I am active, vigorous, able to bear fatigue but not my own emotions,' he wrote in 1887. ' I am becoming very conscious and quite anxious about this. I have frequent palpitations and am often overcome by my efforts to control myself. If my condition deteriorates, it could mean the end of my political career.' After a year in Parliament, Hanotaux had already begun to doubt whether he was emotionally equipped—he never doubted his *intellectual* capacity—to become a minister. The role most suited to him, he concluded, was that of an *éminence grise*, making the statesmen whom he served 'the more or less conscious executors of my policies . . . Nothing could be easier in a parliamentary system where ministers are made and broken so quickly.'[8]

Hanotaux's brief career as a deputy came to an end at the 1889 elections. Although disheartened by his defeat, he soon came to feel that it was for the best. He returned to the Quai d'Orsay as *Sous-directeur des protectorates*, and in 1892 he was appointed *Directeur des affaires consulaires et commerciales*, the second most important post in the ministry. Under Ribot and Develle (Foreign Ministers: 1890–3), he saw himself becoming a French Holstein: 'I have more or less achieved the goal I set myself: to exert a decisive influence on the affairs of state without allowing my influence to be seen.' But his preference for a role behind the scenes conflicted with his craving for public recognition. He wanted not merely diplomatic successes but, as the British ambassador later observed, 'diplomatic successes which will increase his own reputation'.[9] Anonymous power could never provide an adequate substitute for public acclaim. It was this tension between his ambitions and abilities which finally persuaded him, at the end of May 1894, to take the Foreign Ministry in the Dupuy government: a post for which he knew himself to be temperamentally unsuited.

Hanotaux was not Dupuy's first choice. The Prime Minister's original candidate whas his former Under-Secretary for Colonies and a leading member of the *groupe colonial* in the Chamber, Théophile Delcassé. But Delcassé was 'too unsure, too inexperienced, too closely tied to the *parti colonial* whose excesses were to be feared . . .' The post was then offered to Paul Cambon, the ambassador at Constantinople. Only when he refused was Dupuy persuaded to approach Hanotaux. The latter was equally hesitant about accepting. He disliked the new Prime Minister: 'his vulgarity has always repelled me'. The outgoing Foreign Minister, Casimir-Périer, urged him to decline, warning him that 'my knowledge of affairs would never be more than that of a *chef de bureau*; my former colleagues in the ministry, now to become my subordinates, would never accept the change of status; Nisard [the *Directeur des affaires politiques*] would probably resign in order to avoid placing himself under my orders; the representatives of foreign powers, having known me in junior posts, would never accept me as their equal.' But the support of President Carnot and Nisard's pledges of loyalty finally overcame his hesitation.[10]

In fact, Casimir-Périer's forecasts were wrong. Hanotaux's position as a permanent official did not prevent him from establishing his authority over the department; Nisard and most of the senior ambassadors accepted the reversal in rank.[11] His reception by foreign governments and the diplomatic corps in Paris was also favourable. Even Lord Dufferin, who disliked him, recognised the new minister as 'a very clever man, very quick and intelligent'. No Foreign Minister, Cambon later assured him, 'has ever been so well received in Europe or been greeted with so much satisfaction by his colleagues and staff'.[12]

Hanotaux's position in the cabinet was much weaker. His lack of a seat in Parliament did not in itself diminish his influence; indeed, some of his friends considered it a positive advantage, enabling him as it did to remain above party battles. Nor was he without allies among the other ministers.[13] But he was on notably bad terms with those of his colleagues most directly concerned with foreign and colonial affairs. Dupuy had not wanted him in the government, and his feelings could not have been improved by Hanotaux's active campaign against his bid for the Presidency of the Republic after Carnot's assassination in June 1894. Delcassé, the Colonial Minister, must have resented being passed over in favour of a civil servant a year younger than himself, all the more so since Dupuy tactlessly sent him, *gravissant son calvaire*, to offer the post to his successful rival. Casimir-Périer, who succeeded Carnot, might have been expected to show gratitude for Hanotaux's efforts to secure his election. But the new President treated his Foreign Minister as he had treated his *Directeur des affaires commerciales*, and Hanotaux retaliated by refusing to transmit diplomatic correspondence to the Elysée.[14] The conflict between the Foreign Minister on the one hand and the President of the Republic, Prime Minister and Colonial Minister on the other was to have a decisive effect on the evolution of the Fashoda strategy.

Hanotaux's views on foreign policy before he became a minister had not been remarkable for their consistency. For most of the 1880s he was hostile to any association with Russia. *Méfiez-vous de la Russie; elle vous trahira* was the theme of his anonymous newspaper articles in 1887. But by 1891 he had reluctantly concluded that France had no option but to sign the Russian alliance.[15] The real continuities in

Hanotaux's early career were ones of attitude rather than of policy, and of two attitudes in particular. The first; evident in everything he wrote, was a fervent if sentimental nationalism: 'Through her smiling optimism, through the limpid vivacity of her thought, through the light which emanates from her, France radiates upon humanity.' The second was a deep-seated concern for his own prestige, a concern which became all the more marked when he moved to the centre of the stage. 'What he has at heart as Minister for Foreign Affairs', Dufferin concluded, 'is his own personal reputation.'[16]

It was clear when Hanotaux became Foreign Minister that the maintenance of French prestige, to which the French public (despite its general lack of interest in the outside world) attached great importance, would depend above all on strengthening the Russian alliance and on ending the British occupation of Egypt. It was by his success or failure in these two areas of policy that his own reputation would be made or destroyed. The Franco-Russian alliance, finally ratified at the beginning of 1894, was still secret. But the public knew that some sort of understanding with Russia had been reached and had greeted it with 'an excess of Russophilia' which had alarmed even some Russophiles. No French government in the mid-1890s could have survived a visible collapse of the *Franco-Russe*. Equally, no government could acquiesce openly in the continued British occupation of Egypt. Few Frenchmen had any clear idea of the reasons why the occupation should be so intolerable. But all felt vaguely that Britain's domination of a country associated since Napoleon with the *mission civilisatrice* was an affront to national honour which could never be accepted.

Yet no French statesman at the end of the nineteenth century could have achieved either of these objectives. The Dual Alliance had been welcomed in France as relief from the inglorious isolation of the previous twenty years. It had been welcomed more prosaically in Russia as a means of securing access to the Paris money market. As yet, however, the two countries had no real common interests; indeed the Eastern crises of the mid-1890s revealed a basic conflict of interest between them. Having tried and failed to resolve this conflict, Hanotaux was reduced to papering it over. The solution of the Egyptian question was more difficult still. It is clear in retrospect that no British government after 1889 could have agreed to evacuation; and no French government had any chance of forcing it to do so. In seeking to end the British occupation Hanotaux, although he failed to realise it, was attempting the impossible. And here he could not even devise a form of words to provide the illusion if not the reality of success.

The insoluble problems which Hanotaux faced were to lay bare those weaknesses of character which, despite his intelligence, rendered him fundamentally unsuited to be Foreign Minister. He was already aware of one of them: his lack of composure and indecisiveness in a crisis. It was partly this failing which made him so vulnerable to outside pressure, particularly from the *parti colonial*. As Dufferin observed, it needed 'grit' to stand up to the colonialists,[17] and grit Hanotaux did not possess. The second weakness Hanotaux was less willing to acknowledge. Just as his nerve was suspect, so was his critical judgement. And just as crisis and failure broke his nerve, so success tended to destroy his sense of realism. His papers contain one remarkable example. In June 1892, during his happiest and most successful period as a permanent official, he conceived an incredible plan to solve all the problems of continental Europe through the partition of the British Empire and, incidentally, of the Turkish Empire and one or two 'minor' powers as well. The inspiration came to him during a sleepless night, and he treated it at first purely on the level of fantasy. But as he put it down on paper, he began to take it seriously. By the time he finished, he had quite forgotten its fantastical conception. 'The means of execution', he concluded, 'are not in the least chimerical'; and he resolved to put the scheme to Ribot for consideration by the government if it gained a large majority at the 1893 elections.[18] The same lack of realism—if on a less heroic scale—was to show itself during his years as Foreign Minister. His eventual conversion to the Fashoda strategy was merely the most notable example.

II

Hanotaux later claimed that the issue which finally persuaded him to accept the Foreign Ministry was the Anglo-Congolese Agreement of 12 May 1894 and its implications for the Upper Nile: 'It seemed to me that I was really the only one who understood this question of the Congo which, unless it were solved without a moment's delay, would result in a veritable catastrophe for France.' By leasing much of the southern Sudan to King Leopold, the Agreement cut the French off from the Upper Nile. For Hanotaux this was a personal as well as a national affront. Since 1892 he had been struggling to secure a clear French access to the Nile and had taken a consistently tough line in his negotiations with the Congolese authorities. By the spring of 1894 he was threatening to wage a press campaign aimed at 'blowing up the Belgian monarchy'.[19] Unknown to him, however, Leopold had already concluded his agreement with the British. Its publication was thus an open challenge to Hanotaux's skill as a negotoator which he felt he had to answer.

Hanotaux's intransigence on the Congo question sprang more from a concern for his own reputation than from any deep-seated colonialism. 'M. Hanotaux proclaims that he could not care less about French interests in Africa', complained Harry Alis, the Secretary-General of the Comité de l'Afrique Française in December 1892. 'All he considers in these questions is his own personal point of view, which is determined by the likely verdict of public opinion on the decisions which he has to take as a negotiator.'[20] Despite his later professions of colonialist faith, Hanotaux was still sceptical of the value of new additions to the African empire and suspicious of the 'excesses' of the parti colonial. But he knew that the colonialists were committed to reopening the Egyptian question by establishing a French presence on the Upper Nile.

He knew that the *groupe colonial;* which since 1893 had been calling for 'active measures'—a euphemism for force—to clear the Congolese out of the disputed territories, would insist on root and branch opposition to the Anglo-Congolese Agreement. And he knew too that the *groupe colonial* was now the most powerful pressure group in the Chamber, able to command a majority on any colonial issue involving *national* prestige.[21] So he had the strongest parliamentary as well as personal reasons for taking the offensive.

On the other hand, Hanotaux was anxious not to precipitate a new and potentially serious conflict with Britain. Though determined to end her occupation of Egypt, he was resolved to do so by negotiation, not by force. Except during bouts of insomnia, he was not an Anglophobe. Indeed, one of his original fears about the *Franco-Russe* was that it might destroy all hope of reconciliation with Britain and push her into the arms of the Triple Alliance.[22] He hoped to achieve the reputation of a latter-day Richelieu by using the settlement of the Egyptian question to add an English entente to the Russian alliance. His general policy, as he later defined it, was to persuade Britain to negotiate. He himself intended 'to negotiate in good faith, with the firm intention of upholding French rights, but also of sacrificing a great deal for an agreement; . . . to work, through this settlement, for an entente based on mutual respect and dignity.'[23]

These conflicting pressures had their inevitable effect on Hanotaux's nerves. The need to make the first public defence of his policy was a particular source of strain. He dreaded the *groupe colonial*'s interpellation on the Anglo-Congolese Agreement. Conscious that 'I had no experience of public speaking, or to be more frank, that I was not a public speaker', he followed what was to be his usual practice and replied to the interpellation by reading a prepared statement. His subtle mixture of moderation and firmness in rejecting the treaty achieved the remarkable feat of pleasing the colonialists without offending the British ambassador. But Hanotaux himself remained apprehensive. 'I can never describe the agonies which I experienced,' he wrote later. In particular, he feared that colonialist pressure had pushed him too far and that his dismissal of the Congolese leases as *nul et non avenu* would be taken by the British as a virtual declaration of war. For a week he remained 'in a state of real anxiety.'[24]

Hanotaux had satisfied colonialist demands only at the cost of raising colonialist expectations. During the debate, the leader of the *groupe colonial*, Eugène Etienne, had been careful to underline the broader significance of the Congolese question: *Messieurs, c'est la question égyptienne qui s'ouvre ainsi devant vous.* The Colonial Minister, Delcassé, was anxious to arrange the departure of the Monteil expedition to the Upper Nile which he and his colonialist allies had first planned in 1893. To gain the support of the *groupe colonial*, Hanotaux had to promise that Monteil would be sent without delay 'to consolidate our positions [and] . . . to ensure the defence and maintenance of our rights'. This announcement was the most applauded part of his speech

5—CH * *

and led the colonialists to propose the motion of confidence—which the Chamber unanimously approved.[25]

Although the colonialists expected Hanotaux to use Monteil as a means of putting pressure on the British, he had no intention of doing so. When he agreed to the expedition, he was banking on the fact that 'it would take [Monteil] three months to get to the Ubangi, and twice that number of months to the limit of the Congo basin; and that in the meantime it was to be hoped that [the Anglo-French] difference would be peaceably settled'.[26] Hanotaux had two good reasons for caution. First of all, to send a French expedition to the Upper Nile would destroy the legal basis of his opposition to the Anglo-Congolese Agreement, and indeed to the British occupation of Egypt itself: that neither Britain nor any other power had the right to dispose of territory still technically part of the Ottoman empire.[27] Secondly, a confrontation with Britain on the Upper Nile formed no part of his search for an Egyptian settlement, especially not when negotiations over the Anglo-Congolese Agreement might provide 'the opportunity to reopen the whole Egyptian question . . . and rescue us from the morass in which we have been floundering since 1882'. The British government professed itself willing to discuss French objections 'in a most conciliatory spirit'. But Hanotaux's talks with Dufferin soon revealed the gulf between their respective positions. The British were as determined as ever to keep the French off the Upper Nile. On 28 June Dufferin, aware of French plans to force the issue, warned Hanotaux that, if Monteil went into the Nile Valley, 'it would simply mean war between the two countries; and that it would be a terrible thing if we were going to revive in Africa the miserable combats which had deluged India with French and English blood in the middle of the last century'.[28] Hanotaux, who took the warning seriously, now had a third reason for prudence. He realised the political impossibility of cancelling a mission supported by the *groupe colonial* and approved by the Chamber as a whole. But if he could not stop it, he could at least render it harmless. On the eve of Monteil's departure, Hanotaux obtained from him a 'solemn undertaking that he would not send a platoon or even a single man into the Nile Basin', and he wrote this undertaking into Monteil's instructions.[29]

Once the Monteil expedition had been neutralised and the danger of conflict removed, Hanotaux's confidence returned. The lack of progress in his discussions with Dufferin ceased to worry him. Time as well as justice, he was now convinced, were on the side of France. The longer the British delayed, the greater would be the risk for them of having the whole Egyptian question reopened. Abandoning his efforts to undermine the Anglo-Congolese Agreement from the British side, Hanotaux turned instead to the Congolese. As in the previous spring, he adopted the tactics of intimidation, threatening to demand the recall of all Belgian officers in the Congolese administration since their presence was incompatible with Belgium's neutrality. This time Leopold had to give way. 'There was nothing to discuss', the Belgian ambassador to France admitted; 'there was no alternative to surrender.[30] Hanotaux was well pleased with the outcome. The Franco-Congolese Agreement of

14 August was hailed as 'a great success both for France and for you', and all his senior colleagues congratulated him on his diplomatic triumph. He had saved France's honour and enhanced his own reputation. He had put the Colonial Ministry in its place and had done so without impairing his relations with the *parti colonial*. And all this at the cost of 'great nervous tension, a few hours of anguish, and a good deal of sweat'.[31] He had not yet concluded a settlement with the British, but the fact that he had been able to denounce and then to destroy the Anglo-Congolese Agreement convinced him that Britain would always see reason if one had the courage to stand up to her. Success, as usual, left Hanotaux optimistic about the future.

The Franco-Congolese Agreement, by annulling Leopold's leases in the Bahr el Ghazal, removed the barrier between the French Congo and the Nile. 'Our route to the Upper Nile is open once more,' declared the French ambassador in Rome, 'and the British have no legitimate reason for complaint.' But this was a route which Hanotaux still refused to take; on 10 August he had assured the British 'with some vehemence that there was no question of France advancing to the Bahr el Ghazal'. His objective, as always, was to negotiate, and on 11 August he proposed a resumption of talks on all outstanding African questions. This time, Hanotaux and the British *chargé d'affaires*, Phipps, were at least able to reach a provisional agreement to keep out of the Upper Nile Valley until the frontiers of Egypt and the Sudan had been determined. But London repudiated this self-denying ordinance. The unfortunate Phipps was shipped off to South America, and Dufferin returned from leave with instructions to demand a unilateral undertaking that France would not cross the Congo-Nile watershed. Hanotaux flatly refused to give any such assurance, and on 7 November the negotiations collapsed. Hanotaux, it is true, did not lose hope immediately. But when the new French ambassador to London, Baron de Courcel, tried to revive the idea of a mutual self-denying ordinance, 'the depth of pride and intransigence beneath the courteous words of Lord Kimberley' soon discouraged him.[32]

The collapse of the negotiations increased Hanotaux's vulnerability to colonialist pressure. Throughout his talks with Phipps, one of his chief anxieties had been to secure an agreement which would 'conciliate the aspirations of the Colonial party'.[33] The Colonial Party was not, however, in a conciliatory mood. On 25 August a delegation from the *groupe colonial* called on the Egyptian head of state, Khedive Abbas, then on a private visit to Geneva. Both Eugène Etienne, the leader of the delegation, and Francois Deloncle, the *groupe*'s leading spokesman on Egyptian affairs, adopted the role of spokesman for the French government. Parliament and government, said Etienne, were both resolved on a new attempt to end the British occupation. It was therefore vital that Abbas make no concession to the British which might prejudice a French initiative: 'success was only possible if the capitulatory régime were maintained intact.' Abbas was at pains both to reassure and to encourage the delegation. He praised French policy for its 'disinterested sincerity', gave his blessing to 'whatever action'

France might decide upon, and declared himself confident of its success.

Deloncle sent Casimir-Périer an account of the meeting with the Khedive. His aim was doubtless to win over the new President, like Carnot before him, to colonialist policy on the Egyptian question.[34] Casimir-Périer's conversion, if not immediately accomplished, was not to be long delayed. With Delcassé at the Colonial Ministry, the *parti colonial* was also able to exert pressure for its policies from within the government. Despite his decision to cancel the Monteil expedition, Delcassé was still determined to press ahead with the Fashoda strategy.[35] Hanotaux was warned on 15 October by the *directeur politique* at the Colonial Ministry that his Minister was totally opposed to the proposed agreement with the British. A few days later Delcassé himself announced that, on his own authority, he was sending *Commissaire* Liotard to lead an expedition to the Upper Nile. On 26 October the *groupe colonial* issued a public demand for the speedy evacuation of Egypt.[36]

On 17 November the cabinet was forced to choose between the conflicting policies of the Foreign and Colonial Ministers. Delcassé's position was much the stronger. All that Hanotaux could suggest as an alternative to the Liotard mission was the self-denying ordinance which the British had already rejected. Delcassé had the support of the colonialists in the Chamber. He also had the Prime Minister and the President of the Republic on his side. Hanotaux later blamed Casimir-Périer for swinging the rest of the cabinet against him: 'I have since learned that Delcassé had arranged matters with you beforehand. You decided to assert your authority. You did so. I gave way. I could have protested, left, slammed the door. Perhaps it was my duty to resist. I didn't do so—and perhaps I was wrong not to.' For the first time, the French government as a whole authorised the advance to the Upper Nile which the *parti colonial* had been pressing for two years. By this decision, the colonialists momentarily gained control over a vital area of foreign policy, and Hanotaux saw his hopes for an entente with Britain menaced by their intransigence. He could have 'protested, left, slammed the door'. Instead, he suffered a nervous collapse, followed by a severe attack of influenza. For a few days his life seemed in danger.[37] Not until the beginning of January was he well enough to resume his post.

III

Early in 1895 the three men who had been responsible for sending Liotard to the Nile fell from power. On 13 January Casimir-Périer resigned from the Presidency of the Republic and was succeeded by Félix Faure. Following established custom, the Dupuy government also resigned. Ribot returned to form his third administration, and Emile Chautemps replaced Delcassé at the Colonial Ministry. These changes strengthened Hanotaux's position as Foreign Minister in the new government. But the diplomatic problems confronting him were even more serious than before. During the first six months of 1895 he was faced not merely with the collapse of his hopes for a negotiated settlement of the Egyptian question but also, and almost simultaneously, with the threatened collapse of the Dual Alliance.

Hitherto, colonialist pressure for action on the Nile had been exerted largely behind the scenes. Now it became public. In January 1895 Harry Alis of the *Comité de l'Afrique Française* published an article which, as Hanotaux admitted, caused 'a considerable stir', calling for a French presence on the Upper Nile as the only way to force the British out of Egypt. He then went on a lecture tour to stir up opinion in France, while his newspaper, the *Journal Egyptien,* stirred up the Egyptians. Equally embarrassing for Hanotaux was the parliamentary agitation of the *groupe colonial,* 'which had grown conscious of its strength and, under the leadership of men like M. Etienne and Prince d'Arenberg, whipped up opinion and kept up ceaseless pressure on the government'. First Flourens, then François Deloncle, both senior members of the group, mixed denunciations of 'English dreams of African hegemony' with calls for a rapid advance to the Upper Nile. Hanotaux could only reply with embarrassed remarks about the danger of impromptu statements on important diplomatic questions.[38]

Colonialist attempts to dictate official policy became increasingly brazen. In March Deloncle visited Egypt. Although Hanotaux had tried to prevent his visit, Deloncle claimed that he had secret instructions from the Quai d'Orsay and Cogordan, the French Minister in Cairo, was about to be recalled. Even when Cogordan produced letters declaring Hanotaux's confidence in him, some of his staff continued to believe Deloncle. Bouteron, the *administrateur des domaines,* told him: 'The reason why Hanotaux tells you a different story is quite simple. This is a *secret* mission'.[39] During his stay Deloncle called again on the Khedive, renewed his contacts with the 'Young Egyptian' nationalists and promised them that 'England will have evacuated Egypt in ten months'. He also gained control of the *Journal Egyptien* which he then turned over to Aristide Gavillot, a wealthy French journalist and member of the Egyptian financial administration, regarded by the British as 'a creature of Deloncle's whose money will no doubt be used for the purposes of the cause'.[40] Deloncle's parting speech was a violent and threatening denunciation of the British occupation: 'Can one still imagine that, with an army of three million men, we do not have the firm desire to be respected by a power which occupies Egypt with three thousand men?' Cogordan did his best to suppress the speech. Gavillot, however, insisted on publishing it, on the grounds that 'his objective over the past ten years had been precisely to force the hand of the French government . . . besides which he took his orders from M. Deloncle and the *groupe colonial,* whose agent he had agreed to become.'[41] Deloncle continued his campaign after his return to France, denouncing the 'moral tyranny' of the British occupation and promising a new round of interpellations in parliament. He also arranged for Mustafa Kemal, the leader of the 'Young Egyptians' and his 'most fervent admirer and friend', to go on a lecture tour of Paris and the provinces.[42] The colonialists maintained their pressure throughout the summer, using the Havas news service to spread reports that the solution of the Egyptian question was imminent; the *Journal Egyptien* published rumours that a French expedition had actually reached the Upper Nile and had already begun to negotiate with the Khalifa Abdallahi.[43]

Deloncle and his friends inevitably provoked a British reaction. In February Courcel described threats to depose the Khedive which appeared in the British press as 'the brutal reply, *à l'anglaise,* to the somewhat imprudent polemics ... of French papers in Paris and Alexandria'.[44] On 11 March a British M.P. referred to the speeches of Flourens and Deloncle and demanded a firm statement that the Upper Nile was a British sphere of influence. On the 28th he raised the question again, and on the same evening Grey, the Under-Secretary for Foreign Affairs, issued his famous declaration that any French attempt to enter the Upper Nile would be considered an 'unfriendly act'.

Hanotaux, like most French politicians, was not unduly disturbed by the Grey Declaration. It was, he believed, 'not seriously intended and solely for the purpose of avoiding trouble from *les Deloncle d'Outre-Manche*'. All that concerned him was the possibility that Liotard might turn up on the Nile and put the declaration to the test before tempers had had time to cool. The British for their part seemed conciliatory too. Kimberley protested that 'he attached far less value to this question of Egypt than to the maintenance of friendly relations with France'. Dufferin indeed suggested another round of talks. But conciliatory attitudes on both sides did not bring a solution any closer. On 12 June the ambassador had to tell Hanotaux that his government had failed to authorise new negotiations.[45] With the British government unwilling even to discuss the Upper Nile, Hanotaux temporarily had to abandon his plans for a negotiated settlement.

Hanotaux, however, was more worried by the state of the Dual Alliance than by the Egyptian question. The first threat to it came in February with the German invitation to attend the opening of the Kiel Ship Canal the following summer. The Russians accepted without consulting their ally, and the French government had to follow suit in order to preserve the appearance of unity. 'I must tell you,' Hanotaux wrote to Montebello, his ambassador in St. Petersburg, 'that nobody in France at the present time knows what to make of our entente, and that our former confidence in it has been shattered.' The attempt at international mediation in the Sino-Japanese war provided an even more galling demonstration of Russian insensitivity. In March, without bothering to inform the French government, Russia accepted Germany's offer to join with the Dual Alliance in a common peace initiative. Still without consulting France, the Russians then decided to oppose the cession of the Liao-Tung peninsula to Japan, by force if necessary; and Hanotaux felt obliged to endorse their demand. But, as he told Montebello, 'we cannot commit ourselves to any expenditure or to military action *without seeking the approval of Parliament*. This will lead inevitably to a general debate about the Franco-Russian entente. We shall then be obliged to discuss in public the arrangements we have made with Russia against Germany, at the very moment when we shall be asking to go *with* Germany to the assistance of Russia. It's all a perfect mess.'[46]

By the end of May, Hanotaux was completely exasperated. His ambition to become the quasi-permanent Foreign Minister was seriously at risk. The Russians had forced him to embroil himself in Far Eastern affairs, against the wishes of public opinion and merely in order to preserve the alliance. They had forced him to agree to Kiel on the same terms. Now public opinion had had enough. The government had been humiliated—'Are we being duped? If only we were sure that we were! But the worst of it is that we look like dupes.' The Russians had even refused to make the alliance public. Unless some clear demonstration of Franco-Russian solidarity were made, Hanotaux warned Montebello, 'we can all pack our bags'.[47]

The interpellation on the alliance which Hanotaux so dreaded took place on 10 June. To save itself, the government had for the first time to reveal the existence of a *treaty* of alliance. 'It was not merely necessary,' Hanotaux explained to Montebello, 'it was vital. The fate of the Cabinet and the whole future of Franco-Russian relations were at stake.' But with the Russians anxious for another loan, the alliance suddenly took on a new lease of life. Much to Hanotaux's surprise, the Czar enthusiastically approved his revelations. He also agreed that the two fleets should rendezvous beforehand and arrive at Kiel together, thus—in French eyes at least—turning a potential embarrassment into a naval demonstration of the alliance in German waters. The need for military action in the Far East never materialised, and the conclusion of peace between China and Japan was also recognised as 'a great success for our policy', and for Hanotaux personally: 'Europe knows it, and hers, after all, is the opinion which makes Foreign Ministers' reputations.'[48]

What finally restored Hanotaux's faith in the Dual Alliance was the visit of Prince Lobanov to France in September. Few Foreign Ministers have ever been so taken with each other. Both fancied themselves great historians as well as great diplomats. Lobanov, Cambon complained, exercised over Hanotaux *une attraction dominante*, and the attraction was mutual. 'Lobanov's ideal is Hanotaux,' wrote the German Foreign Minister, 'and Hanotaux seems to have found his weak spot. The Prince never tires of describing their first meeting when they stayed up till two in the morning talking about books, with never a word about politics.' By the end of the visit Hanotaux was convinced of the sincerity of Lobanov's repeated assurances that 'so long as he remained in office, Russia would remain faithful to the policy of Alexander III [the founder of the alliance]'.[49] The first of his ambitions as Foreign Minister—the consolidation of the Dual Alliance—seemed on the point of realisation.

But his other ambition—the settlement of the Egyptian question—

appeared as remote as ever. The massive Conservative victory at the British General Elections of June 1895 made the prospect of an Anglo-French agreement gloomier than ever. Courcel had forecast as early as February that the Tories would be even more committed to the isolation of France than the Liberals. In July he warned that 'the revival of the spirit of British imperialism could become very dangerous for other nations, and we might well find the British government not merely intransigent but positively aggressive'.[50] On 21 August Curzon, the new Foreign Under-Secretary, ruled out the possibility even of discussions about the evacuation of Egypt. Hanotaux now had either to abandon his Egyptian ambitions or to devise a new Egyptian strategy.

IV

In the autumn of 1895 three influences—the Colonial Party, Jean-Baptiste Marchand and the international situation—pushed Hanotaux towards an acceptance of the Fashoda strategy. The colonialists had drawn optimistic conclusions from Germany's co-operation with the Dual Alliance in the Far East. Citing articles in the semi-official Russian press, the *Bulletin du Comité de l'Afrique Française* predicted that '[this] entente . . . will not limit itself simply to the solution of Sino-Japanese affairs but will shortly attempt the solution of the Egyptian question'. As usual, increased British intransigence over Egypt led to increased colonialist pressure on the foreign minister. During the debate on the Russian alliance in June Hanotaux had to declare that the Egyptian question was 'still open', and Flourens demanded: 'Can we not ask Russia to return the services we have rendered her . . . by co-operating with us in the liberation of Egypt?' Immediately afterwards, a new pressure group, the *Comité de l'Egypte*, was formed. The presence of Deloncle and Gavillot among its officers gave some indication of the policies it would follow. The presence of Etienne and Arenberg as Honorary Presidents, and of some twenty colonialist deputies among its members, was a guarantee of its influence. By the time Hanotaux left office in November, the *Comité de l'Egypte* felt satisfied enough with the results of its pressure on him to pass a vote of thanks 'for the sympathy which he has shown towards our activities'.[51]

The colonialists, however, found it more difficult to maintain their pressure for an advance to the Nile. The slow and expensive progress of the Madagascar campaign made all colonial expeditions temporarily unpopular in the summer of 1895. The increasingly chaotic finances of military expansion in West Africa made parliament unwilling to authorise any new expenditure. Chautemps sought to placate the Chamber by cutting his Estimates to the bone. Although Liotard had still not reached the Congo-Nile watershed and could not make further progress without reinforcements, the Colonial Minister dared not ask for the necessary credits. 'Any idea of serious action on the Upper Nile', he told the Budget Commission on 18 June, 'is to be dismissed . . . On the Upper Ubangi, we must limit our expenditure to the strict minimum needed to maintain our existing positions.'[52] But by the autumn the prospects for a new intitiative on the Nile were much brighter. Once the Madagascar campaign came within sight of success, all the old enthusiasm for it revived. In September the government felt compelled to make its peace terms even harsher than it had originally intended, for the sole purpose of 'placating public opinion' and 'flattering national pride'. Not even the imposition of a rigorous protectorate satisfied the *groupe colonial*, which demanded outright annexation. On 23 October Le Myre de Vilers, the *groupe*'s spokesman on Madagascar—and the man in charge of the final negotiations with the Hovas in October 1894—resigned from the foreign service in order to campaign against Hanotaux's protectorate policy. Having badgered the Foreign Minister over Egypt, the colonialists were getting ready to give him a 'disagreeable' time over Madagascar as well.[53] Hanotaux would have to be careful how he responded to their pressure for another expedition to Fashoda.

The idea for such a mission in the summer of 1895 came from a Captain in the *infanterie de marine*, Jean-Baptiste Marchand. Despite his junior rank, Marchand possessed considerable political influence. He was a member of the *officiers soudanais,* a tightly-knit group of colonial officers who had already carved out a virtually private empire for themselves in the western Sudan. Through them, he could count on the support of several militarist deputies, most notably René Le Hérissé, a prominent member of the *groupe colonial* and the chief spokesman for Sudanese military interests in Parliament. He could also rely on the *Comité de l'Afrique Française* which had supported his mission to the northern Ivory Coast in 1893 and now backed his plans for an expedition to the Nile. Arenberg, the *Comité*'s president, later claimed that 'they, the colonial party, had purposely instigated, planned and started the Marchand expedition'. By a fortunate coincidence, Marchand also had 'easy access' to Hanotaux through their mutual friends, the Ménard family. It was at the home of Louis Ménard, Hanotaux's doctor, that the two men met for the first time in 1892 and discussed Marchand's forthcoming mission to the Ivory Coast. From then on, Hanotaux claimed, the two of them were 'linked by a close friendship'. The force of Marchand's own personality and his indefatigable energy were also of great importance. 'You will never believe,' he told Liotard later, 'what a desperate campaign I waged in Paris for thirteen months ... The number of deputies, senators, ministers—*all the ministers*— I saw. The number of hours, days, months, I spent fighting with recalcitrants, pushing journalists, collecting supporters ...'[54]

Marchand probably made his first approach to Hanotaux on 18 July, just after the minister's successful defence of the Franco-Russian alliance and the collapse of his talks with Dufferin.[55] Significantly, despite his previous opposition to any action on the Upper Nile, Hanotaux did not dismiss the project out of hand. Instead, he encouraged Marchand to elaborate his scheme and submit it to the Ministry of Colonies. Marchand's reception at the *Pavillon de Flore* was more enthusiastic. He already had an important ally in Colonel

Louis Archinard, the Ministry's Director of Defence and his former commanding officer in the Sudan. Chautemps himself seemed most taken with the scheme. 'One must be able to say,' he declared after their first interview, 'that Captain Marchand *a pissé dans le Nil en amont de Khartoum.*'[56]

Marchand submitted his detailed plans on 11 September. The lengthy document was cleverly drafted to appeal both to the Ministry's extravagant ambitions on the Upper Nile and to its immediate financial preoccupations. The long-term objective, as Marchand defined it, was to forestall a British master-plan to dominate the whole of the African interior by linking the Cape with Cairo and the Gulf of Benin with the Red Sea. To this 'British theory of the African cross,' Marchand opposed 'the more modest junction of the Congo with Obock by way of the Bahr el Ghazal and Ethiopia . . .' In this way, France could not only thwart British schemes for African hegemony but also participate effectively in the eventual partition of the Sudan, 'secure the Nile hinterland for the French Congo', and, implicitly, hasten the evacuation of Egypt. 'I make no secret of the fact,' he added, 'that Fashoda is the principal objective of my mission.' But Marchand did not intend to occupy Fashoda or any other point in the Nile Basin. His objective, once across the Congo-Nile watershed, was simply 'to make alliances . . . and extend French influence', which he could do with less than fifty men. This in itself would be a guarantee against any conflict with the Mahdists. And the expedition as a whole would be cheap. Its total cost, spread over three years, was estimated at only 600,000 francs (£24,000 in contemporary English terms). Chautemps, however, was too frightened to accept responsibility for an expedition even on this scale, and Archinard also agreed that 'we must reduce our expenditure as far as possible'. So they sent Marchand back to see Hanotaux, giving his scheme their blessing but stressing that 'the further extension of our sphere of influence . . . in the direction of the Nile . . . [is] even more a question of general foreign policy than of purely colonial interests'.[57]

> Time and again I visited the Quai d'Orsay which soon . . . came out energetically in my favour . . .
> The ministry studied my project (thanks to the easy access which I had to M. Hanotaux). On 20 October, in the office of M. Benoît [the *sous-directeur des protectorats*], I received the order from M. Nisard to condense my report into something more theoretical, more substantial, and shorter—100 lines. On the 25th, I submitted my *note analytique complémentaire*—it simply contained the *théorie des gages*, with this theory quite explicitly spelled out . . .
> The two ministers [Chautemps and Hanotaux] meet. At last, my mission is approved. Chautemps promises me that I shall receive my instructions on 29 October. Crash! The ministry falls on the 28th. I have to start everything all over again . . .
> [But] it must be said that M. Hanotaux had prepared everything and merely left room for a signature before he left the Quai d'Orsay . . .[58]

Admittedly, this account contains several discrepancies. The date of the *note complémentaire* is the least significant. Although the copy of the note in the Foreign Ministry files is dated 10 November, not 25 October, it is entirely probable that Marchand resubmitted his project to the incoming government. More serious is the fact that the ministerial meeting which he mentions did not take place.[59] And although the Ribot government did fall on 28 October, Hanotaux still had time to sign Marchand's instructions before he finally handed over to his successor on 2 November. Only his scruples as a *ministre démissionnaire* would have prevented him from doing so. He could certainly not have been seeking to avoid responsibility for the final decision, since on 1 November he was still expecting to remain as Foreign Minister in the new government.[60]

But Marchand's claims about the support which he received from the Quai d'Orsay ring true. Certainly, he planned his campaign at the Foreign Ministry as carefully as at the Pavillon de Flore. Just as his original project had been designed to appeal to Chautemps, so his *note analytique complémentaire* was designed to appeal to Hanotaux. There was no mention in it that the Bahr el Ghazal might eventually be added to the French empire. On the contrary, Marchand specifically recognised the province as part of the Egyptian Sudan and hence an Egyptian possession. The only purpose of his mission, therefore, was to obtain 'sureties in the Nile basin for the restitution to Egypt of territories which once formed part of the Egyptian Sudan and have been momentarily occupied, under whatever pretext, by one or more European powers'. The relatively innocuous character of his activities was still more heavily emphasised. Once in the Bahr el Ghazal, he claimed, his mission would become 'a sort of anonymous visit made by a group of European travellers, without any official character or instructions, to the inhabitants of territories neighbouring the Upper Ubangi with whom they wish to establish friendly commercial relations'. There was of course no need for concern about the Mahdists; there was no need to worry about other Europeans either. If another European expedition were encountered, the two commanders would simply 'greet each other with all due courtesy ... and let their respective governments decide what the consequences should be'. The ultimate objective was also more clearly stated: 'In the final analysis, it is, by peaceful but certain means, to make it necessary for Britain to accept, if not to summon herself, a European conference to determine the future of the Egyptian Sudan, i.e. the Nile Valley. In addition to the importance of such a result for French colonisation in Africa, whose future is so gravely menaced by British pretensions, may we not hope that the question of the evacuation of Egypt would flow quite naturally from that of the Sudan and bring itself with a new urgency to the attention of the conference?'[61]

There were several reasons why such a plan should have appealed to Hanotaux. He was already under severe colonialist pressure, on Egypt, on Madagascar, and also because of his attempts to settle an Anglo-French dispute over Siam, where the very prospect of an agreement 'would always be regarded with suspicion by the wild men of the

colonial party'.[62] He could not lightly risk adding to his troubles by
rejecting their demands for action on the Upper Nile. Nor could he
ignore Marchand's insistence on the dangers of British expansion.
There were rumours of an impending British advance into the Sudan,
and by August even the Khedive's Foreign Minister, hitherto a staunch
opponent of any European presence on the Upper Nile, was calling
for a French occupation of the Bahr el Ghazal as the only way to forestall a British takeover.[63] Marchand's expedition would provide a
defence against British aggression. It might even provide a way out of
the Egyptian impasse. Hanotaux need not have rejected it on principle.
'With the British,' he believed, 'one must always negotiate, but one
must always act as well,' for British negotiators only took concrete
facts seriously. He later claimed that he had achieved surprisingly good
results 'by suddenly presenting, during the course of a negotiation, the
homme du fait. He did not have to speak; his presence alone was
enough'.[64] Only an optimist, of course, could have seen the Marchand
expedition as a possible solution to the Egyptian question. But by
October 1895 Hanotaux was in a highly optimistic mood. Lobanov's
visit had completely erased the memory of his troubles with the Russians
in the spring and had restored all his faith in the solidity and effectiveness of the alliance. Lobanov, an inveterate Anglophobe who could never
mention the British 'without breathing fire', was just the man to urge
him on. Cambon at least was convinced that 'the famous Marchand
expedition was jointly decided on by Lobanov and Hanotaux'.[65] Certainly, after the Prince's visit Russia began to support French policy in
Egypt with unaccustomed vigour.

By the time Hanotaux left office he was talking, with the careless
abandon he often showed when optimism had gone to his head, about
'retaking Egypt from the British with our victorious troops from Madagascar'.[66] Such wild talk does not necessarily mean that Hanotaux had
finally committed himself to the Fashoda strategy. But his senior officials
certainly had. Marchand was full of praise for their 'true political
courage . . . At the Foreign Ministry, opinion has not changed with the
minister; only here, happily, does one find such firmness'.[67] Nisard and
Georges Benoît, the Sous-directeur des protectorats, were the officials
most concerned with examining Marchand's plans, and they were the
most ardent champions of a forward policy on the Upper Nile. Nisard
had consistently favoured an advance since 1892; Benoît seemed at
times closer to the expansionists at the Pavillon de Flore than to his own
superiors at the Quai d'Orsay.[68] It was the support of these men, as
much as that of Hanotaux, which Marchand needed and set out to
acquire; for Hanotaux was indulgent towards his subordinates and
allowed them wide powers of initiative.[69] At the end of October 1895,
it was the support of these men which Marchand undoubtedly enjoyed.

V

On 28 October 1895 the Ribot government resigned. It had not been a successful ministry; the only minister 'whose reputation has certainly improved during his tenure of office' was Hanotaux. Hanotaux hoped to remain at the Quai d'Orsay in the new Bourgeois government and was confident that he could dictate his own terms. But Bourgeois, trying to form the first genuinely Radical administration of the Third Republic, had no time for prima donnas and passed him over.[70]

The loss of Hanotaux was to be a serious blow for the new government. The ex-Foreign Minister retained not only the support of the public but also the loyalty of the ambassadors and the officials at the Quai d'Orsay.[71] It was impossible to find a satisfactory replacement. Having tried and failed to appoint another professional diplomat, Bourgeois was eventually forced to accept the offer of the distinguished chemist, Marcellin Berthelot (originally chosen for the Ministry of Public Instruction) to take over the Quai d'Orsay. The transfer of power at the Colonial Ministry was equally complicated. Chautemps, like Hanotaux, wanted to remain in the government but was persuaded not to by Ribot. Bourgeois then approached Jules Siegfried, a Moderate and a leading member of the *groupe colonial*, who refused to serve in a Radical government. In the end, he had to choose another academic, the Egyptologist Paul Guieysse.[72]

From its formation, the Bourgeois ministry was faced with the simultaneous opposition of the Moderates, the *Ralliés* and the Right, all of whom expected its early demise. Berthelot's position at the Quai d'Orsay was particularly weak. Although 'singularly intelligent', the 'old chemist' was completely inexperienced in foreign affairs. Cambon despised his lack of control over the Ministry; Courcel on his visits to Paris consulted his 'confidant and kindred spirit' Hanotaux more than he did the titular head of the Quai d'Orsay.[73] To make matters worse, Berthelot's daughter died a few days after his appointment, leaving him so distraught that he virtually abandoned his post, refusing to see ambassadors or to conduct any business. On 20 November he submitted his resignation. Although he soon recovered sufficiently to resume charge of his department, he was never able to assert his authority over it. By the end of February even Dufferin, the most favourably disposed of the ambassadors, admitted that Berthelot was 'almost paralysed by the work of his new unaccustomed office. Innumerable questions are being forced on his attention, with the details of which he is unacquainted, and the labour of working them up appears too much for his energies, which have been enfeebled by bad health and lately unnerved by domestic affliction.'[74]

The first and most important question 'forced on his attention' was Fashoda. The initiative came from the Colonial Ministry. The appointment of Guieysse, a political unknown, had taken the colonialists by surprise, but his sympathy for their objectives soon became apparent. Marchand himself paid tribute to the new minister's 'spirit of decision —a rare thing to find in a colonial minister'.[75] On 8 November, four days after Guieysse had taken office, the *Pavillon de Flore* asked Berthelot for an immediate decision about the Marchand expedition. On the 10th, Marchand resubmitted his *note complémentaire*. On the 13th,

Benoît underlined the need for speed. At the cabinet meeting of 21 November, Guieysse himself pressed Berthelot for his answer, and the Foreign Minister, who was in no state to make a reasoned judgement, said he was willing to approve the mission. On the 30th Guieysse pressed him again, assuring him that 'the mission would not occupy any territory, would not even sign any political treaties, but its presence in the Bahr el Ghazal may enable us to intervene effectively in the settlement of the question of the Egyptian Sudan and may even hasten that settlement'. On the basis of these assurances, Berthelot gave his formal approval.[76]

Before Marchand could receive his detailed instructions, however, the Colonial Ministry learned that Liotard had at last begun to resume his advance. This news enabled the *Directeur politique*, Etienne Roume, to argue that Liotard's mission had a number of advantages over Marchand's: in particular, it would give France access to the Upper Nile in an area where he alleged, Egypt had no claim and to which France could establish secure title by alliance with local rulers. But Archinard forcefully argued his protégé's case and eventually won the Minister over. On 3 February Guieysse saw Marchand once more, and on the 11th he and Berthelot put the expedition to the cabinet for its approval. On the 24th, Marchand's instructions were finally signed. Although he was firmly subordinated to Liotard, the main lines of his original project were approved. The mission was to be much more than the simple non-political exploration which Berthelot had agreed to in November. Its objective was 'to secure binding alliances and indisputable claims on the White Nile for the day when the fate of these provinces will be decided', and Liotard was told in no uncertain terms that 'the government attaches the greatest importance to the realisation of M. Marchand's programme, if not in its entirety, at least in its essentials; it is absolutely determined to see his proposed "raid" carried out'. Guieysse sent a copy of these instructions to Berthelot, who made no comment on them.[77]

Dufferin was right to doubt whether Berthelot had 'grit enough to run counter to the colonial party'. On West African affairs, the ambassador found him 'evidently disinclined to apply his own independent judgment to a question to which he knows the Colonial Group in the Chamber attach great importance'.[78] He was no more able to withstand colonialist pressure on the Upper Nile. The *Comité de l'Afrique Française*, through Archinard, was undoubtedly instrumental in getting the mission approved, and Marchand thanked it profusely for 'all you are doing for me . . .' The *groupe colonial* was equally active. Blowitz, the Paris correspondent of *The Times*, warned his readers that 'the action of the group should be attentively watched. It pursues with a persistence not very common here a far-reaching scheme which is finally being adopted by government circles, for the men who have conceived and who pursue it know what they are about and what they want.' Deloncle boasted in two letters to Blowitz, both published in *The Times*, that Britain would be forced, 'whether she likes it or not', to leave Egypt 'in a comparatively near future'.[79]

Although Berthelot allowed himself to be drawn into an anti-British policy on the Upper Nile, his natural inclination was to improve Anglo-French relations. He made no attempt to exploit the South African crises which the Jameson Raid and the Kruger Telegram precipitated in January 1896, and he rejected Germany's offer of a colonial entente to limit 'the insatiable appetites of England'. Instead, he assured the British that France 'had no interests of her own involved in the Transvaal', and no desire to intervene.[80] Britain's difficulties in South Africa and the settlement of the Siamese dispute combined to create a general confidence that negotiations about Egypt, too, could shortly be resumed. Egypt, Dufferin reported on 16 January, 'is in every French mouth'. With the encouragement of Faure, and probably of Hanotaux, Courcel tried to reopen discussions in February, and on this occasion at least Salisbury seemed willing to listen. Hopes for a settlement continued to mount. 'There is no doubt,' wrote Dufferin on 19 March, 'that for some weeks past the French have been living in a fools' paradise and have imagined that their dispute with us about Egypt was on the point of reaching a satisfactory solution.'[81]

On 13 March these illusions were rudely dispelled by the unexpected announcement of an Anglo-Egyptian advance up the Nile to Dongola. All hope of continuing the discussions about Egypt again vanished. The British, Courcel told Faure, 'have certainly tricked us'. For once, France seemed to have the power to make an effective protest; legally, the use of Egyptian revenue to pay for the Dongola expedition needed the unanimous consent of the *Caisse de la Dette*, on which France and Russia were both represented. Under strong pressure from public opinion, Berthelot had to take a firm stand. On 19 March he formally objected to the invasion of the Sudan on the grounds that it would indefinitely prolong the occupation of Egypt, and he threatened to veto any request for funds unless Britain gave him positive assurances of her intention to evacuate.[82] For all his public demonstrations of firmness, however, Berthelot was still anxious to avoid an open breach. Although he maintained his veto on the allocation of funds, he considerably weakened the force of his original protest by accepting Salisbury's assurance that the Dongola campaign in no way altered the temporary nature of the British occupation.[83]

Berthelot's weakness over Egypt led directly to his fall. His position as Foreign Minister had already been undermined by his evident lack of authority and by the equally evident hostility of Russia. Russians and Radicals did not in any case get on, and their relations had been further strained during the diplomatic crisis which followed the Armenian massacres. On 5 December 1895 Lobanov had asked the French what assistance Russia could expect if she decided to occupy the Bosphorus, and Berthelot had been forced to warn him that France could not offer military support unless she saw an opportunity for regaining the Lost Provinces.[84] Since the Russian alliance remained the cornerstone of French foreign policy, it became imperative to avoid any further misunderstandings. Accordingly, when the Dongola campaign was announced, the cabinet unanimously decided 'to remain utterly and completely in step with Russia', and merely to 'take note' of Salisbury's assurances. Ignorant of the fine distinction between 'accepting' an assurance and 'taking note' of it, the unfortunate Berthelot inadvertently contravened the cabinet's decision. Faure was furious. Lest Russia think 'that we were satisfied with banal phrases and had ceased to act in concert with her', he demanded the Foreign Minister's resignation. And when the Russians themselves complained, Berthelot had to go. At Faure's insistence, Bourgeois took over the Quai d'Orsay and gave Lobanov the most abject assurances of future loyalty.[85]

It was now impossible for Bourgeois to maintain a dialogue with Britain; the risk of offending the Russians was too great.[86] Nor could he halt the Marchand expedition. He fully recognised the dangers of 'a situation which might be altered ... in a way most prejudicial to our interests, by Britain's initiative in the Sudan'. But the British invasion had merely intensified the demands of the colonialists, and the determination of the Colonial Ministry, for countermeasures on the Upper Nile. Although Guieysse accepted the need for caution, he insisted that there was no reason 'to fall back to the Congo'. On 18 April Bourgeois did see Marchand and made him confirm his pledges about the peaceful character of his mission. But this was as far as his precautions went.[87] Bourgeois's interview with Marchand was one of his last acts as Foreign Minister. On 23 April the government was forced to resign. On the 25th, Marchand's advance party left for the Congo. On the 29th, Hanotaux returned to the Quai d'Orsay as Foreign Minister in the Conservative government of Jules Méline.

VI

Both Hanotaux and the new Colonial Minister, André Lebon, (himself a member of the *groupe* colonial), later maintained that the Méline government, even had it wanted to, could not have cancelled the Marchand expedition. 'The Colonial Party, then so fervent', wrote Hanotaux, 'would scarcely have agreed to abandon, because of future complications which might never occur the hopes which ... the energetic Captain had inspired in them'.[88] Méline's immediate preoccupation on taking office was to maintain his parliamentary majority, if necessary by 'pandering to interest groups, even those of a rather disreputable nature'. He was conscious from the start of his dependence on colonialist votes and anxious to conciliate the leaders of the *groupe colonial*. In July 1896 he agreed to replace the Governor-General of Algeria, Jules Cambon, whom Etienne and his fellow Algerian deputy, Thomson, found insufficiently subservient. Although Cambon's transfer to the foreign service and his replacement by a colonialist nominee took several months to engineer and caused several cabinet rows in the process, Méline considered the manoeuvre indispensable for securing 'the votes of Thomson, Etienne and company'.[89] Having taken so much trouble to acquire the colonialists' support, Méline was not likely to incur their wrath by countermanding Marchand's instructions.

By the time Marchand left for Africa in June 1896, the leaders of the *groupe colonial* were confident of overwhelming parliamentary support for the expedition. Marchand himself had done much to ensure it. 'Now ... *all the party leaders are committed*,' he told Liotard, 'and if the question comes before the Chamber or the Senate, there will be speakers ready and willing to assert our rights on the Nile in the face of the English, ministers ready to accept what they say, and an immense majority of deputies ready to vote for action.' Marchand's optimism was justified; in December 1896 the credits for his expedition were approved, without discussion, by a majority of 477 to 18. As Marchand implied, he had won over the politicians chiefly by appealing to their sense of nationalism; even a majority of the Socialists proved susceptible to his arguments. 'It is not a political vote that we shall take,' Jaurès proclaimed, 'but a national one.' Interestingly, the opposition was led by a dissident colonialist opposed not to the aims of the expedition but to its methods. Such realists were, however, a minority in the Colonial Party, without influence on the leaders of the *groupe colonial* and the *Comité de l'Afrique Française*.[90]

Marchand had at least three committed supporters within the government: Hanotaux, Lebon, and Cochery, the Minister of Finance.[91] Hanotaux had returned to the Quai d'Orsay in an expansive mood, claiming that the timid diplomacy of the Bourgeois government had thrown away 'the magnificent position' achieved during his first term of office. He talked grandiloquently about the ambitious initiatives he would have taken in the Near East, and of his plans for intervention in Syria to meet any threat to the Turkish Empire. 'Under the circumstances,' Dufferin concluded, 'it has become necessary for Hanotaux to make some striking "coup" in order to justify the expectations of his admirers. Naturally it is at our expense that he will try to win these anticipated laurels.'[92]

After three meetings the Méline cabinet, 'under the direction, naturally, of M. Hanotaux, supported by M. Lebon and M. Cochery', approved the Marchand expedition, and on 23 June Lebon signed the final instructions. Although Archinard had less influence with Lebon than with Chautemps or Guieysse, the new *éminence grise* at the *Pavillon de Flore*, Léonce Lagarde—*l'ami Lagarde* as Marchand called him—was an equally reliable ally. Contrary to Hanotaux's later assertions, the Méline government in no way altered the objectives of the expedition as defined by Guieysse on 24 February. Indeed, Liotard was specifically ordered 'strictly to maintain the policy which you have pursued ... for almost two years, and of which our establishment in the Nile Basin must be the culmination'. And when Hanotaux saw Marchand for the last time, he told him: 'Go to Fashoda. France is firing her pistol shot!'[93]

From the moment that Marchand left France until the early months of 1898 his colonialist backers remained unwaveringly confident about the success of his mission. There were two reasons for this optimism. The first was the conviction, 'which cannot be too often repeated, that the question of Egypt is, at root, one of the main preoccupations of the European concert'. French colonialists simply refused to believe that any imperial power could fail to appreciate the vital importance of breaking the British stranglehold on Egypt and the Suez Canal. They were confident that Germany in particular, however equivocal her attitude for the moment, was bound to see that her own imperial future was at stake once Marchand reached the Nile and reopened the Egyptian question. As Delafosse told the Chamber in April 1896: 'It is inevitable that the Triple Alliance, if consulted about a conflict between Britain and France, would take a stand against us ... But put the question differently; ask Austria, Italy and Germany if they accept the permanent British occupation of Egypt and ... they will answer no, because it is impossible for them to give any other answer.'[94]

The second reason for optimism was what, after Adowa, the colonialists believed to be Ethiopia's dominant position on the Upper Nile: 'Ethiopia, this impregnable eagle's nest, with its 250,000 soldiers, is and must remain the most important military force in Africa, guardian of the peace on the Upper Nile.' The *groupe colonial* was confident that Ethiopian support would make it impossible for the British to challenge Marchand, even if they succeeded in overcoming the Mahdists. Marchand himself had been counting on this support when he had drafted his original report in September 1895. And Arenberg later admitted to the British military attaché that 'the idea [of the Marchand expedition] was to establish connexion with Menelik and the Ethiopians'.[95]

Hanotaux shared the optimism of most colonialists. He was naturally confident of Russian support—Lobanov's continuance in office was guarantee enough of that—and he too believed that everything would depend on Germany's attitude. Despite his suspicions about a possible Anglo-German understanding over Egypt, he did not think that Germany had finally made up her mind. He therefore persuaded the Russians to test the ground in Berlin. For the next few months Courcel also tried to persuade his German colleague in London that a solution to the Egyptian question was 'of vital importance for all our interests in Africa without exception', and Hanotaux himself made a number of unofficial overtures, most notably through his veteran confidential agent, Jules Hansen.[96] Even when all these advances were rebuffed, he did not despair. Like Delafosse, he did not expect Germany to side with France in a purely Anglo-French quarrel, but he was sure that her attitude would change once the Marchand expedition had succeeded in provoking an *international* conference. 'The Egyptian question,' he wrote, 'must be posed in terms which—by the very nature of things— will one day bring the major powers to recognise the identity of their interests with ours. It is the European character of the Egyptian question which gives us our most solid grounds for hoping the Nile Valley can be freed from the régime against which we have never ceased to protest—in the interests of everyone.'[97]

Hanotaux was equally confident that once Marchand was established on the Upper Nile, the Ethiopians would protect him from any possible British attack. Khartoum, he told Dufferin, 'was not the Sudan; it was merely the gateway to the Sudan, and Abyssinia would prove a fortress dominating the Upper Nile and a power which would preclude any foreign nation from establishing itself on its headwaters'.[98] His optimism was not unreasonable in the summer of 1896. Relations with Ethiopia had been cordial ever since the French had begun to support Menelik's attempts to resist the imposition of an Italian pro- tectorate and to supply him with arms. By 1893 the two countries seemed to be moving towards an unofficial alliance. By then, too, Delcassé was confident that, when the time came, Menelik would 'establish a post for us on the Nile'.[99] When Delcassé returned to the Ministry of Colonies in June 1894, he defined 'the independence of Menelik and his eventual alliance with France' as 'the objective of any Nile policy'. Once the Negus had occupied the right bank of the Upper Nile, he would be able, 'with our support, to resist the encroachments of England'. Hanotaux approved the Colonial Minister's efforts to reach an understanding with Menelik.[100] At the same time, he refused to give the Italians any pledge about official action to halt the supply of arms. In March 1895 Menelik offered the French what Hanotaux described as *une véritable traité d'alliance*: the renewal of a commer- cial treaty first concluded in 1843, with additional clauses whereby France recognised, and Menelik undertook to preserve, Ethiopia's independence. Hanotaux could hardly respond until the outcome of the Italo-Ethiopian war was known, but the rout of the Italian army at Adowa on 1 March 1896 completely transformed the situation. The end of the war and the establishment of Ethiopia as a major African power now made it highly advantageous for the French to conclude a formal understanding with her, and on 3 June they accepted Menelik's proposals for an alliance.[101]

In the weeks after Marchand's departure, the objectives of French policy toward Ethiopia became more clearly defined. At the end of September Hanotaux's *direction politique* stressed the need to 'gather the fruits of our policy by establishing lasting ties with the sovereign of an empire whose future, by virtue of its geographical position, affects . . . the territories of the Upper Nile into which we are now penetrating . . . and where, very shortly, questions of great political importance may be posed'. Hanotaux accepted this as his own official policy and set out to obtain Russian support for a joint effort 'to attach Menelik to us'. The Ministry of Colonies was equally enthusiastic. On 1 November Lebon reminded Hanotaux of Ethiopia's importance for the success of the Marchand mission: 'We may soon have to rely on the goodwill of the Negus to supply our advance posts on the Upper Nile . . . It is therefore in large part through the ruler of Ethiopia that we shall have to try to establish our influence in these regions, if we wish that influence . . . to play an important part in the settlement of the Sudan and Nile questions.'[102]

On 24 November 1896 the cabinet decided to send Lagarde (the usual envoy to Menelik) on another mission to the Ethiopians. According to Hanotaux's later account, his mission was to have three objectives: '1. To organise French missions of exploration which will join up with Marchand on the Nile ... 2. To persuade Menelik to occupy the territories traditionally claimed by Ethiopia on the Nile ... 3. To establish, above all, relations of friendship and trust between France and Ethiopia, capable of influencing, when the time came, the negotiations which were to decide the future of these regions.' Lagarde's official instructions, signed on 30 November, covered the third of these objectives. A *Note spéciale* signed by Lebon on 18 December covered the first. The second, and the most secret of all, was not included in any written instructions, but there can be no doubt that Lagarde was aware of it before he left France.[103]

In one sense, Hanotaux was even more optimistic than the *parti colonial* about the settlement of the Egyptian question. Most colonialists had lost all hope that Britain would ever leave Egypt of her own free will. Hanotaux, however, assumed that the difficulties of the occupation, now compounded by the decision to reconquer the Sudan, were gradually making the British more disposed to consider evacuation. On 11 June, a fortnight before Marchand's departure, he assured Dufferin that 'he was ready to encourage us to advance up the Nile, for he believed that the undertaking in which we were now engaged would compel us to come to an understanding with France. The Soudan from earliest times had been a morass and had become the grave of every adventurer who had tried to subdue it.'[104] Although unwilling for the moment to resume serious discussions about Egypt, largely for fear of upsetting the Russians, Hanotaux remained anxious not to break off talks completely, and he repeatedly hinted at his desire of a settlement. He later insisted that, when Marchand left France, he was still hoping to negotiate a settlement with Britain before the expedition reached its destination. His apologia for Fashoda is not always reliable. But on this occasion the tone of his conversations with Dufferin and the 'reiteration' of his 'strong desire to be friends with England' support his later version of events.[105] The Fashoda expedition could either be used to increase the pressure on Britain for a negotiated settlement or, if that failed, to force her hand through an international conference.

VII

It would have been quite out of character if Hanotaux's determined optimism had continued unabated throughout his term of office. He was as prone as ever to erratic changes of mood, which gave rise in turn to erratic changes of policy. By the beginning of 1897 his optimism of the previous summer had given way to a deep depression.

This pessimism, although it influenced his Egyptian policy, was not due principally to Egypt. It had two main causes, each closely related to the other: the state of the Russian alliance and the internal troubles of the Turkish Empire. Hanotaux's first concern on resuming office was to repair the damage done to the alliance by the Radicals and to provide another demonstration of Franco-Russian amity by persuading the Czar to include France in his tour of Western Europe during the autumn of 1896. Nicholas II's state visit, the first by any foreign head of state since the Franco-Prussian war, thus acquired tremendous symbolic significance. Hanotaux made himself ridiculous by his attempts to avoid the slightest offence to the Emperor's susceptibilities. When the director of the *Comédie Française* included a scene from Hamlet in the programme for a gala evening, Hanotaux immediately struck it out: 'You surely don't intend to put on a play in front of the Czar in which a sovereign is killed—and written by an Englishman too!'[106]

As was to be expected, the success of the visit went to Hanotaux's head. He knew that 'the stumbling block in Franco-Russian relations has always been the Eastern Question'. But he was naïvely confident of his ability to reconcile the basic conflict of interest between the allies in the Near East by devising a joint policy for curing the disorders of the Ottoman Empire. The basis of this policy was to be close Franco-Russian co-operation on a strengthened Ottoman Debt Commission which, through its control of the Sultan's purse-strings, would force him to undertake a comprehensive programme of reforms.[107] Only in one of his most optimistic moments could Hanotaux have convinced himself that Russia would ever agree to limit her freedom of action in this way. Faure warned him that 'any measures likely to place the European powers on an equal footing with Russia would be rejected by St. Petersburg', but Hanotaux paid no heed. Not even the death of Lobanov on the eve of the Czar's arrival dampened his enthusiasm. He put his plans to Nicholas on 6 October, the first day of the state visit, and the Czar, out of politeness to his hosts, agreed in principle. But Hanotaux's triumph was short-lived. Within a few weeks the Russians went back on their agreement and refused to appoint a representative to the Debt Commission. Having, in Faure's words, 'committed the serious mistake of boasting much too loudly about Nicholas's initial agreement', Hanotaux found the Czar's apparent change of policy all the more difficult to accept. 'He was absolutely distraught,' wrote Faure. '. . . According to him, everything had collapsed; nothing was ever again to be relied on.'[108]

Worse was to follow. During the winter of 1896–7, the Ottoman Empire seemed at last on the point of collapse. After the intermittent massacres of the past two years, statesmen from London to St. Petersburg expected its imminent disintegration, and the Russians began to prepare for the seizure of the Bosphorus. Although ignorant of the details, Hanotaux knew the outline of their plans and took them seriously. He therefore warned the Russians that they could expect no help from France for any assault on the Straits.[109] But if Russia lacked the support of her ally, Hanotaux feared that she might well be aided and abetted by her traditional enemy. By the autumn of 1896 Britain had abandoned her long-standing commitment to preserve the Ottoman Empire. Although Salisbury still regarded the inevitability of Russian control over the Straits with distaste, both Hanotaux and Courcel believed that he was positively anxious for a partition in order to make Britain's position in Egypt finally secure.[110] Hanotaux knew that the dissolution of the Ottoman Empire—particularly if it were precipitated by a Russian assault on the Straits—would result in the effective end of the Dual Alliance and the permanent British occupation of Egypt. Everything he had set out to achieve as foreign minister would be destroyed. All France could hope to receive in compensation was the strategically worthless Syria. 'If the Russians get the Straits and England Egypt', he concluded, 'we will gain nothing.'[111]

Although none of Hanotaux's worst fears materialised, the strain of the crisis told heavily on him. In December the new British ambassador to Paris, Sir Edmund Monson, found him 'possessed of a feverish restlessness and anxiety to be making a coup of some kind or another'. At the end of the month, as was so often the case during a crisis, he fell ill. By January President Faure thought he was heading for a nervous breakdown: 'I am really frightened to see the control of our foreign affairs in his hands. He is in such a nervous state that he sometimes loses control of himself and speaks without caring about what he said the previous day, and without considering the sense or the consequences of his words.'[112]

Scarcely able to cope with the Eastern Question, Hanotaux found it almost impossible to deal simultaneously with Egypt. As Monson later complained, 'it is very inconvenient that he should be so much the man of one idea and so disinclined to occupy himself with anything but the Eastern Question'.[113] He still referred to 'persistent action on the Powers, and especially Russia' as an element of his Egyptian policy, and he did discuss Egypt with Count Muraviev when the new Russian Foreign Minister visited Paris in January 1897. But they merely decided to continue with 'the policy of resistance which we have been following, . . . especially on financial questions'. Hanotaux certainly had no intention of 'making a coup' here. Indeed, he deliberately avoided the Egyptian question in his talks with Monson. 'My belief', Monson told Salisbury, 'is that he knows quite well the inutility of discussing Egypt at this moment; and he is only anxious to divert public attention from his neglect to do so . . .'[114]

The passive nature of Hanotaux's Egyptian policy was unlikely to commend itself to the colonialists. The *parti colonial* felt a growing sense of frustration at the gradual worsening of the diplomatic situation during a year which had begun so promisingly for them. They felt in particular that an opportunity to secure Germany's support had somehow been missed. In November 1896 Henri Pensa, the Secretary-General of the *Comité de l'Egypte*, again stressed the need for an understanding between the Dual Alliance and Germany on ways to 'help' Britain leave Egypt. During the debate on the Foreign Affairs budget, Deloncle complained: 'I don't know why, but the confidence felt last April about our action in Egypt seems to have disappeared. There are doubts, hesitations, fears, all of which are ably exploited by our adversary . . .' Deloncle stopped short of a direct attack on Hanotaux's policy. Indeed, he made it clear that he wanted to avoid a public quarrel between the colonialists and the Foreign Minister: 'I am not here to ask you for any reply to my questions; I am here to ask you for swift and decisive action.' In private, however, Hanotaux was subjected to 'fierce pressure' by Deloncle and the *groupe colonial* who, the Italian ambassador reported, would have no compunction about drawing France into an open conflict with Britain.[115]

Colonialist dissatisfaction with Hanotaux's passivity came to a head early in 1897. On 6 February Hicks-Beach, the Chancellor of the Exchequer, made a speech asserting British rights in Egypt with an aggressiveness which Salisbury privately deplored. Two days later, Deloncle replied by attacking British policy with a violence which prompted several deputies to protest: *C'est excessif*. Although Hanotaux tried to placate him by insisting that his resolve to end the British occupation remained as strong as ever, he also expressed a desire to avoid 'one of these bouts of interparliamentary polemics'. Once again, the colonialists avoided a public attack on the Foreign Minister. Etienne, however, privately berated him for the weakness of his speech. Monson found Hanotaux 'extremely excited' after Etienne's visit. 'The Colonial group,' he warned Salisbury, '... are powerful and very bitter against us ... Hanotaux knows that his position is shaken, and that it is on the cards that he and his colleagues may be turned out.' Simultaneously, the colonialist press intensified its demands for an understanding with Germany. 'Every opportunity,' Monson told Salisbury, 'seems to be taken by a certain class of journalists to accustom the French public to the idea that it is worth a certain amount of sacrifice to enlist Germany in a Franco-Russian campaign against us, and that the task of persuading her may not be so difficult after all.'[116] In March, Deloncle launched his own campaign to whip up popoular feeling by concocting a series of fictitious press reports about British misdeeds in Egypt, which he then passed off as the despatches of the *Havas* correspondent in Alexandria. The campaign made life imposisble for Cogordan, who bitterly denounced the *enragés* of the Colonial Party—*le parti agité français*.[117]

Early in 1897 the diplomatic focus of the Eastern Crisis shifted from the Armenians to the Cretans, traditionally among the Sultan's most rebellious subjects. The Cretan insurrection and the Greek invasion of the island in February reduced Hanotaux to an even deeper state of depression than the Armenian massacres of the previous year. Once more he had to face the imminent prospect of the Turkish Empire's dissolution, and with it the collapse of the Dual Alliance and his hopes for settling the Egyptian question. His fears were increased by Russia's failure to preserve even the appearance of a common front with her ally. Muraviev, he complained, 'launches circular after circular without ever consulting us in advance'. Growing parliamentary criticism of his apparent inactivity in the Near East also affected his morale. From November 1896 onwards, he had to deal with a number of increasingly hostile interpellations from both sides of the Chamber. Hanoteaux had never felt at ease in Parliament, and the strain of defending his policy now proved too much for him. All he could do was to read prepared statements—often interrupted by taunts of *Lisez Lisez*—and then hand over to the Prime Minister for the rest of the debate. The crisis even threatened to damage his literary career. Lobbying had already begun for the next election to the *Académie Française*, for which he was a leading candidate. As he later admitted, Crete very nearly cost him 'immortality'.[118]

From the beginning of the Cretan crisis, Hanotaux's policy went through a series of erratic changes which reached their climax in mid-March. At a cabinet meeting on the 9th, he spoke of the danger that Germany might abandon the Triple Alliance and try to settle the fate of the Turkish empire with Russia. On the following day, basing himself on a solitary and inaccurate press report, he jumped to the conclusion that Germany, so far from abandoning her allies, was inciting Italy to prepare simultaneous expeditions against the Greeks in Crete and the Turks in Albania. By the 16th he was quite hysterical: 'He declared successively that Germany would march with and against Turkey, that Russia would support Turkey and fight her, that England would take the Dardanelles and Russia the Bosphorus . . . , that Turkish forces were overwhelmingly strong, that Turkey herself would soon be overwhelmed, that the crisis would last a long time and one shouldn't expect a solution within a year. That Cambon is a traitor, that Muraviev is a villain, etc. etc. All this is becoming very dangerous for the country and Hanotaux will have to be closely watched. I [Faure] spoke about it to Méline . . . and he is of the same opinion.'[119]

Just when Hanotaux could no longer bear the strain of the Eastern crisis, an Egyptian crisis threatened to break on him as well. At the end of February he had been disturbed by the announcement of a British mission to Ethiopia. Menelik, he told Lebon, must be warned not to 'lose sight of the fact that England's scheme . . . to become mistress of the Upper Nile would prevent the expansion of Abyssinia towards the great African river'.[120] Then on 10 March he received a telegram from Cogordan transmitting an unconfirmed report that a French expedition had actually reached the Upper Nile. The report was, of course, inaccurate, but both Cogordan and the Ministry of Colonies thought it likely to be true. According to Lebon, even if Liotard or Marchand were not yet on the Nile, their arrival must be imminent. By this time, Hanotaux was 'entirely absorbed in the Creto-Greek question' and quite incapable of devoting his attention to any other subject.[121] The initiative therefore passed to the *Pavillon de Flore*.

Looking at the situation in a narrowly colonial context, Lebon was confident about the success of the Fashoda enterprise. It would, he claimed, be 'easy' to persuade Menelik to occupy the right bank of the Upper Nile. But the Negus would only act if he were assured, 'if necessary by a convention', that the French intended 'to keep the territories which the Liotard and Marchand missions were to place under our influence, . . . the Nile being destined to serve as the frontier between our possessions and his empire'. This policy, Lebon added, 'has always been that of the French government and the objective of the negotiations which we have been pursuing with Ethiopia until now'. Cogordan was equally optimistic. Once established on the Nile, a French expedition, especially if reinforced through Ethiopia, would 'form a barrier which England could not cross except by going to war—which is virtually out of the question—or by making concessions which it would be up to us to specify'.[122]

Hanotaux did not wish to commit France to a partition of the Upper Nile with Ethiopia until the outcome of the Fashoda expedition was known for certain. But neither the state of his morale nor his weakened position in the cabinet enabled him to insist. On 11 March the cabinet approved the Colonial Minister's proposals, and on the 14th Lebon wired the necessary instructions to Lagarde. Before they could reach him, however, Lagarde announced the conclusion of a secret *Convention pour le Nil Blanc*, whereby 'His Majesty the Emperor of Ethiopia, establishing his authority over the right bank of the White Nile from 14°N southward, will assist, as far as possible, the agents of the French government on the left bank between 14°N and 5°N. In return, the French government will, as far as possible, assist His Majesty . . . to maintain himself solidly on the Nile. His Majesty's flag will be flown on the right bank and the French flag on the left bank of the White Nile.'[123] While Lebon busied himself with the consolidation of French power in the Upper Nile valley, Hanotaux did his best to pretend that the Egyptian question had ceased for the moment to exist. He sent no instructions to Courcel or Cogordan, and he deliberately left Egypt off the agenda for his talks with Salisbury at the end of March. 'I know the conditions in which we could negotiate,' he minuted beforehand, 'but the time is not ripe.'[124]

Until the outbreak of the Greco-Turkish war in April, Hanotaux lived in a state of acute nervous tension. On 17 March, the day after his hysterical outburst in the cabinet, he called on President Faure to apologise. Three days later he suffered a relapse. He now told the cabinet that he had found a foolproof way to restrain the King of Greece from precipitating war by offering him 'a financial deal'. The ministers, wrote Faure, 'could not believe their ears. Quite clearly, Hanotaux is daily losing more of his authority; for my part, I find him at his wits' end. The burden is too much for him, and I think he will soon resign.'[125]

As in the previous winter, Hanotaux believed that the Russians planned to use the Eastern crisis as a pretext for seizing the Straits. He even suspected, although the precise nature of his suspicions varied from day to day, that Russia might be seeking the secret approval of Germany. 'I cannot but conclude,' wrote Monson on 21 March, 'that he is beginning to dread an evolution which will be practically the reconstruction of the original "Dreikaiserbund".'[126] Muraviev himself did nothing to lessen Hanotaux's anxieties. At the beginning of April he asked for a clarification of French policy should Russia become involved in a Near Eastern war. Hanotaux had to give the same reply as Berthelot before him: 'We are and shall remain the faithful friends of Russia . . . but anything more than diplomatic support would not be understood in France unless the question which has plagued us for twenty-five years [Alsace-Lorraine] were clearly involved.'[127] To Hanotaux, both the survival of the Ottoman Empire and the peace of Europe now seemed balanced on a knife's-edge. He feared another round of Christian massacres; and if that happened, he believed, European intervention and a Russian assault on the Straits would become inevitable. Although Muraviev continued to proclaim his peaceful intentions, Hanotaux did not trust him. 'He has a persecution mania,' wrote Faure, 'and he sees traitors everywhere.'[128]

Hanotaux's sense of persecution stemmed not merely from his bitterness at the behaviour of the Russians but also from the constant criticism levelled against him in the press, in parliament, and even in the foreign service. His particular *bête noire* was Paul Cambon, whose scarcely veiled attacks on his lack of energy drove him to distraction. 'M. Cambon,' he wrote on one of the ambassadors's despatches, 'now has the sole aim of proving that we should have acted "last year".' On 13 April Hanotaux again lost control of himself in cabinet. He insisted that Paul Cambon was organising a campaign against him, that both the Cambon brothers were personal enemies, and that he could no longer allow Jules Cambon into the foreign service. Méline in turn insisted that the bargain with Thomson and Etienne must be kept, to which Hanotaux replied: 'Choose between Cambon and me!' Thereupon, Méline threatened to resign unless Hanotaux honoured his promise to make a place for Jules Cambon. Squalid and trivial though the affair was, Faure thought it would bring down the government. 'Secretly, Hanotaux would not be sorry to go,' he added, 'since he knows he has no honourable way out of the present crisis.'[129] With the prospect of war in the Near East and the consequent failure of all his ambitions staring him in the face, Hanotaux must have felt that resignation was the only way out. And with his 'immortality' guaranteed by his election to the *Académie* on 30 March, he could now return to his other career as a writer.

VIII

On 16 April Hanotaux submitted his resignation. On the following day Greek troops invaded Macedonia. Méline refused to accept the resignation, probably because the outbreak of war made a change of Foreign Minister inopportune, and Hanotaux gave way.[130] The unexpected outcome of the war dispelled many of the fears which had preyed on Hanotaux's mind since the previous winter. In only a month, the Greeks suffered a humiliating defeat. The Ottoman Empire did not disintegrate but was positively strengthened by its victory. Most surprisingly of all, Russia and Austria-Hungary, the two major powers most likely to be drawn into the conflict, agreed to put the Balkans 'on ice'. Freed from his anxieties about a partition of the Turkish Empire, Hanotaux could once again take a more rational view of Near Eastern affairs. By 12 May he had recovered sufficiently to patch up his quarrel with Paul Cambon.[131] When the crisis on the Upper Nile failed to materialise—Liotard and Marchand were nowhere near Fashoda in the spring of 1897—Hanotaux recovered his composure on this question too. On 21 May he congratulated Lagarde on the success of his mission; three days later, the *Convention du Nil Blanc* was ratified by Presidential Decree, countersigned by Hanotaux and Lebon.[132] With Menelik's support now assured, there was every reason for Marchand to 'speed up his advance to the Nile', and on 30 June Lebon ordered him to do so.[133]

Not all the Foreign Minister's troubles, however, were at an end. He continued to be attacked for his pusillanimous Eastern policy, and his defence in the Chamber on 22 May was conducted amid continuous uproar. Hanotaux could not 'say two or three words, let alone a sentence, without being interrupted'. According to Monson's information, 'many of the supporters of M. Méline are much chagrined at having been compelled to vote as they had done when the foreign policy of the Quai d'Orsay has been discussed'.[134] The Eastern crisis permanently weakened Hanotaux's position as a minister. The stormy debates of the winter and spring cruelly exposed his inability to answer hostile critics in parliament. He never fully recovered his authority in the cabinet either, and he remained scarcely on speaking terms with Méline.[135]

It would have been uncharacteristic of Hanotaux not to contemplate some dramatic initiative to restore his damaged reputation. His first scheme was to secure the appointment of a Frenchman as Governor of Crete. Since the Powers, at his own suggestion, had previously agreed to the appointment of a neutral governor, his plans clearly had no chance of acceptance, and on 17 August the cabinet rejected them. 'It probably means the loss of all our influence in the Eastern Mediterranean,' he complained pompously to Nisard. 'In any other circumstances I should have resigned. That would have made them change their minds since the fate of the cabinet depended on it. But on the eve of our trip to Russia even this course was denied to me.'[136] The state visit to Russia, however, provided a better opportunity for Hanotaux to recoup his losses. Having silenced his critics in June 1895 by revealing the alliance, he left for Russia in August 1897 'with the firm intention of proclaiming the alliance publicly'. The dinner on board the *Pothuau* at the end of the visit was the setting he chose. Muraviev was decidedly cool about using the official toasts for such a purpose. But the Russians had always been willing to satisfy their allies in matters of form if not of substance, and at Hanotaux's insistence both the Czar and the President drank to the union of *les deux nations amies et alliées*.[137] Satisfactions of form again had their desired effect. Monson at least was sure that the toasts 'ought to strengthen the Méline ministry in general and Hanotaux's position in particular'.[138]

Hanotaux came back from Russia with his morale fully restored, brimming with renewed self-confidence. And as his morale improved, so his whole diplomatic outlook changed. In September, he tried to revive his scheme for the appointment of a French governor in Crete.

In October, he tried to revive his plans for Ottoman financial reform which the Russians had rejected a year before.[139] All his old optimism about the Egyptian question returned as well. By now, even Lebon doubted whether Menelik's promises of support could be relied on, but Hanotaux did not share his doubts. He had discussed 'securing Menelik's assistance against the English' with Muraviev during the visit, and he remained convinced that French and Russian influence with the Negus 'promises to achieve the most important results'.[140] He became equally optimistic about the prospects of German support. Although he still doubted whether Germany would join in an immediate Franco-Russian initiative, he was sure that, once the Egyptian question was actually reopened, 'Germany, skilfully handled, may be of great service to us'. In November 1897 he told Cogordan that France was assured of 'the faithful support of Russian diplomacy' in Egypt and predicted that 'other powers will in their turn come to recognise their common interest with us in this part of the Middle East, and that all the questions relative to Egypt will thus one day come to be decided by Europe as a whole'.[141] The beginning of German *Weltpolitik*, signalled by the seizure of Kiaochow and the introduction of Tirpitz's naval bill, strengthened his confidence that Germany could not allow Egypt and the Suez Canal to remain indefinitely in British hands.

Confidence in the support of Germany and Ethiopia also increased Hanotaux's optimism about the chances of a negotiated settlement with Britain. In September, he interpreted the unexpectedly easy settlement of the Tunisian question, 'which only a few months before had seemed so intractable', as evidence of Britain's readiness to settle all outstanding differences with France in the same conciliatory manner.[142] In October, the resumption, after a break of eighteen months, of negotiations over West African boundary disputes increased his optimism still further. The British, he later claimed, already knew that Marchand was nearing his destination, and it was therefore reasonable to assume that they had also decided to resolve the eventual crisis on the Upper Nile by negotiation. Hanotaux was determined to seize the opportunity. On West Africa, Monson found him 'feverishly anxious to set to work with me at once . . . [and] in a hurry to come to a settlement'. There was a particular reason for his haste. Both Hanotaux and Lebon later maintained that the West African negotiations were intended to serve as 'the necessary prelude to the settlement, at the proper time, of the question of the Upper Nile'. This almost certainly *was* Hanotaux's intention, and in November he told Monson of his hope that the talks about West Africa would lead to a 'general settlement of all the questions at issue'.[143]

Hanotaux's belief in the possibility of Anglo-French negotiations about the Upper Nile was not entirely unreasonable. In November 1897 Cromer still found it 'impossible to foresee in what precise manner the difficulties which will . . . ensue [when the French reached Fashoda] will be capable of solution'. He even doubted 'whether it is desirable, merely in order to forestall the French on the Upper Nile, to send an expedition to Khartoum'. 'All that can be said,' he concluded, 'is that it is difficult to believe that a settlement of some kind will be impossible.' Salisbury too found it difficult to predict the outcome: 'If ever we get to Fashoda the diplomatic crisis will be something to remember, and the "what next" will be a very interesting question.' But he too expected the crisis to end in a '[negotiated] settlement of some kind'.[144]

By the end of 1897, however, neither Salisbury nor Hanotaux were free agents. Both of them had to contend with an increasingly volatile public opinion and, on West Africa in particular, with their aggressive Colonial departments. 'I doubt Hanotaux's giving in,' Monson reported in October, 'not because he is not intelligent enough to see that he might easily do so, but simply because he dare not.' This time, however, the intransigence of the *Pavillon de Flore* and the *parti colonial* was more than matched by the bellicosity of the British Colonial Office. Chamberlain took charge of the West African negotiations, determined to make the French 'eat dirt publicly'—at gunpoint if necessary. He almost succeeded. At the beginning of February Hanotaux was seriously alarmed by the very real possibility of an armed clash in West Africa, and convinced that the British were deliberately seeking a conflict.[145] By the end of March, the mounting tension had again shattered his nerve. On the 29th, he lectured the cabinet for an hour about the imminent prospect of a war with Britain, all because of an anonymous report that British forces in Northern Nigeria had wiped out a French expedition which, they claimed, had crossed the Say-Barruwa line and entered the British sphere.[146] What should have worried Hanotaux most was Britain's increasingly obvious intransigence on the Upper Nile. At the end of November he had offered to recognise British influence south of the Say-Barruwa line in return for the recognition of French influence over the north and east banks of Lake Chad. According to his later account, the purpose of this offer was 'indirectly to raise the question of Marchand'. But Salisbury's reassertion of British claims to the whole of the Upper Nile valley was so harshly uncompromising that Hanotaux had to abandon his hope of discussing the Upper Nile until the West African disputes were out of the way.[147]

Incredibly, however, the Egyptian question and the possible consequences of the Marchand expedition seemed to worry him least. In January Cogordan, always susceptible to rumour, reported that the British were planning to declare a protectorate over Egypt within a few weeks. But Hanotaux was not disturbed by this 'typical English bluff'. 'Our interest,' he minuted, 'is not to push things too far ... [but] to maintain the existing situation as long as Europe has not opened her eyes. Besides, the expense and danger of a profitless occupation may one day or another bring British statesmen and public opinion to their senses.'[148] For all his fears about the danger of war in West Africa, Hanotaux never envisaged the possibility of war on the Upper Nile. He was convinced that Britain would never fight France and Russia at the same time: ' "Two enemies are better than one" would be a strange formula to adopt in military tactics or diplomacy.' He knew that Russia would not support France in a West African conflict; but he was sure that Russia was bound to intervene if the conflict were over Egypt, where her own vital interests were at stake.[149]

The colonialists voiced the same confidence more stridently. They too were convinced that Germany, now embarked upon the creation of an Asian empire, would have a greater interest than ever in opposing Britain's 'universal pretensions'. On 7 February 1898 Deloncle denounced British claims to 'an option on the whole world' and warned that her days in Egypt were numbered. France, he boasted, was assured of Ethiopian support on the Upper Nile and with it could reopen the Egyptian question, when all the continental powers would take her side. Delcassé even claimed the responsibility—and the credit —for the whole Fashoda strategy. It was not his fault, he declared, if Marchand had not yet reached the Upper Nile.[150]

By the summer, colonialist optimism had vanished. Now that the crisis was finally drawing near, they were no longer confident about Germany's support. The resumption of Kitchener's advance in February had aroused their suspicion that the Germans had given Britain 'carte blanche' on the Nile in return for British support in the Far East. At first, these suspicions only strengthened their determination to make sure of German support. But in April, William II's congratulations to Kitchener on his decisive victory at Atbara confirmed their worst fears about the existence of an Anglo-German deal. 'Doubtless,' commented the *Bulletin du Comité de l'Afrique Française*, 'the Kaiser wanted to erase the memory of the Kruger Telegram.' Having lost faith in Germany, the colonialists began to despair about the Fashoda strategy itself. And, despairing of the strategy, they began to consider an alternative solution to the Egyptian question, that of territorial compensation for France elsewhere in Africa.[151]

But Hanotaux remained confident, and in June whatever doubts he may have had about the final success of his policy were resolved. On the 14th, the Anglo-French Agreement on West Africa was finally signed. The Niger convention, he believed, 'rings down the curtain on a whole series of international difficulties (Siam, Madagascar, Tunis, China . . .) which England could use to answer our Egyptian claims by pressing grievances and claims of her own'. Now, only the Egyptian question remained to be settled, and Hanotaux expected to have 'three or four months' to prepare for the negotiations which would inevitably follow Kitchener's capture of Khartoum and his meeting with Marchand on the Nile. At exactly the same time, the so-called Münster Note confirmed his confidence in Germany's support. He saw Germany's proposal for 'parallel action' to prevent the cession of the bankrupt Portugal's East African territories to Britain as incontrovertible evidence of the basic antagonism of German and British interests in Africa. On 21 June he told Cogordan that all the elements needed for the solution of the Egyptian question were at hand: Lagarde and an Ethiopian mission were on their way to France with authority to continue discussions about 'the possession of both banks of the Nile'; Marchand was about to reach the river, where he would make contact with Menelik's envoys; Anglo-Russian tensions in the Far East were already running high, Anglo-German tensions in South Africa would soon be high; the capture of Khartoum would lead to a conference in which 'all the Powers with interests in Egypt will participate'. All that remained was to 'collect . . . the various elements which may be of use for the peaceful discussions which will probably soon take place about those great international interests which Europe in general and France in particular have never ceased to defend in Egypt'.[152]

Incredible as it may seem, Hanotaux seriously expected the Egyptian question to solve itself. Although the Méline government had fallen on 15 June and Hanotaux had become a *ministre démissionnaire*, he was determined not to lose the opportunity of presiding over the settlement which was to 'crown' his diplomatic career. On 19 June, the day he received the Münster Note, he sent Hansen to tell Dupuy and other possible leaders of the new government of the need to maintain continuity at the Quai d'Orsay and of his willingness to serve under them. When his offers were rejected, he sought instead to have himself appointed ambassador to London.[153] Only if he were supremely confident of success would he have tried so desperately to remain at the centre of the stage.

Nor was Hanotaux's confidence peculiar to himself. Marchand approached his destination in a mood of growing elation. In his first despatch to the *Comité de l'Afrique Française* after his arrival at Fashoda, he reported jubilantly: 'Political situation here *excellent*—have confidence, complete confidence.'[154] The permanent officials at the Quai d'Orsay were also full of opitimism. Nisard and the *Direction politique* were convinced that the Münster Note revealed a fundamental conflict between German and British colonial ambitions which boded well for the forthcoming international conference on the Egyptian question. On 18 July, three weeks after Delcassé had become Foreign Minister, the *Direction politique* was still predicting that, with Marchand at Fashoda, 'we shall have an excellent bargaining counter with which to await the opening of negotiations'. It even revived a fanciful plan, first drawn up in February 1897, for making the evacuation of Egypt more acceptable to Britain by offering her most of the Sudan, including Darfur, Kordofan, the right bank of the Upper Nile and an outlet to the Red Sea.[155] Hanotaux was not the only man capable of self-deception on the grand scale.

The following weeks brought the Fashoda strategists unceremoniously down to earth. The Germans, of course, had never intended to support France in Egypt and had said as much more than once. Not even the Münster Note was genuinely meant; its real purpose was to increase pressure on Britain for a settlement.[156] With the Anglo-German Agreement on the Portuguese territories in August, one major premise of the Fashoda strategy was seen to have collapsed. Menelik was an even bigger disappointment. With Ethiopian support, the Marchand expedition might have been more difficult to evict from Fashoda, for Salisbury was determined to avoid 'by all possible means, any collision with the forces of the Emperor Menelik'.[157] But the Negus had never intended to help Marchand, and he deliberately hamstrung the expeditions which Lagarde sent to the Nile. By the spring of 1898 even Hanotaux had begun to have his doubts, although renewed assurances of Menelik's friendly intentions soon overcame them.[158] His successor could not afford to be so credulous. By the time news of Marchand's arrival reached Paris, Delcassé had already concluded: 'There is no reason to expect the practical and effective assistance which we once hoped to receive from Ethiopia.'[159] A second major premise of the Fashoda strategy was seen to have collapsed.

When Kitchener met Marchand at Fashoda on 19 September, the French discovered that they had no 'bargaining-counter'. Might if not right was overwhelmingly on Britain's side. Marchand confronted the advance guard of an Anglo-Egyptian army with 150 *tirailleurs*. The French navy confronted British battleships with a 'fleet of samples', and the French government was forced to recognise the 'absolute impossibility of carrying on a naval war, even with Russian help'.[160] Salisbury himself still favoured a negotiated settlement, but amid the passions aroused by the confrontation at Fashoda, the majority of his cabinet supported the intransigent Chamberlain. On 2 November Delcassé reluctantly accepted the inevitable and ordered Marchand's unconditional withdrawal from the Nile. The Fashoda strategy itself had now collapsed.

IX

In retrospect, Delcassé and most colonialists agreed that the crucial reason for the failure of the Fashoda strategy was diplomatic: the lack of German support for reopening the Egyptian question. By implication, the *Comité de l'Afrique Française* put most of the blame on Hanotaux: 'To believe . . . that the mere presence of a few French soldiers at Fashoda would permit the reopening of the Egyptian question in favourable conditions, and would be enough to make England retreat, was the most inexcusable folly. The Marchand mission seems to have been so totally ignored by our diplomacy that it might just as well have been no more than an incident in our Congolese policy, an idea of the Colonial Ministry unknown to the Foreign Ministry.'[161] Yet by concentrating on the failure to obtain German support, the colonialists missed the point. The basic error had been to believe that German support could be obtained in the first place. This error was partly due to Germany's skill in wielding the Egyptian baton to threaten England and attract France. It was also a consequence of wishful thinking, of an inability to realise that Egypt and the Suez Canal did not have the significance for Germany which they had for France.

The Fashoda expedition, however, was a gamble which would probably have been taken anyway, whatever the attitude of Germany (or indeed of Ethiopia). Marchand described his mission as the result of a 'decision to confront England boldly on the Upper Nile—*no matter what the consequences*'.[162] The gambler's mentality which produced the

Fashoda strategy was itself a product of the African partition. The success of French expeditions in carving out a vast empire on the Niger encouraged a willingness to take similar risks on the Upper Nile. But the colonialists, and eventually the government, took the risk only because they believed that Britain would never go to war. As Cogordan ruefully admitted after the withdrawal, 'intelligent men never expected us to fight for the Nile when we did not fight for the Rhine; but almost everyone accepted as a self-evident truth that Britain would never go to war . . . , that her commercial interests would always prevent her from placing her communications . . . at risk . . .'[163] The French gamblers at Fashoda were bluffing. And they believed that the British were bluffing too. This was their fatal miscalculation. They failed to understand that, by the 1890s, Britain's vital national interests *were* at stake in Egypt, and when the British raised the stakes on the Upper Nile accordingly, the French had to throw in their hand.

The failure of the Fashoda strategy threw into sharp relief the contradictions inherent in the international position of the Third Republic. At the end of the nineteenth century, as under the *Ancien Régime*, France was in the unique position of being both a great continental and a great colonial power. In the eighteenth century, the strain of simultaneously maintaining supremacy in Europe and waging a protracted struggle with England overseas had driven the *Ancien Régime* to bankruptcy and had helped to bring it down. A century later, French aims in Europe were again to conflict with her ambitions in the outside world. Her great enemy in Europe was Germany; her great rival outside Europe was Britain. As a European power, she needed British support against Germany; as a colonial power, she needed German support against Britain. She could not reasonably hope to challenge Germany's right to remain in Alsace-Lorraine while at the same time challenging Britain's right to remain in Egypt. And the fact that the Lost Provinces were always, in the last resort, more important than the Nile would always make genuine co-operation with Germany—and hence a serious challenge to Britain—impossible.

Hanotaux bears much of the responsibility for the failure at Fashoda. He staked both his nation's interests and his own reputation on a hopeless gamble. He never had any chance either of persuading Britain to leave Egypt or of obtaining the German support which alone could have forced her hand. In his attempt to emulate his hero, Richelieu, he also embarked upon the impossible task of regaining French primacy both in Europe and in the outside world. Fashoda demonstrated the futility of his attempt to challenge Britain's pre-eminence overseas. Russia's simultaneous disregard of French interests on the Rhine demonstrated the hollowness of the alliance with which he hoped to challenge Germany's mastery in Europe.[164] His failure on both counts ended his political career. Hanotaux left the Quai d'Orsay in 1898 at the age of 45. He never again held major public office.

But the miscalculations which led to Fashoda were not the responsibility of any one man; the fundamental fault lay in the very nature of French policy-making. Cabinet control over foreign and colonial policy hardly existed. Most ministers cared little for the affairs of the outside world, and their apathy was compounded by an almost total ignorance of the African continent. Few members of the governments which authorised the Fashoda expedition had more than the vaguest idea of where Marchand was going. Chautemps, when he first became Colonial Minister, was alleged to have confused 'Madagascar with Gibraltar [and] Gabon with the Sudan'.[165] The abdication of cabinet responsibility placed excessive power in the hands of the Foreign and Colonial Ministers—even when, as in the case of Hanotaux, the Minister was an erratic and unstable individual. By the spring of 1897 both Faure and Méline recognised that Hanotaux's continuance in office was becoming 'dangerous for the country', yet neither made any attempt to unseat him. And just as the weakness of the cabinet left too much power in the hands of an individual minister, so the weakness—or ignorance—of a minister left too much power in the hands of his permanent officials. Nisard and Benoît at the Quai d'Orsay, Archinard and Lagarde at the *Pavillon de Flore*, all played their part in the evolution and implementation of the Fashoda strategy. Finally, the weakness of government both at cabinet and at ministerial level placed too much power in the hands of the *parti colonial*. The colonialists devised the Fashoda strategy, and they exerted much of the pressure which secured its acceptance by three different governments. Significantly, the two most fateful expeditions in the history of French African expansion—the Marchand mission and the expedition to Fez in 1911—were first authorised by two of the feeblest cabinets in the history of the Third Republic, the Bourgeois and Monis ministries. In each case, the effectiveness of colonialist pressure was directly proportional to the weakness of the government.[166]

The influence of the *parti colonial* also depended on the latent nationalism of public opinion. In themselves, colonial affairs were quite incapable of attracting the attention let alone the enthusiasm of the French public. The secret of the colonialists' influence, both in Parliament and in the country, was their ability to present colonial issues as ones involving France's *national* interests. French nationalism was all the easier to exploit because it was an ignorant nationalism. Like Salisbury, Frenchmen knew as much about the Upper Nile as about 'the other side of the moon'. But, as Marchand discovered, all they needed to be convinced of its importance was to be told that it was necessary 'to assert our rights on the Nile in the face of the English'.

French imperialism itself was little more than the extension of a previously continental nationalism into the colonial field. By the end of the nineteenth century, Africa allowed freer play to European rivalries than Europe itself. In Europe, the risks of war were obvious and real, and the restraints on policy were correspondingly great. All French governments between the Franco-Prussian and First World Wars were committed to the recovery of the Lost Provinces, yet none of them would ever have dreamt of making a forcing bid on the Rhine. In Africa, however, the ground rules of the great power game had still to be established. In Africa, as in Europe, they could only be learned through experience. Not until the gamble taken at Fashoda had failed would further gambles be discredited. Fashoda, however, was to mark a turning point. When Delcassé later tried to take the same risks with Germany over Morocco that he had taken with Britain over Egypt, the very colonialists who had earlier urged him on now tried to hold him back. Fashoda had much the same effect on public opinion in France that the Boer War was soon to have in Britain. 'Before the Boer war,' wrote Sir Edward Grey in 1906, 'we were spoiling for a fight . . . Now this generation has had enough excitement, and has lost a little blood . . .'[167] After Fashoda, French opinion too 'lost a little blood'. Without Marchand's heroic but futile gesture on the Upper Nile, the French people could never have been reconciled to the sacrifice of Egypt. Fashoda, followed by the Boer War, made possible the Entente Cordiale.

NOTES

Abbreviations used in the notes:

A.E.	Archives du Ministère des Affaires Etrangères.
A.N.S.O.M.	Archives Nationales (Section Outre-Mer).
B.C.A.F.	*Bulletin du Comité de l'Afrique Française.*
Carnets	G. L. Jaray (ed.), 'Carnets de Gabriel Hanotaux', *Revue des Deux Mondes*, 1 Apr.–15 May 1949.
D.D.F.	*Documents Diplomatiques Français*, 1ère série.
Fachoda	G. Hanotaux, 'Fachoda', *Revue des Deux Mondes*, XLIX (1909), pp. 481–512, 721–55.
F.F.	Félix Faure, 'Notes Personnnelles', in the possession of M. François Berge.
G.P.	*Die grosse Politik der europäischen Kabinette, 1871–1914.*
H.P.	Hanotaux Papers, Archives du Ministère des Affaires Etrangères.
J.O. D.P.C.	*Journal Officiel, Débats Parlementaires, Chambre.*
S.P.	Salisbury Papers, Christ Church, Oxford. (Consulted by permission of the fifth Marquess of Salisbury).

1. The origins of the Fashoda strategy are most fully discussed in J. Stengers, 'Aux origines de Fachoda: l'expédition Monteil', *Revue belge de philologie et d'histoire*, XXXVI (1958), 436–50, XXXVIII (1960), 366–404, 1040–65. The most detailed study of the Fashoda strategy as a whole is G. N. Sanderson, *England, Europe and the Upper Nile* (Edinburgh, 1965). See also: idem, 'The Origins and Significance of the Anglo-French Confrontation at Fashoda', in P. Gifford and W. R. Louis (eds.), *France and Britain in Africa* (Yale, 1971). The best study of the Marchand mission itself is M. Michel, *La Mission Marchand* (Paris, 1972). On the Fashoda crisis and its consequences, see: C. M. Andrew, *Théophile Delcassé and the Making of the Entente Cordiale* (London, 1968).

2. For a recent attempt to place the Fashoda strategy in its 'domestic setting', see: R. G. Brown, *Fashoda Reconsidered* (Baltimore, 1970). Brown's attempt to relate the development of the Fashoda strategy to the course of the Dreyfus affair is, in our view, unconvincing.

3. G. Hanotaux, *Mon Temps* (Paris, 1933–47), II, 1–2, 127–8; V. S. Vetter, 'Gabriel Hanotaux', in B. E. Schmitt (ed.), *Some Historians of Modern Europe* (Chicago, 1942), 173.

4. *Mon Temps*, II, IV, passim.

5. *Mon Temps*, IV, 203–4.

6. Hanotaux, Journal, June 1887, 21 Aug. 1887, H.P. 1, ff. 25, 28–9.
7. Monson to Salisbury, 17 Mar. 1897, S.P. A/115.
8. Hanotaux, Journal, 21 Aug. 1887, June 1887, H.P. 1, ff. 28, 24.
9. Ibid., 18 Dec. 1893, f. 59; Dufferin to Salisbury, 9 July 1895, S.P. A/114.
10. *Carnets*, 13 Feb. 1895, 390–2.
11. The ambassador to London, Decrais, was the only one with whom he failed to establish a smooth working relationship, and Decrais soon resigned. See: Decrais to Nisard, 11 Sept. 1894, H.P. 21.
12. Decrais to Hanotaux, 31 May 1894, H.P. 22; Dufferin to Salisbury, 9 July 1895, S.P. A/114; Cambon to Hanotaux, 4 Mar. 1896, H.P. 19.
13. Poincaré, the Minister of Finance, Barthou, the Minister of Public Works, Leygues, the Minister of Public Instruction, and Hanotaux were all members of the *déjeuner des neuf*, a dining club of political friends. Poincaré was particularly close to Hanotaux. F.F., V, Oct.–Nov. 1895; Lavertujon to Hanotaux, 14 June 1896, H.P. 24.
14. *Carnets*, 13 Feb. 1895, 10 Mar. 1895, 390, 399–401.
15. Hanotaux, Journal, 21 Aug. 1887, 24 Aug. 1891, H.P. 1.
16. Vetter, 'Gabriel Hanotaux', loc. cit., 189; Dufferin to Salisbury, 15 May 1896, S.P. A/114. cf. Monson to Salisbury, 12 Oct. 1897, S.P. A/115: 'His avowed ambition is to be able to claim a series of diplomatic successes at frequent intervals.' Monson was much more favourably disposed to Hanotaux than Dufferin.
17. Dufferin to Salisbury, 20 Jan. 1896, S.P. A/114.
18. Hanotaux, Journal, 22 June 1892, H.P. 1.
19. *Carnets*, 13 Feb. 1895, 390; Sanderson, op. cit., 158.
20. Alis to Etienne, 4 Dec. 1892, Bibliothèque de l'Institut, Terrier MSS 5891. Alis, by then in the pay of King Leopold, was even more angry at Hanotaux's intransigence towards the Congolese.
21. Millet to Hanotaux, 10 June 1894, H.P. 25; *Politique Coloniale*, 11 May 1893. See also: C. M. Andrew and A. S. Kanya-Forstner, 'The French "Colonial Party": Its Composition, Aims and Influence, 1885–1914', *The Historical Journal*, XIV (1971), 99–128.
22. Hanotaux, Journal, 23 Aug. 1892, H.P. 1.
23. *Fachoda*, 497.
24. *Carnets*, 15 Feb. 1895, 395; Note du Ministre, 11 June 1894, *D.D.F.* XI, no. 139.
25. *J.O. D.P.C.*, 7 June 1894.
26. Dufferin to Kimberley, 30 June 1894, cited in Stengers, 'Aux origines de Fachoda', loc. cit., 1045.
27. Hanotaux, Note, 28 May 1894, cited in ibid., 381.
28. Cambon to Hanotaux, 14 June 1894, H.P. 19; Dufferin to Hanotaux, 6 June 1894, *D.D.F.* XI, no. 133; Dufferin to Kimberley, 30 June 1894, cited above, note 26.
29. Delcassé to Monteil, 13 July 1894, *D.D.F.* XI, no. 191, and 277, n. 2.
30. Hanotaux to Decrais, 15 July 1894, *D.D.F.* XI, no. 193; Beyens to Lambermont, 18 Aug. 1894, cited in Stengers, 'Aux origines de Fachoda', loc. cit., 1064.
31. Cambon to Hanotaux, 23 Aug. 1894, H.P. 19; Billot to Hanotaux, 16 Aug. 1894, H.P. 17; Jusserand to Hanotaux, 17 Aug. 1894, H.P. 24; Nisard to Hanotaux, 18 Aug. 1894, H.P. 27; *Carnets*, 13 Feb. 1895, 395.
32. Billot to Hanotaux, 16 Aug. 1894, H.P. 17; Phipps to Kimberley, 11 Aug. 1894, cited in Sanderson, op. cit., 191; Note du Ministre, 7 Nov. 1894, *D.D.F.* XI, no. 272; Courcel to Hanotaux, 19 Dec. 1894, H.P. 20.
33. Phipps to Kimberley, 5 Sept., 18 Oct., 26 Oct. 1894, cited in Sanderson, op. cit., 194, 205.
34. Deloncle to Casimir-Périer, 9 Sept. 1894, enclosing procès-verbal of meeting with the Khedive on 25 Aug., A.E. Casimir-Périer MSS. (We are greatly indebted to Mr. John Parsons for this reference.) In May 1893 Carnot and Delcassé had decided to send Monteil to the Upper Nile without

consulting, or even informing, Hanotaux's predecessor as foreign minister, Develle.

35. The reasons for Delcassé's decision to divert the Monteil expedition from the Congo to the Ivory Coast have been generally misunderstood. In fact, Delcassé was extremely reluctant to recall Monteil and did so only on the urging of his *directeur politique*, Jacques Haussmann, who told him that Hanotaux was strongly in favour of it. Subsequently, Hanotaux was highly critical of the decision, but not because he still hoped to use Monteil for putting limited pressure on the British during the negotiations. He wanted to keep Monteil on the Upper Ubangi because he feared that the Congolese were planning to violate the agreement and refuse to evacuate the ceded territories. See: Bourée (French ambassador, Brussels) to Hanotaux, 21 Aug. 1894, *D.D.F.* XI, no. 225; Haussmann to Hanotaux, 22 Aug. 1894, H.P. 32; Nisard to Hanotaux, 21 Aug. H.P. 27 cf. Sanderson, op. cit., 189–91.

36. Note du Ministre, 30 Oct. 1894, *D.D.F.* XI, no. 260; B.C.A.F., Nov. 1894. The Liotard expedition was partially financed by the *Comité de l'Afrique Française*. See: Andrew and Kanya-Forstner, 'The French "Colonial Party" ', loc. cit., 112.

37. *Carnets*, 10 Mar. 1895, 402; Billot to Hanotaux, 20 Dec. 1894, H.P. 17; Cambon to Hanotaux, 28 Dec. 1894, H.P. 19; cf. M. Paléologue, *My Journal of the Dreyfus Affair* (London, 1957), 30, 36. There is no evidence for R. G. Brown's suggestion that Hanotaux was overruled in cabinet because his authority had been shaken by the Dreyfus affair.

38. *B.C.A.F.*, January, March, 1895; *Fachoda*, 504; *J.O. D.P.C.*, 1 Feb., 28 Feb. 1895.

39. Hanotaux to Cogordan, 31 Mar. 1895, A.E. Egypte 138; Hanotaux to Cogordan, 13 Apr. 1895, A.E. Egypte 139; Cogordan to Hanotaux, 6 Apr., 20 Apr., 11 May 1895, H.P. 18; Cogordan to Hanotaux, 27 Apr. 1895, A.E. Egypte 139; Cogordan to Reinach, 18 May 1895, Bibliothèque Nationale, n.a.fr. 13534, Reinach MSS. Deloncle was in the habit of passing himself off as Hanotaux's emissary. In July he turned up in Brussels, claiming to have the Foreign Minister's approval for a plan to install Leopold as *gendarme* of the Upper Nile and eventually as the guarantor of Egypt's neutrality. In December he turned up again, claiming that Menelik intended to seek the King's good offices in his conflict with the Italians, which could in turn lead to the neutralisation of Ethiopia under Leopold's patronage. See: L. Ranieri, *Les relations entre l'Etat Indépendant du Congo et l'Italie* (Brussels, 1959), 78–81.

40. Cogordan to Hanotaux, 23 Mar. 1895, A.E. Egypte 138; Cogordan to Hanotaux, 12 Apr., 22 May 1895, A.E. Egypt 139; Rodd to Salisbury, 7 Sept. 1895, S.P. A/108. Gavillot had accompanied the delegation from the *groupe colonial* which saw the Khedive in September 1894. Harry Alis, the previous owner of the *Journal Egyptien*, was killed in a duel on 1 March 1895.

41. Cogordan to Hanotaux, 16 Apr., 17 Apr. 1895, A.E. Egypte 139.

42. *Eclair*, 21 Apr. 1895 (interview with Deloncle); Cogordan to Hanotaux, 15 June 1895, A.E. Egypte 140; Cogordan to Berthelot, 1 Dec. 1895, A.E. Egypte 141. On the relations between Deloncle and Mustafa Kemal, see: A. Goldschmidt, 'The Egyptian Nationalist Party: 1892–1919', in P. M. Holt (ed.), *Political and Social Change in Modern Egypt* (London, 1968), 313–15.

43. Corgordan to Hanotaux, 7 June, 8 June 1895, A.E. Egypte 140; Boutiron to Hanotaux, 24 July 1895; Hanotaux to Boutiron, 6 Sept., 30 Oct. 1895; Rodd to Salisbury 7 Sept. 1895, S.P. A/108; Cogordan to Berthelot, 7 Nov. 1895, A.E. Egypte 141. According to Boutiron, Cogordan's second-in-command, the aim of the reports sent out by the new Havas agent in Cairo, Vayssié, was 'to keep up agitation about Egyptian affairs in line with the ideas put about by M. Deloncle during his stay'. Boutiron had no doubt that Havas reports on Egypt reflected the policy of the *groupe colonial*. Rodd, Cromer's deputy, believed that Vayssié had been personally installed by Deloncle as his 'private agent' to send out 'a series of mendacious telegrams which are published under the aegis of Havas in the French press'. In fact, Vayssié had

been posted in Cairo on the recommendation of René Millet, the future
Resident-General in Tunisia and a prominent member of the *parti colonial*.
Hanotaux had finally to intervene personally with the Director of the Havas
Agency in order to moderate its Egyptian reports.

44. Courcel to Hanotaux, 10 Feb. 1895, in G. L. Jaray (ed.), 'France et
Angleterre en 1895', *Revue Historique*, CCXII (1954), 44.

45. Hanotaux to Courcel, 29 Mar., 2 Apr. 1895; Courcel to Hanotaux,
2 Apr., 11 May 1895; Note du Ministre, 12 June 1895, *D.D.F.* XI, nos. 416,
424, 423, XII, nos. 3, 62; Hanotaux to Courcel, 29 June 1895, A.E. Angleterre
905.

46. Hanotaux to Montebello, 3 Mar., 25 Apr. 1895, *D.D.F.* XI, nos.
389, 483.

47. Hanotaux to Montebello, 24 May 1895, *D.D.F.* XII, no. 32.

48. *J.O. D.P.C.*, 10 June 1895; Hanotaux to Montebello, 12 June 1895;
Montebello to Hanotaux, 5 June, 27 June 1895, *D.D.F.* XII, nos. 61, 49, 76;
Courcel to Hanotaux, 30 June 1895, 'France et Angleterre en 1895', loc. cit.,
50.

49. Cambon to his wife, 1 Sept. 1896, P. Cambon, *Correspondance,
1870–1924* (Paris, 1940–6), I, 411; Marschall to Münster, 23 Apr. 1896, *G.P.*
XI, no. 2848; *Carnets*, 578.

50. Courcel to Hanotaux, 2 Feb., 17 June, 15 July 1895, 'France et
Angleterre en 1895', loc. cit., 41, 47, 54.

51. *B.C.A.F.*, August 1895; *J.O. D.P.C.*, 10 June 1895; *Bulletin du
Comité de l'Egypte*, no. 1 (July 1895), 2 (1896), referring to a resolution passed
on 6 November 1895.

52. A. S. Kanya-Forstner, *The Conquest of the Western Sudan* (Cambridge, 1969), 235–6; Procès-Verbaux de la Commission du Budget, 18 June
1895, Archives Nationales, C 5548, f. 74.

53. F.F. V, October 1895; Le Myre de Vilers to Hanotaux, 23 Oct. 1895,
H.P. 24; Hanotaux to Courcel, 21 Oct. 1895, *D.D.F.* XII, no. 180.

54. Marchand to Mangin, 24 Apr. 1896, cited in Michel, op. cit., 36;
Kanya-Forstner, op. cit., 233–4; Mission Marchand en Côte d'Ivoire, Terrier
MSS 5930; D. F. Dawson, *A Soldier-Diplomat* (London, 1927), 243–4, also
cited in Brown, op. cit., 39; Hanotaux, *Mon Temps*, I, 238–9; Hanotaux, *Le
général Mangin* (Paris, 1925), 1–3; Marchand to Liotard, 17 Nov. 1896, M.
Michel (ed.), 'Deux lettres de Marchand à Liotard', *Revue française d'histoire
d'outre-mer*, LII (1965), 50.

55. In an interview given to the *Matin* in 1905, Marchand claimed he
first saw Hanotaux on 14 June. But in his unpublished *Journal de Route*,
written in February 1896, he gave the date as 18 July. See: Michel, op. cit., 26.

56. Ibid., 30.

57. Marchand, Projet de Mission, 11 Sept. 1895, A.N.S.O.M. Afrique III
32/a; Archinard, Note pour le Ministre, 16 Aug. 1895, A.N.S.O.M. Gabon-
Congo XVI 13; idem, Note pour le Ministre, 12 Sept. 1895, A.N.S.O.M.
Gabon-Congo IV 14/a; Chautemps to Hanotaux, 21 Sept. 1895 [drafted by
Archinard], *D.D.F.* XII, no. 152.

58. Marchand to Liotard, 16 May 1897; Journal de Route, 25 Feb. 1896,
cited in Michel, op. cit., 40–1.

59. Note pour le Ministre, 13 Nov. 1895, *D.D.F.* XII, no. 197: 'A meeting between M. Hanotaux and M. Chautemps on this subject was due to take
place when the ministerial crisis intervened.'

60. See below, 73.

61. Marchand, Note analytique complémentaire, 10 Nov. 1895, *D.D.F.*
XII, no. 192. The final sentence of this *note* was placed in quotation marks,
and the editors of the *Documents Diplomatiques* wrongly assumed that it was
borrowed from his original project. It was most probably taken from an earlier
draft which he had submitted to the Quai d'Orsay.

62. Courcel to Hanotaux, 23 Oct. 1895, *D.D.F.* XII, no. 181. Cf.
Defrance [Bangkok] to Hanotaux, 4 Nov. 1895, H.P. 2: 'You are right to
find the state of mind of our "colonialists" exaggerated...'

63. Boutiron [Cairo] to Hanotaux, 27 Aug. 1895, *D.D.F.* XII, no. 142.
64. *Fachoda*, 496.
65. Eulenburg to Hohenlohe, 28 Aug. 1896, *G.P.* XI, no. 2747; Cambon to his son, 10 June 1904, *Correspondance*, II, 143. Cambon's suspicions were confirmed by a talk with Mackenzie Wallace, the editor of *The Times* and a former tutor to the Czar.
66. F.F. LIX, Nov.–Dec. 1898, subsequently published as Félix Faure, 'Fachoda (1898)', *Revue d'histoire diplomatique*, LXIX (1955).
67. Marchand, Journal de Route, 25 Feb, 1896, cited in Michel, op. cit., 41.
68. For Nisard's attitude, see: Nisard to Ribot, 5 Aug. 1892, A.E. Ribot MSS 4; Nisard to Hanotaux, 18 Aug., 21 Aug. 1894, H.P. 27. In August 1894, Benoît was leaking confidential information from the Quai d'Orsay to Jacques Haussmann, the *directeur politique* at the colonial ministry. See: Nisard to Hanotaux, 21 Aug. 1894, H.P. 27.
69. Cambon to Hanotaux, 21 Oct. 1895, H.P. 19: 'With the exception of Jules Ferry, I have never known a minister give so much freedom of action to his agents as you do.' Even Benoît was soon forgiven for his indiscretions.
70. Dufferin to Salisbury, 31 Oct. 1895, S.P. A/114; F.F. V, Oct.–Nov. 1895.
71. E.g. Billot to Hanotaux, 1 Nov. 1895, H.P. 17; Cambon to Hanotaux, 6 Nov. 1895, H.P. 19; Courcel to Hanotaux, 2 Nov. 1895, H.P. 20.
72. F.F. V, Oct.–Nov. 1895.
73. Dufferin to Salisbury, 2 Nov. 1895, S.P. A/114; Cambon to his mother, 25 Dec. 1895, *Correspondance*, I, 397; Marschall to Hatzfeldt, 27 Feb. 1896; Holstein to Saurma, 15 Apr. 1896, *G.P.* X, no. 2691, XI, no. 2846.
74. F.F. V, Nov. 1895–Jan. 1896, subsequently published as F. Berge (ed.), 'Le ministère Léon Bourgeois et la politique étrangère de Marcellin Berthelot au Quai d'Orsay', *Revue d'histoire diplomatique*, LXXI (1957). Dufferin to Salisbury, 3 Mar. 1896, cited in J. D. Hargreaves, '*Entente Manquée*: Anglo-French Relations, 1895–6', *Cambridge Historical Journal*, XI (1953), 81.
75. Marchand, Journal de Route, 25 Feb. 1896, cited in Michel, op. cit., 41. Guieysse's professional background may well have predisposed him to favour a more active Egyptian policy. French scholars traditionally regarded Egyptology as a peculiarly French science and Egypt as a French sphere of influence.
76. Note du Ministre des Colonies, 8 Nov.; Marchand, Note Analytique, 10 Nov.; Note pour le Ministre, 13 Nov.; Note de M. Guieysse, 21 Nov.; Roume to Quai d'Orsay, 22 Nov. 1895, *D.D.F.* XII, nos. 190, 192, 197, 210, and n. 1; Guieysse to Berthelot, 30 Nov. 1895, cited in Michel, op. cit., 4; Berthelot to Guieysse, 30 Nov. 1895, *D.D.F.* XII, no. 219.
77. Guieysse to Marchand, 24 Feb. 1896, A.N.S.O.M. Afrique III 32/a; Guieysse to Liotard, 24 Feb. 1896, *D.D.F.* XII, no. 312. For the conflict between Archinard and Roume, see: Michel, op. cit., 42–9.
78. Dufferin to Salisbury, 20 Jan. 1896, S.P. A/114; same to same, 3 Mar. 1896, cited in Hargreaves, '*Entente Manquée*', loc. cit., 81.
79. Marchand to Terrier, 16 Mar. 1896, Terrier MSS 5904; *The Times*, 27 Jan., 3 Feb. 1896.
80. Herbette to Berthelot, 1 Jan. 1896; Berthelot to Herbette, 7 Jan. 1896, *D.D.F.* XII, nos. 254, 262; Dufferin to Salisbury, 11 Jan. 1896, S.P. A/114. Although the Germans specifically excluded Egypt from the proposed entente, Herbette, the French ambassador in Berlin, did think that the Egyptian question could now be usefully raised with them.
81. Dufferin to Salisbury, 16 Jan. 1896, S.P. A/114; F.F. IX, March 1896; Marschall to Hatzfeldt, *G.P.* X, no. 2691; Courcel to Berthelot, 19 Feb. 1896, *D.D.F.* XII, no. 306; Dufferin to Salisbury, 19 Mar. 1896, S.P. A/114.
82. F.F. IX, March 1896; J.O. D.P.C., 19 Mar. 1896. Berthelot's statement was approved both by the Chamber and by the *Comité de l'Egypte*. See:

Bulletin du Comité de l'Egypte, no. 3 (1896), referring to a resolution of 24 March.

83. Courcel to Berthelot, 20 Mar., 21 Mar., 22/23 Mar. 1896; Berthelot to Courcel, 22 Mar., 24 Mar. 1896, *D.D.F.* XII, nos. 335, 341, 342, 346, 347.

84. Montebello to Berthelot, 6 Dec. 1895; Berthelot to Montebello, 20 Dec. 1895, *D.D.F.* XII, nos. 225, 241.

85. F.F. IX, March 1896; Bourgeois to Montebello, 28 Mar., 29 Mar. 1896, *D.D.F.* XII, nos. 356, 358.

86. Montebello to Bourgeois, 31 Mar., 2 Apr. 1896, *D.D.F.* XII, nos. 361, 365. Lobanov insisted that Russia too had a vital interest in securing freedom of passage through the Suez Canal and hence the British evacuation of Egypt.

87. Bourgeois to Guieysse, 7 Apr. 1896; Guieysse to Bourgeois, 16 Apr. 1896, A.N.S.O.M. Afrique III 32/a; Bourgeois, Note, 18 Apr. 1896, cited in Michel, op. cit., 54.

88. *Fachoda*, 511. cf. A. Lebon, 'La mission Marchand et le cabinet Méline', *Revue des Deux Mondes*, 15 Mar. 1900, 280.

89. F.F. XVIII, 13 Apr. 1897. See also: Hanotaux to Faure, 23 Dec. 1896, F.F. Correspondance Diplomatique; Méline to Hanotaux, 25 Dec. 1896; Hanotaux to Méline, 25 Dec. 1896, H.P. 25. Hanotaux was extremely reluctant to approve the manouvre.

90. Marchand to Liotard, 17 Nov. 1896, Michel, 'Deux lettres', loc. cit., 52; *J.O. D.P.C.*, 8 Dec. 1896. The leader of the opposition to the Marchand expedition was Bazille, a member of the *Comité de l'Egypte*. One other member of the *groupe colonial*, Rameau, voted with him. Only one other known member, Gerville-Reache, was among the 61 deputies who abstained. The strongest opposition came in the press from the *Politique Coloniale*, which in attacking Marchand was pursuing a long-standing campaign against military influence in the colonies.

91. Marchand to Liotard, 17 Nov. 1896, Michel, 'Deux lettres', loc. cit., 51. All three were members of the *déjeuner des neuf*. Lebon had been a passionate opponent of the British occupation of Egypt since 1882. See: A. Lebon, *L'Année Politique*, 1882, v.

92. F.F. XVII, January 1897; Dufferin to Salisbury, 15 May 1896, S.P. A/114.

93. Marchand to Liotard, 17 Nov. 1896, Michel, 'Deux lettres', loc. cit., 51-2; Lebon to Liotard, 23 June 1896, *D.D.F.* XII, no. 411; Mangin to General des Garets, 6 Nov. 1898, *Revue des Deux Mondes*, 6 Nov. 1931, 277. By now, the Ministry of Colonies was openly referring to its plans for territorial expansion to the Nile, e.g. Lebon to Quai d'Orsay, 11 July 1896 [transmitting news from Liotard], A.N.S.O.M. Gabon-Congo I 61: '[Liotard] also hopes to be able to establish a post on the Nile itself whenever he receives reinforcements. The measures which my department has taken during the last few months will hasten the final success of his efforts.' The Quai d'Orsay made no comment when it acknowledged the letter.

94. *J.O. D.P.C.*, 7 Feb. 1898 [speech by Deloncle]; 2 Apr. 1896 [speech by Delafosse].

95. *J.O. D.P.C.*, 7 Feb. 1898; Monson to Salisbury, 4 Oct. 1898 [enclosing report by Colonel Dawson], S.P. A/117; Marchand, Project, 11 Sept. 1895, A.N.S.O.M. Afrique III 32/a. Marchand was even hoping that Ethiopia would become 'either our protectorate or that of our ally [Russia]'.

96. Hanotaux to Montebello, 7 May, 12 June, 15 June 1896, *D.D.F.* XII, nos. 382, 404, 408. See also: Andrew, op. cit., 159.

97. Hanotaux, Affaires d'Egypte, 30 Sept. 1896, H.P. 9.

98. Dufferin to Salisbury, 11 June 1896, S.P. A/114.

99. Delcassé to Quai d'Orsay, 15 June 1893, cited in Michel, op. cit., 139; cf. Lagarde to Delcassé, 15 June 1893, *D.D.F.* XI, no. 65, *n*. Delcassé was hoping to reinforce the Monteil expedition from Ethiopia and, with the help of the *Comité de l'Afrique Française*, was planning to send a mission under Casimir Maistre to reach the Nile from the east. The leaders of the *parti*

colonial were also interested in a fantastic scheme for a railway from Jibuti to Fashoda. With their encouragement a French businessman, Léon Chefneux, obtained a concession from Menelik in March 1894 for a railway to Fashoda through Ethiopia. Deloncle sent Casimir-Périer the procès-verbal of a meeting between Chefneux and the Khedive on 24 August 1894 at which the railway project was discussed. Deloncle to Casimir-Périer, 9 Sept. 1894, A.E. Casimir-Périer MSS.

100. Delcassé, Note, 6 June 1894, cited in Michel, op. cit., 138; Hanotaux to Delcassé, 6 Oct. 1894; Delcassé to Lagarde, 6 Oct. 1894, A.N.S.O.M. Côte Française des Somalis 1016. We are grateful for these references to Professor G. N. Sanderson.

101. Note du Ministre, 23 July 1895, *D.D.F.* XII, no. 99; Lebon, 'La mission Marchand', loc. cit., 286–7; *D.D.F.* XIII, 63, n. 1.

102. Note pour le Ministre, 30 Sept. 1896, *D.D.F.* XIII, 63, n. 1; Hanotaux, 'Politique à l'egard de l'Abyssinie', n.d. (Sept./Oct. 1896), H.P. 9; Lebon to Hanotaux, 1 Nov. 1896, A.N.S.O.M. C.F.S. Affaires Politiques 142.

103. *Fachoda*, pp. 738–9; Hanotaux to Lebon, 30 Nov. 1896 (enclosing Lagarde's instructions), *D.D.F.* XIII, no. 35; Lebon to Lagarde, Note spéciale d'instructions, 18 Dec. 1896, A.N.S.O.M. C.F.S. Affaires Politiques 142. Although this *note spéciale* was not countersigned by Hanotaux, there can be no doubt that he knew of its contents. He spoke to Bonvalot, the leader of one of the expeditions involved, and was told of his objectives. See: Note on Lebon to Bonvalot, 18 Jan. 1897, A.N.S.O.M. C.F.S. 17. On the second objective of Lagarde's mission, see below: p. 85 and note 123.

104. Dufferin to Salisbury, 11 June 1896, S.P. A/114. Courcel shared Hanotaux's confidence. Courcel to Hanotaux, 9 May 1896, *D.D.F.* XII, no. 384: '[The Egyptian question] is nothing like a major element in either their present worries or in their views about the future. It is not even impossible to foresee that, with the passage of time, it may lose much of its importance for them.'

105. Hanotaux to Cambon, 1 July 1896, *D.D.F.* XII, no. 418; *Fachoda*, 721. cf. Dufferin to Salisbury, 11 June 1896; Monson to Salisbury, 4 Dec. 1896, S.P. A/114.

106. Boisdeffre to Hanotaux, 23 May, 1 June 1896, *D.D.F.* XII, nos. 389, 397; J. Claretie, '28 ans à la Comédie Française', *Revue des Deux Mondes*, 1 Oct. 1949, 433.

107. Hanotaux, Note (for President Faure), n.d. (Sept./Oct. 1896), H.P. 2; F.F. XIV, Nov. 1896–Jan. 1897. The plan was not Hanotaux's. It was suggested to him by Nagelmaekers, a Belgian businessman with interests in the Ottoman empire, but he then passed it off to Faure as his own.

108. Note du Ministre, 12 Oct. 1896, *D.D.F.* XII, no. 472; F.F. XIV, Nov. 1896–Jan. 1897.

109. Montebello to Hanotaux, 26 Dec. 1896; Note du Ministre, 30 Dec. 1896, *D.D.F.* XIII, nos. 51, 54.

110. Courcel to Hanotaux, 18 Jan. 1897, *D.D.F.* XIII, no. 68; cf. Courcel to Hanotaux, 20 June, 3 Oct. 1896, *D.D.F.* XII, nos. 410, 468.

111. Hanotaux to Montebello, 31 Jan. 1897, *D.D.F.* XIII, no. 87; Hanotaux to Cambon, 13 Dec. 1896, H.P. 19.

112. Monson to Salisbury, 18 Dec. 1896, S.P. A/114; Hanotaux to Faure, 23 Dec., 25 Dec. 1896, F.F. Correspondance Diplomatique; F.F. XVII, Jan. 1897.

113. Monson to Salisbury, 20 July 1897, S.P. A/115.

114. Monson to Salisbury, 18 Dec. 1896, S.P. A/114.

115. *B.C.A.F.*, November 1896; *J.O. D.P.C.*, 21 Nov. 1896; Tornielli to Visconti-Venosta, 20 Dec. 1896, *I Documenti Diplomatici Italiani*, 3rd. ser. I, no. 313.

116. Courcel to Hanotaux, 11 Feb. 1897, *D.D.F.* XIII, no. 100; *J.O. D.P.C.*, 8 Feb. 1897; Monson to Salisbury, 10 Feb., 12 Feb., 13 Feb., 19 Feb. 1897, S.P. A/115.

117. Cogordan to Reinach, 16 Apr. 1897, B.N. n.a.fr. 13534 Reinach MSS; Cogordan to Hanotaux, 14 Apr. 1897, A.E. N.S. Egypte 19.

118. Mohrenheim to Hanotaux, 14 Mar. 1897, *D.D.F.* XIII, no. 150; Hanotaux to Courcel, 27 Mar. 1897, H.P. 2; *J.O. D.P.C.*, 3 Nov., 21 Nov. 1896, 22 Feb. 8 Mar., 9 Mar., 15 Mar., 3 Apr. 1897; Monson to Salisbury, 17 Mar. 1897, S.P. A/115; *Mon Temps*, II, 68: '...the Cretan question, which so disturbed my life, and which almost cost me (who would believe it) my election to the Académie Française.'

119. F.F. XXIII, 16 Mar. 1897.

120. Hanotaux to Lebon, 24 Feb., 28 Feb. 1897, *D.D.F.* XIII, nos. 126, 133; Lebon to Lagarde, 3 Mar. 1897, A.N.S.O.M. C.F.S. 17.

121. Cogordan to Hanotaux, 17 Mar. 1897 [referring to a telegram of 10 March]; Lebon to Lagarde, 14 Mar. 1897, *D.D.F.* XIII, nos. 149, 154; Monson to Salisbury, 19 Feb. 1897, A/115. All Hanotaux did was to ask the *direction politique* to draw up a note about 'the generally active attitude adopted by England (Niger, Gold Coast, Egypt, Transvaal, Abyssinia). All this while Europe is preoccupied with the Eastern Question'. Note du Departement, 12 Mar. 1897, *D.D.F.* XIII, no. 148, n. 1.

122. Lebon to Hanotaux, 5 Mar. 1897; Cogordan to Hanotaux, 17 Mar. 1897, *D.D.F.* XIII, nos. 137, 154.

123. Nisard, Note, 11 Mar. 1897, on Lebon to Hanotaux, 5 Mar. 1897; Lebon to Lagarde, 14 Mar. 1897; Convention pour le Nil Blanc, 20 Mar. 1897, *D.D.F.* XIII, nos. 137, 149, 159. Lagarde could not possibly have received Lebon's instructions of 14 March before the Convention was signed on the 20th. But he must clearly have had instructions to negotiate such an agreement before he left Paris; he could hardly have committed the government on his own initiative.

124. Hanotaux, Note, n.d. [ca. 25 Mar. 1897], H.P. 2, also published in *Carnets*, 212.

125. F.F. XXIV, 20 Mar. 1897.

126. Mohrenheim to Hanotaux, 14 Mar. 1897; Montebello to Hanotaux, and minute by Hanotaux, 27 Mar. 1897, *D.D.F.* XIII, nos. 150, 168; Monson to Salisbury, 21 Mar. 1897, S.P. A/115.

127. Montebello to Hanotaux, 3 Apr. 1897; Hanotaux to Montebello, 10 Apr. 1897, *D.D.F.* XIII, nos. 176, 193. Hanotaux, in fact, was simply quoting from a letter which Faure had written to Montebello during the crisis in December 1895, cf. Faure to Montebello, 25 Dec. 1895, F.F. Correspondance Diplomatique.

128. Minute by Hanotaux on Cambon to Hanotaux, 15 Apr. 1897; Hanotaux to Montebello, 15 Apr. 1897, *D.D.F.* XIII, nos. 200, 201; F.F. XXV, 30 Mar. 1897; XXVII, 13 Apr. 1897.

129. Minute by Hanotaux on Cambon to Hanotaux, 15 Apr. 1897, *D.D.F.* XIII, no. 200; F.F. XXVII, 13 Apr. 1897.

130. T. M. Iiams, *Dreyfus, Diplomatists and the Dual Alliance* (Geneva, 1962), 145, n. 33.

131. Ibid.

132. Hanotaux to Lebon, 21 May 1897, A.N.S.O.M. C.F.S. 17; *D.D.F.* XIII, no. 159, n. 1.

133. Lebon to *Commissaire du Gouvernement*, Libreville, 20 June 1897, A.N.S.O.M. Missions 44. This despatch has led to several misunderstandings. When he received it, Marchand wrote: 'Very important order from the government to advance. I have received a letter from the *haut protecteur* of the mission. At last! The occupation of Fashoda by France has been decided.' On the strength of this, it has been claimed that Lebon's orders amounted to an important departure in policy, undertaken without the approval of Hanotaux. It is clear that they did not. The occupation of the Upper Nile valley had been accepted by the Méline government from the start, and the occupation of Fashoda too was implicitly accepted by Hanotaux when he countersigned the Upper Nile Convention in May.

134. *J.O. D.P.C.*, 22 May 1897; Monson to Salisbury, 17 Aug. 1897, S.P. A/115.

135. Further rows between Méline and Hanotaux, on subjects as diverse as protectionism and bimetallism, are described in F.F. XXVIII, 25 May 1897; F.F. XXX, 22 June 1897.

136. Hanotaux to Nisard, 18 Aug. 1897, H.P. 11. cf. Hanotaux to Noailles [Berlin], 22 June 1897, *D.D.F.* XIII, no. 256.

137. Hanotaux, Notes, published as 'Voyage de M. Felix Faure en Russie', *Revue d'histoire diplomatique*, LXXX (1966), 228–30. According to the German ambassador in St. Petersburg, the Russians agreed to the toast only in order to keep Hanotaux in office. Even so, the formula: *nations amies et alliées* was a compromise; both Hanotaux and Faure wanted to use the actual word *alliance*. Radolin to Hohenlohe, 29 Aug. 1897, *G.P.* XIII, no. 3448.

138. Monson to Salisbury, 31 Aug. 1897, S.P. A/115.

139. Hanotaux to La Boulinière (Constantinople), 20 Sept., 21 Sept. 1897; Note du Ministre, 23 Oct. 1897, *D.D.F.* XIII, nos. 329, 332, 343. Neither of these initiatives had any practical result.

140. Lebon to Lagarde, 27 Sept. 1897, *D.D.F.* XIII, no. 334; Hanotaux, 'Points à aborder dans entretiens avec Muraviev', Aug. 1897, H.P. 2; Hanotaux to Vauvineux, 10 Sept. 1897; Note du Ministre, 23 Oct. 1897, *D.D.F.* XIII, nos. 321, 343.

141. Note du Ministre, 23 Oct. 1897; Hanotaux to Cogordan, 16 Nov. 1897, *D.D.F.* XIII, nos. 343, 360.

142. *Fachoda*, 725. Nor was Hanotaux the only one to reach this conclusion. The *Bulletin du Comité de l'Afrique Française* referred to 'a general view that all the outstanding difficulties between France and England would soon be settled', and added: 'We have never wanted to see [these] difficulties go on forever. Indeed, we hope for the best possible relations between our two countries.' *B.C.A.F.*, October 1897.

143. *Fachoda*, 726; cf. Lebon, 'La mission Marchand', loc. cit., 295–6; Monson to Salisbury, 12 Oct., 19 Nov. 1897, S.P. A/115.

144. Cromer, 'The Sudan Question', 5 Nov. 1897; S.P. A/110; Salisbury to Cromer, 29 Oct. 1897, S.P. A/113.

145. Monson to Salisbury, 22 Oct. 1897, S.P. A/115; minute by Salisbury, cited in Sanderson, op. cit., 318; Hanotaux to Courcel, 1 Feb. 1898, *D.D.F.* XIV, no. 35; Kanya-Forstner, op. cit., 246–8.

146. F.F. L, 30 Mar. 1898. The report was not entirely implausible. At the end of February, when protesting against the alleged invasion of the British sphere, Salisbury had threatened to drive the invaders out by force if necessary. By the middle of March, Courcel was transmitting reports that Salisbury had lost control of the wild men in his cabinet, and that the situation was critical. Monson to Hanotaux, 21 Feb. 1898, A.N.S.O.M. Afrique IV 38/c; same to same, 25 Feb. 1898, *D.D.F.* XIV, no. 65; Courcel to Hanotaux, with enclosures, 12 Mar. 1898, *D.D.F.* XIV, no. 80.

147. *Fachoda*, 727–9; Monson to Hanotaux, 10 Dec. 1897; Hanotaux to Monson, 24 Dec. 1897, *Livre Jaune*, Affaires du Haut-Nil et du Bahr el Ghazal, 1897–8, nos. 1, 2.

148. Cogordan to Hanotaux, 9 Jan., 13 Jan. 1898 (and minute by Hanotaux), *D.D.F.* XIV, nos. 6, 11.

149. Minute by Hanotaux on Courcel to Hanotaux, 28 Jan. 1898, *D.D.F.* XIV, no. 32. The growth of Anglo-Russian tension in the Far East after the occupation of Port Arthur and Wei-Hai-Wei seemed to confirm his assessment. See: Hanotaux to Montebello, 6 Apr. 1898, *D.D.F.* XIV, no. 134.

150. *B.C.A.F.*, December 1897; *J.O. D.P.C.*, 7 Feb., 8 Feb. 1898.

151. *B.C.A.F.*, February, April, May 1898; Andrew, op. cit., 49 ff.

152. Hanotaux to Cogordan, 21 June 1898, *D.D.F.* XIV, no. 236; minute by Hanotaux, 15 June 1898, H.P. 11. For the Münster Note and Hanotaux's reaction to it, see: Hanotaux to Noailles, 22 June 1898, *D.D.F.* XIV, no. 238,

and n. 1; Münster to Auswärtiges Amt, 19 June 1898, *G.P.* XIV, no. 3814. cf. F.F. LIX, Nov.–Dec. 1898.

153. 'Politique extérieure du cabinet Méline', n.d. [post 1909], H.P. 2; note by Jules Hansen, 19 June 1898, A. E. Hansen MSS.; Pierre Bertrand to Hanotaux, 2 July, 4 July, 7 July 1898, H.P. 17.

154. Marchand to Terrier, 10 July 1898, Terrier MSS 5904.

155. Note pour le Ministre, 30 June; Note du Département, 18 July 1898, *D.D.F.* XIV, nos. 245, 258; Horric de Beaucaire, Projet de règlement des questions pendantes dans le nord-est africain, (10) Feb. 1897, H.P. 10.

156. Bülow to Hatzfeldt, 17 June, 22 June 1898, *G.P.* XIV, nos. 3812, 3818.

157. Salisbury to Cromer, 2 Aug. 1898, *British Documents on the Origins of the War, 1898–1914,* I, no. 185.

158. Minute by Hanotaux on Lebon to Hanotaux, 15 Apr. 1898, *D.D.F.* XIV, no. 157; Lagarde to Hanotaux, 8 Mar. 1898, H.P. 24; same to same, 22 May/11 June 1898; Hanotaux to Lagarde, 17 June 1898, *D.D.F.* XIV, nos. 216, 229.

159. Delcassé to Trouillot, 7 Sept. 1898, *D.D.F.* XIV, no. 329.

160. Andrew, op. cit., 102–3.

161. *B.C.A.F.*, November 1898.

162. Marchand to Liotard, 17 Nov. 1896, Michel 'Deux lettres', loc. cit., 51.

163. Cogordan to Delcassé, 21 Nov. 1898, *D.D.F.* XIV, no. 531.

164. This disregard was graphically demonstrated by the Czar's call for an international disarmament conference in August 1898. 'If the Czar's manifesto means anything', commented *The National Review* in October, 'it would make the Treaty of Frankfurt the basis of European peace.'

165. *Politique Coloniale,* 22 June 1895, citing attacks on Chautemps in *Figaro, Siècle, Paris, Justice.*

166. On the later history of the Colonial Party, see: Andrew and Kanya-Forstner, 'The French "Colonial Party" ', loc. cit.; idem, 'The French Colonial Party and French Colonial War Aims, 1914–1918', *The Historical Journal,* XVII (1974), 79–106; idem, '*The Groupe Colonial* in the French Chamber of Deputies, 1892–1932, ibid., 837–66; Andrew Kanya-Forstner, and Grupp, 'Les coloniaux français de 1890 à 1914,' forthcoming in *Revue Française d'Histoire d'Outre-Mer.*

167. G. M. Trevelyan, *Grey of Fallodon* (London, 1937), 115.

The Imperial Factor in South Africa in the Nineteenth Century: Towards a Reassessment

by

A. Atmore and S. Marks*

In their much quoted and by now classic article on 'The Imperialism of Free Trade' in 1953,[1] Professors Robinson and Gallagher remarked on the diversity of interpretation of imperial theory and pointed out in their usual acute fashion that every imperial historian is 'at the mercy of his own particular concept of empire; his final interpretation rests upon the scope of his original hypothesis'. In South Africa this problem is compounded by the sheer complexity of its nineteenth-century history, and by a historiography which starkly follows the bitter contemporary socio-political cleavages, whether between Afrikaner and English, black and white, nationalist, liberal or radical.[2]

In what follows we cannot claim to have escaped either from our own particular concept of empire, or from these socio-political cleavages, though by concentrating upon impact rather than upon motive, by adopting a multiple-factor rather than a single cause analysis (and perhaps by somewhat mischievously raising questions we ourselves cannot answer, but which we feel are essential if we are to escape the limitations imposed on themselves by previous historians by the nature of the readily accessible and easily digestible evidence they have used), we hope to reopen the debate on a—perhaps *the*—crucial area of South Africa's nineteenth-century history.

The tangle of relationships between Britain and South Africa in the nineteenth and early twentieth centuries has been a happy hunting ground for imperial historians: British policy on the Cape Eastern frontier in large measure led to Professor Galbaith's hypothesis of 'the turbulent frontier' as a factor in imperial expansion;[3] it was on British withdrawal from the interior in the 1850s that much of the myth of mid-Victorian anti-imperialism[4] was based; and there is little doubt that Hobson's entire conceptualisation of the nature of late nineteenth-century imperialism[5] was profoundly shaped by his knowledge and experience of South Africa. According to Koebner, indeed, the very term only achieved wide currency, together with its pejorative connota-

* Respectively Secretary, The Centre of International and Area Studies, University of London and Lecturer in History, Institute of Commonwealth Studies and School of African and Oriental Studies, University of London. This article was originally written in 1972–3. Since then a certain amount of new material has appeared, particularly on late nineteenth century South Africa; nevertheless, the broad outlines of this piece still hold.

tions, during the South African war.[6] The official sources, in London, Cape Town and Pretoria, have provided historians of the South African war, including Marais, Robinson and Gallagher, Le May and Thompson, Gann and Duignan,[7] with sufficient evidence to refute Hobson's theory, and to put in its place what might be termed (in shorthand) a 'diplomatist' interpretation of the war.

Perhaps one of the reasons for the confusion that clutters the concept of imperialism in the historiography of South Africa is the tendency to pick one 'cause'—or cluster of causes—from an apparently inexhaustible bin of factors. This one 'cause' is thereby considered by the historian to encompass all the other possible causes, or he rejects them, and also rejects the hypotheses erected upon other such causes. The reason for individual historians alighting upon a particular cause seems to be the result of two interrelated elements: one the presuppositions of the writer, his ideology, and the other—rather unfortunately but none-the-less understandably—the nature of the main body of documents with which he is dealing. This feature is unfortunate because it tends to lead at the worst, to outright distortion, or at the least, to a limited interpretation. Because of distorted, or limited, interpretations, the picture presented of these complex relations between Britain and South Africa is not only monocausal but is also static. We do not mean to imply that scholars of the stature of Galbraith, Goodfellow, Le May, Robinson and Gallagher, and Wilson and Thompson, have ignored change in their examinations of various areas and problems of Anglo-South African relations: they certainly have not—indeed much of their work is a study of the fluctuating nature of these relations. We suggest that they have spotlighted—and thereby isolated—one aspect, and have proclaimed this one aspect, and the changes which it has undergone, to be predominant. And because of presuppositions which are not always stated, and therefore might be unintentional, and because of the nature of the sources used—in so many cases, official documents and papers—this predominant factor is taken to be political, or more precisely, policy: and the reasons for both the consistencies and inconsistencies, the continuities and the changes, of British 'policy' towards South Africa is, in the last report, frequently ascribed to the decisions, or even the whims, of personalities.

Probably the most glaring lacuna in any consideration of imperialism in South Africa throughout the nineteenth century has thus been the almost total oblivion to economic history, and in particular to the changing economy of Britain itself. Thus even Robinson and Gallagher, in writing about the imperialism of Free Trade, while at one time rightly stressing the point that in many respects what was important was not whether Britain had extended its formal empire, but whether it was able to protect its interests better by informal or formal means, at the same time obscure the very considerably changed nature of these interests between the era when 'Cotton is King' and the period of railway building, of steamships and of overseas investment. In this context, moreover, what is frequently missed is that South Africa's role, particularly in the later nineteenth century, is far more analogous to that of the 'white dominions'—in terms for example of the export of capital and of labour—than to the rest of Africa.

Clearly in the space of a single article it is impossible to do justice to the complexities of the changing relationships between Great Britain and the various British colonies, Afrikaner republics and African polities which made up nineteenth-century South Africa, even were we fully equipped to undertake this daunting task. All we can hope to achieve is to highlight some of the critical areas of debate, to show how and where recent research, on the one hand in British economic history and on the other in African history,[8] leads us to challenge earlier hypotheses, and to suggest ways in which the debate needs to be developed further.

In particular, a number of interpretations of the effects of British imperialism upon South Africa are pertinent to much of our argument. These are the basically complementary views of, on the one hand, liberal South African historians such as Macmillan and de Kiewiet,[9] that the activities of the agents of British imperialism—missionaries, administrators, and in the last resort, the military—were generally beneficial to the African peoples of South Africa, and on the other hand, the views of many Afrikaner historians that in attempting to interfere in South African affairs, often with the stated purpose of protecting African rights or interests, British imperialism was negrophile, and was hostile to and had detrimental effects upon the Afrikaner people.[10] Indeed, the conventional wisdom of both liberals and Africaners attribute most of the origins, and much of the historical development, of Afrikaner nationalism to the machinations at various stages of South African history of Perfidious Albion.[11] It should be noted here, however, that at least one of the historians whom we would categorise as 'liberal'—Professor Galbraith—considers that British intervention on the Cape Eastern frontier from the 1820s to the 1860s was definitely not beneficial to African interests.[12]

Also relevant to the debate between liberal and Afrikaner historians over the effects of British imperialism is an argument propounded most strongly and notably by Gann and Duignan. They maintain the superiority in such areas as military capability, state organisation and 'national' cohesion, of the white colonist societies, and in particular the Afrikaners, over all the people they term the Bantu. They assign this superiority basically perhaps to racial characteristics, but more immediately to rather vague concepts such as 'dynamism' and 'ideological initiative'.[13] Gann and Duignan appear to adopt a Hegelian interpretation of historical forces, and in such an interpretation British imperialist intervention in South Africa (whether viewed by liberals or by Afrikaners) consistently backed the wrong horse in opposing Afrikaner expansion.

Our argument, which is partly a response to such contentions, is briefly as follows:

1. Most of the historical evidence suggests that, contrary to Gann and Duignan's thesis, until the 1870s–80s (with the exception of the

Cape), the various societies in South Africa were more evenly balanced than is generally appreciated.

2. After the 1870s and 80s, the balance of political and economic power swung rapidly in the favour of the white colonist societies.

3. The crucial tipping of the balance of power was the outcome of British imperialist intervention more than of any other single factor. This was the case not only after the 1870s and '80s, when most of the colonist societies did achieve a predominant position, but also for the earlier period, and was intimately connected with the growth of the capitalist economy in South Africa.

4. Far from being humanitarian, though it inevitably 'wore humanitarian garb'[14] in the nineteenth century, the British intervened to protect their own interests in South Africa. And while these interests were in part designed to protect the sea-route to India, they were essentially, although not invariably, related to the development and demands of the British economy.

So we would deny Gann and Duignan's assertion of white colonist superiority, before the changes brought about by the exploitation of minerals; we would argue that a major reason for the inadequacy of the 'liberal' interpretation of the role of the imperial factor in South Africa lies in its generally unquestioned assumption that 'progress' and 'civilisation' were incompatible with the independence of either African chiefdoms or Afrikaner republics—and that 'progress' and 'civilisation' were synonymous with Christianity and a capitalist economy: assumptions which are as firmly embedded in volume II of *Oxford History of South Africa*[15] as they are in the work of historians in the 1940s and '50s. While we agree with Galbraith in seriously questioning the beneficient effects of imperialist intervention (or 'protection') upon African societies, we would maintain that, broadly speaking, all white colonist societies gained in economic and political power as against Africans as a direct result of such intervention; white colonist superiority is inseparable from the intimate involvement of metropolitan imperialist power in South Africa. Although white colonists, especially in the Cape, had gained immeasurably greater power by the late nineteenth century, and with the unification of South Africa in 1910 the growth of their superiority became to a considerable extent self-sustaining, it can be argued that even today the position of white settlers in southern Africa is at least in part dependent on external support.

In some ways our argument is an extension—or a re-evaluation in the specific South African context—of the well-known Robinson and Gallagher complex of ideas about the need for, and the nature of, collaborating groups and local or sub-imperialisms, and about the responsibilities forced upon an imperial power by having to form and maintain special relationships with the chosen collaborators.[16] The relationship between Britain and the Cape, as we see it, is fairly straightforward; Natal always presented a peculiar and rather special case; whilst Anglo-Afrikaner relationships were complex, and, by the end of the nineteenth century, crucial in determining the course of

South African history. The conflict between Britain and Afrikaners, which culminated in the South African war and the reconstruction of the Transvaal, was basically the result of the failure of the Afrikaner societies to fulfil the role of collaborating groups to the satisfaction of the gold-mining industry, which was, largely, controlled by British capital and capitalists. During the century of imperial relationships there were only a few, and comparatively short-lived, examples of Africans or coloured people even marginally becoming collaborating groups.[17] In most cases, the price of white colonist collaboration was African subjugation.

By the beginning of the nineteenth century the tiny Dutch outpost established by the Dutch East India Company at the Cape in 1652 had grown into a sprawling multi-racial colony in which some 22,000 settlers of mainly European descent occupied a privileged position over a labouring class of some 25,000 slaves and an indeterminate number of the indigenous hunter-gathering and pastoralist Khoisan inhabitants. By this time the Khoisan had been largely deprived of their cattle and of their grazing and hunting lands within the confines of what was considered the colony. There were, moreover, significant divisions within the ranks of the white colonists, divisions between the merchants of Cape Town who constituted a metropolitan enclave and who were thereby integrated within the European-world economy, the wine and wheat farmers of the western Cape (who owned the greatest numbers of slaves), and the cattle-farmers who traded, raided and raised cattle in the interior for the cattle market at the Cape, but who were far less market-oriented than their kinsmen closer to the metropolitan enclave.

The great expansion in the demand for meat in the second half of the eighteenth century, and the unequal nature of this trade (in the course of which the Khoisan people lost what remained of their cattle), meant that by the time the British arrived, the Dutch *trekboers* or cattle-farmers were in close contact with the most westerly of the Bantu-speaking Africans—the Xhosa—whose main body extended from the Fish River eastward in a dense bloc of population covering most of the well-watered areas of south-east Africa suitable for pastoral farming and mixed agriculture. To the north of the colony, the cattle trading frontier was beginning to reach out to the Griqua and Tswana peoples, north of the Orange river.

By the turn of the century the westernmost Xhosa had fought three wars against the vanguard of the expanding white pastoralists in the frontier zone known as the Zuurveld, wars closely relating to the increasing demands of the colonial economy. As the British had reason to know, the last of these wars—between 1799–1802, which occurred during their first, temporary, occupation of the Cape—was the most disastrous, because the Zhosa were joined by an uprising of Khoisan servants whose conditions on the colonists' farms and cattle ranges were in some respects worse than those of the slave population. Deserting their employers with guns and horses and possessing considerable technological expertise, the result of 150 years' experience of colonial rule, they were formidable foes.[18] And the result of the 1799–1802 war,

8—CH * *

as of the previous two wars, was a stalemate: the colonists were unable on their own to oust the Africans from the disputed lands, and before the British left in 1803 there was even talk that the eastern districts of the colony would be abandoned.[19] Although the British 'bought off' further Khoisan opposition by granting lands and promises of fairer treatment to their leaders, and the Batavians further shored up the situation during their brief rule at the Cape (1803-6), the problems of the eastern frontier and relations between masters and servants were as acute as ever when the British returned to a permanent occupation in 1806.

Despite Afrikaner and pro-settler historiography which suggests that the impact of the British missionaries and imperial authorities upon this situation was to favour servants at the expense of their masters, and Africans at the expense of settlers—and despite liberal historians who look back at the early nineteenth century in order to defend missionaries and imperial officials from these onslaughts, and see mainly 'the high motives' and 'worthy ends' in British intervention in South Africa[20]—the impact of the British on the Cape Colony was essentially conservative. In the Western Cape they were concerned to secure and regulate the supply of labour for the farmers, and on the frontier they were anxious to protect colonists against Africans, and were increasingly drawn into frontier conflict in the wake of their subjects. The evidence does not support Gann and Duignan's contention that 'left to themselves, the Afrikaners would have become the undisputed masters of South Africa'.[21]

It is far more likely that, if 'left to themselves' (whatever this might mean), the various societies of South Africa would have undergone an even more unstable and disorderly history than in fact they did have to suffer in the course of the nineteenth century; and it is possible that, 'in the long run', considerable numbers of white colonists, especially the Afrikaners, would have become merged with the majority population of these various societies, as did the Portuguese *prazeros* in the Zambezi valley,[22] or the half-caste Griqua on the Orange river. For many observers from Europe at the beginning of the nineteenth century, the white *trekboers* were coming to resemble their African neighbours in many aspects of their life style.[23] Although, by and large, they were critical of the extent to which Afrikaners had 'degenerated', to a less culture-bound generation their description of the *trekboer* way of life shows its remarkable adaptation to a difficult environment. Without the constant injection of capital and technological skills from the metropolis itself or from the metropolitan enclave at the Cape, to say nothing of the impositions of its ideological norms on the 'frontier'[24], Afrikaner society, whether on the Cape's eastern frontier, or later on in the Voortrekker republics of the interior, would have had a very different history to that envisaged by Gann and Duignan—whether for better or worse is not for the historian to judge.

It is only when the extent of the setback on the eastern frontier at the turn of the century is understood and the almost total stalemate which followed until the arrival of British troops on the frontier in

1811, that the true nature of British intervention can be measured, and the reasons for it assessed. Thus, the two British occupations of the Cape, with the Batavian interlude, raise all kinds of questions, which must form the foundation for an overall assessment of Anglo-South African relations, though apart from a useful article by W. Freund on the Eastern frontier during the Batavian period,[25] there is a lacuna in the recent research in this crucial area. Neumark's conclusions hardly do justice to his most interesting and lucidly presented material,[26] while the writings of John Barrow,[27] in some ways one of the most perceptive of the contemporary observers of the Cape, have been strangely neglected, perhaps because historians have been in collusion with de Mist in regarding him as 'an enemy of the inhabitants'.[28] Freund's reassessment of the Batavian period, however, and his stress on the economic aspects of the political decision making, is surely suggestive for the early British period as well. Whatever the political and/or strategic motives both the Batavians and the British (and, it could be added, the French during their 'occupation' of 1781–4) may have had for conquering the Cape in the first place—could it be that the sea-route to India argument has been taken for granted rather too long?—there is little doubt that economic considerations soon weighed extremely heavily with metropolitan governments when faced with the necessity of trying to make the Cape Colony pay. Like the Batavians, who set out imbued with liberal ideals but were rapidly converted by the exigencies of the situation,[29] the British were convinced this could only be done through sustaining the white economy.

Once the British decided to remain at the Cape they needed both to establish an administration and to finance that administration. Theoretically of course, they could have displaced the 'native' ruling groups in any colonial situation, and imposed their own administrators and entrepreneurs. By and large, this was too expensive, and even in those areas they controlled formally, the British attempted to find a local group of collaborators who could fulfil these functions. Also the British hoped that the colony would bring economic benefits, through the production of raw materials and the purchase of British manufactured goods; at worst, it would not be a burden to the British treasury. It was necessary therefore to ensure that certain basic economic demands be met.

The British appear to have followed Batavian precedent in the decision to employ the Cape Dutch as the collaborating class when in 1806 they took over the colony (and this policy was continued after its formal acquisition in 1814), as an inspection of the civil lists for the period until the 1820s, both at Cape Town and in the Eastern frontier districts, confirms. As H. A. Reyburn pointed out in the 1930s,[30] almost all the officials and judges involved in the Slachters Nek affair were Afrikaners.[31] The British lacked their own personnel, and simply accepted the realities of political power at the Cape.

The obvious collaborators were the already existing wealthy Dutch-speaking merchant class, many of whom had interests in trade and land speculation in the interior. These were the people who were becoming increasingly enmeshed in the European-dominated world market, and who benefited immediately from the free trade policies and the more securely based financial system which followed in the wake of the British occupation. Certainly there could be no question of employing the subordinated Khoisan or slaves in this respect; their function as a labouring class was quite clearly defined in the developing economy of the Cape.

As the number of British settlers increased after 1820, both on the frontier—where initially the British also took over much of the already existing administrative machinery, such as it was—and in the Western Cape, they augmented the Dutch as the collaborating group, and in some important respects came to supplant them, especially over the control of capital. This British control over colonial capital was to have far reaching effects later in the century, when the British settlers came to dominate commercial wool farming: [32] though the Batavians were aware of the potential of the eastern Cape[33] for sheep-farming, this only got under way after the arrival of substantial numbers of British settlers in 1820.

Their decision in 1820 to bring in 5,000 British immigrants to settle on the Cape Eastern frontier provided the most sudden and dramatic increase in the English-speaking population of the colony. The superficial and generally accepted reasons for this settlement scheme are obvious, but some of the underlying causes remain obscure. Although the traditional historiography[34] ascribes the 1820 settlement very largely to Somerset's defence policy on the Eastern frontier, this skill leaves a large number of crucial questions concerning the settlement unexamined. The plans for, and the actual patterns of, British settlement, in 1820 and subsequently, in the Cape and in Natal—and for that matter, patterns of British settlement later on in the industrialising areas of the Transvaal—reveals a great deal about what kind of colonial society it was hoped to establish, what kind of colonial society was actually established, and how, ideally and in practice, this colonial society was related to the metropolitan power, and how it reflected the social structure of the home country.

The value to Britain of the Cape as a trading colony was advocated during the first British occupation,[35] and in 1813 Colonel Graham, an officer on the Eastern frontier, urged the settlement of the Zuurveld by Highland crofters—this was at the time of the Highland Clearances, which were so socially and economically destructive.[36] As R. N. Ghosh has pointed out, the widespread economic distress in Britain after the Napoleonic Wars was generally attributed—following Malthus—to a population explosion. As a result, a number of economists were beginning to consider the emigration of surplus population to the colonies as a remedy.[37] In 1814 a London merchant, Richard Fisher, who had by then established commercial interests in the Cape, and who was a friend of Governor Cradock, published a pamphlet, *The Importance of the Cape of Good Hope as a Colony to Great Britain:* he proposed a programme of economic development for which a major stimulus would be British labour transported to the Cape. It is no coincidence perhaps that Sir Charles Somerset, who had the most ambitious schemes for developing the Cape, wrote in his first communication to the Secretary for War and Colonies shortly after his appointment as future Governor of the Cape advocating British emigration to increase its white population.[38]

Similar schemes for assisted labour transportation, as distinct from land settlement, were advocated during the next few years—in 1818 one proponent, Henry Nourse, submitted to the Colonial Office a scheme 'for the relief of the numerous distressed objects who crowd our streets'.[39] Nourse proposed that a careful selection should be made of persons of good character and ability who would be conveyed to the Cape. On arrival, their indentures, embodying certain conditions, should be put up for sale. Nourse argued that lack of labour in the colony was so chronic that these indentures would fetch anything from £30 to £100. The amount of the original expenditure on clothing and transport, totalling about £20, should be immediately returned to an emigration fund, the surplus profit being retained at the Cape for the support of emigrants awaiting employment. By this time, however, Lord Liverpool's government had come out in favour of the alternative notion, namely the establishment of a land settlement. A 'proprietor' would be granted 100 acres for every settler whom he engaged—a minimum grant would be 1,000 acres for 10 such 'followers', and the government would then provide a free passage for these settlers. The proprietor was to deposit £10 for every follower or dependent, which would be repaid as soon as 'his people' had been located on the land assigned to him.[40] It is of course well known that in the face of serious initial difficulties, Liverpool's scheme proved a dismal failure. Apart however from a number of somewhat uncritical descriptive accounts of the 1820 settlers,[41] there has been little serious attempt to assess the impact of the British settlers upon the societies or society of the Cape, and vice versa. Most of the examinations into nineteenth-century British colonisation projects have been located within a framework of elitist—or whig—interpretations of British history. Yet these settlement schemes also relate to those other aspects of British history illuminated by such works as E. P. Thompson's *The Making of the English Working Class*.[42] The various exponents of the Cape emigration schemes gave evidence to the 1819 Select Committee of the Commons on the Poor Law—a Committee concerned to lessen the burden of the Poor in as cheap and as 'safe' (i.e., so as not to provoke further militancy) a manner as possible.

Though it is clear that by the 1820s, with the advent of Wilmot-Horton as Under-Secretary of State for War and the Colonies (in December 1821), colonization came to be seen increasingly as an answer to Britain's economic problems, even before this the 1820 settlement appears to have been motivated in part by some of these considerations: the acquisition of the Cape with its sparse population in the east gave Britain an opportunity to dispose of its own 'surplus' numbers, alleviate destitution, relieve parishes from some of the burden of providing Poor Law relief, perhaps also to draw the teeth of a growing militancy and radicalism. Though the authorities at the Cape were clearly concerned to create a 'buffer' of fairly close British settlement to prevent the incursions of the barbarian from without, the concern to establish a class society modelled on the British ideal generally associated with Wakefield's 'systematic colonization' appears to have earlier echoes here.

There are other, older echoes too in official attitudes to South Africa. Robinson and Gallagher have drawn our attention to the range of assumptions or ideologies 'shared by the aristocratic castes of Europe', though it may be that the British upper classes were rather different from those of Germany or France.[43] Many of these attitudes had been formed by centuries of colonial experience—in Wales to some extent, but very powerfully in Ireland and in Scotland. The colonization and exploitation of Ireland and of Highland Scotland by the English upper classes (which in fact became British by incorporating sections of the Irish and Scottish aristocracies) was the nursery of much subsequent British imperialism,[44] and it has specific parallels in South Africa: parts of the Eastern Cape and the Cape Midlands and much of the highveld were cleared/improved/exploited, and fairly self-sufficient peasant communities were replaced by sheep-runs,[45] in a process not dissimilar to the Highland clearances.

Ireland and Scotland did not, however, merely provide models for successful colonization and exploitation; in these alien lands, the invading English formed long-lasting racial attitudes. Dr. Kay (or Kay-Shuttleworth), close associate of Chadwick, of Poor Law fame, for example, refers to the Irish labourers in England as a 'colonisation by savage tribes'.[46] There is a lot of 'feed-back' here—between attitudes established by the English exploiters of Ireland, attitudes formed by English employers of Irish labour, and non-Irish colonial situations. Some recent works touch on this situation, but the core of the situation has as yet not really been investigated.[47]

There was one particular aspect of the South African situation which was affected by pre-conditioned British (or English) racial and class attitudes that should be mentioned here: this is the general and at times virulent anti-Afrikaner attitudes displayed by various British visitors, officials and settlers. It was not only Coloured or African peoples who bore the brunt of British racialism. Many of the nastier remnants of this racialism committed to writing were directed against Afrikaner communities, rather than against non-white peoples. In South Africa, the Afrikaners seemed to play the role for the English that the Irish and Scots played in Britain; thus, in some cases, it appears that while the social distance between white and black prevented the worst excesses of racism, and gave rise to the image of 'the noble savage', the measure of social propinquity ('whiteness', similarity in religion, language) encouraged them.

This behaviour pattern can be traced from the notoriously anti-Dutch Barrow through even so renowned a radical as Olive Schreiner, who during the South African war became an outspoken pro-Boer. She was able to look back on her childhood and write (in the introduction to *Thoughts on South Africa*):

> I started life with as much insular prejudice and racial pride as it is given to any citizen who has never left the northern island to possess ... I cannot remember a time when I was not profoundly convinced of the superiority of the English, their government and their manners over all other peoples.[48]

She retells anecdotes which reveal an antipathy to Boers only slightly less than that felt towards Africans:

> To have eaten sugar [age four] that had been in the hand of a Boer child would have been absolutely impossible to me.
> I remember it as often a subject of thought within myself at this time [as a child], why God had made us, the English, so very superior to all other races, and, while feeling it was very nice to belong to the best people on earth, having yet a vague feeling that it was not quite just of God to have made us so much better than all the other nations. I have only to return to the experiences of my early infancy to know what the most fully developed Jingoism means.[49]

Latter-day anti-Afrikaner rascism is discernible in more recent attitudes to apartheid, which tend to point on accusing, moralizing finger only at the Afrikaners in South Africa; many of its roots are to be found in missionary writings ostensibly designed to rouse righteous indignation against the Afrikaner handling of 'native affairs' and to encourage British annexation of both Afrikaner and African societies.

There are many indications that, as elsewhere, the 'agents of imperialism' at the Cape—administrators, missionaries, landed proprietors, merchants, and traders—were attempting to turn the colony into a replica of the metropolitan power.[50] The possibilities however of creating a 'fragment' of the old society in Natal were very much greater than at the Cape, especially when the majority of Dutch settlers trekked out of the colony after the British annexation: and indeed much of A. F. Hattersley's work is devoted to portraying Natal society in these terms[51]. Again, the concern in Britain with capitalist control over land, its proper survey and intensive exploitation, so contrary to the practice of both African and Afrikaner pastoralists, has to be seen in terms of Wakefield's systematic colonization: and within Natal itself, it can be argued that notwithstanding Governor Harry Smith's impetuous grant to the trekkers of 6,000 acre farms, the effects of their withdrawal in Natal—land speculation and land shortage—were what Wakefield had advocated; closely settled centres with division of labour as in the mother country, and social stratification, though with Africans and Indians occupying the bottom rungs of the ladder, instead of the British immigrants envisaged by Wakefield.[52]

At the centre of the relationships and conflicts at the Cape was the question of labour, and this was amongst the first problems the British set themselves to solve. Closely linked with colour and class stratification, it was complicated by the anti-slavery movement in Britain. As we have already seen, in addition to 25,000 slaves at the Cape, there were large (but generally scattered) numbers of Khoisan servants, who were extremely poorly paid—not by any means all in money—had little security of position or freedom of movement, and no legal rights.[53] Many had deserted their masters, especially during the series of conflicts at the turn of the century, and these had still not returned. After the abolition of the slave trade in 1807, the actions of the British were to tie Khoisan even more firmly to their white masters, by means of the Codes of 1809 and 1815. These provided that servants could only leave their masters if they had the latters' written permission on a document known as a pass; if they failed to produce this on demand they could be arrested as vagrants. Secondly, the codes provided that the children of servants could be 'apprenticed' to white masters up to the age of 25.[54] In addition, except within mission reserves, Khoisan were not allowed to own land. This is another neglected field of study in the early history of the British colony at the Cape, and we do not know in any detail the relationship between these labour codes, and other Cape ordinances, based on Roman-Dutch precedents and the equally harsh contemporary British/Irish Masters and Servants Laws, vagrancy laws and laws against riotous assembly and sedition.

While these initial attempts to regulate master and servant relations were almost wholly in favour of the masters, Khoisan *were* given access to the courts. In 1828, moreover, in the law known as Ordinance 50, a more serious attempt to improve their position was made when in particular Khoisan were relieved of the need to carry a pass, and an area of land on the Kat River was set aside for their independent occupation. Ordinance 50 and the Kat River settlement caused a furore amongst the white colonists, many of whom were anxious also over the status of their slaves: it was clear that emancipation was in the offing, and it followed in 1833. Despite the fact that the colonists felt severely threatened by these changes—so much so that they were among the factors which led some 10,000 Afrikaners to leave the confines of British rule, between 1836 and 1840, in a migration known as the Great Trek—both the emancipated slaves and Khoisan (the two groups became merged as the Cape Coloured population) were soon re-incorporated in the economy as semi-servile labourers subject to new forms of coercion. The 1841 Masters and Servants Ordinance, though it made no mention of race, made breach of contract a criminal offence, and this largely affected the coloured population;[55] vagrancy and other laws passed later on also had the effect of immobilising coloured labour.

Thus though humanitarian pressures—to abolish the slave trade, to improve the legal position of Khoisan servants and to protect African land-rights—were important at the Cape, they had only limited success. The ambiguity of humanitarians, the divisions between missionaries (the effective agents of philanthropy in the colony), their overall philosophy that civilization and industry went hand in hand, and their notion that industry was limited either to cash-crop production or to working for white colonists meant that they were never as consistently pro-African or pro-Coloured as either the settlers or present-day liberal historians would have us believe.[56] Their role in undermining the fabric of African life in the process of creating what they considered to be a better, Christian, society is fundamental to any understanding of the impact of imperialism on African societies in South Africa and of the shape of contemporary South African society.

In this respect, we need fresh investigations into the ideologies and activities of the missionaries in South Africa. E. P. Thompson (in *The Making of the English Working Class*) provides a valuable starting point with his detailed—and controversial—treatment of the Methodist and other Free Church movements in England. Thompson draws attention to what he calls 'the cultural shock entailed in the transition to mature industrialism. Methodism's function as a carrier of work-discipline was shared by Evangelism more generally, but in no other church is it to be seen so clearly. The Wesleyans . . . repeatedly sought for outright confrontation with the older, half-pagan popular culture, with its fairs, its sports, its drink, and its picaresque hedonism.'[57] This kind of approach to the late eighteenth-century religious revival in Britain seems also to be highly suggestive when applied to the missionary situation in South Africa: in Britain and in South Africa the spread of missionary Christianity was ambiguous in the extreme— potentially it was a radicalizing, even revolutionary, force; in both cases its exponents used religion to bring about changes, but in a manner as acceptable to, and least destructive and dangerous to, the established social order. As Galbraith has remarked, evangelicalism and humanitarianism 'did not imply a reordering of the social and economic hierarchy; they did not attack the validity of the immutable laws of economics'.[58]

The reactionary and conformist elements in missionary Christianity are nowhere more evident than in education. Here an article in 1970 by Richard Johnson is of great comparative interest. This mainly concerns the educational activities of Dr. Kay, the social reformer, whom we have already quoted. Kay's outspoken and unashamedly biased castigation of 'the Poor' is a correlative to the attitudes held by most missionaries—and, perhaps in slightly different terms, by administrators and colonists—towards Africans. In South Africa, the initiation ceremonies took the place of the English public houses, which were the places of resort 'for the pleasure of talking obscenity and scandal, if not sedition, amidst the fumes of gin and the roar of drunken associates'. Kay describes 'the natural progress of barbarous habits' among the poor, but he believed that by 'judicious management' such habits might be 'entirely' removed. They were temporary embarrassments by which the natural influence of manufactures was 'thwarted'. 'A system which promotes the advance of civilisation, and diffuses it over the world . . . cannot be inconsistent with the happiness of the great mass of the people.'[59] The parallel quotations one could cite from representatives of all the missionary societies at work in South Africa are legion.

If missionary attitudes to Africans were shaped in part by their attitudes to the poor, this view of the social order was predicated on their conviction that 'the extension of trade', the close settlement of land, cash crop production, 'industry' were all part of 'Christian civilisation', and as Monica Wilson has pointed out, in the nineteenth century African peasant communities sprang up around mission stations all over South Africa.[60] In the absence of white settlers, this fostering of African peasant agriculture was also supported by the imperial authorities and their officials in South Africa, who saw in African cash crop production a way of getting newly annexed territories to pay their way. In this they were supported too by the not inconsiderable mercantile class of Cape Town and Grahamstown.[61]

But in area after area this initial encouragement of African peasant prosperity turned sour as settlers increased their hold over the political machinery of the colonies of South Africa. The process has been most clearly delineated in the Eastern Cape, but it is equally evident in Griqualand West, Natal, Lesotho, the Orange Free State and Transvaal at different times but at parallel phases in their development.[62]

Missionaries not only coincided with the other imperial agents for change in their encouragement of economic development; their role in advocating imperial expansion can hardly be over-estimated. A John Philip or a Bishop Colenso might couch their demands for the extension of formal empire in humanitarian terms; their outspokeness over 'settler injustices' against African peoples should not obscure the fact that all over Southern Africa missionaries were in the forefront of demands for the annexation of African territories, and the end of African independence in the interest of 'progress' and civilization.

As the London Missionary Society proudly proclaimed in its Centenary Report in 1895:

> The only way to get a just estimate of the missionary history of the past century is to read with it the story of material progress and of territorial expansion . . . The extension of trade, the facility of colonization, the enlargement of territory, the scientific knowledge of the world and its peoples, the suppression of internal wrongs, the possibility of free and useful intercourse between the different races have been largely helped by the earnest labour of the band of unassuming missionaries.[63]

By far the most penetrating examination of the extension of imperial control is J. K. Galbraith's account of British policy on the South African frontier, 1834–54 the subtitle of his *Reluctant Empire*.[64] Galbraith weighs humanitarian and financial influences on this policy in Britain, and missionary influences in South Africa, and explores the 'mechanisms' in the Colonial Office and the men who worked them. In rejecting Macmillan's John Phillip[65] as the predominant personality who influenced events during these twenty years, Galbraith gives pride of place to James Stephen, who became Permanent Under-Secretary of State at the Colonial Office in 1836, but had worked in the Office since 1813, and to his political masters, notably Earl Grey. These statesmen, says Galbraith

> seemed condemned to everlasting frustration in their efforts to achieve order in South Africa ... They failed not because they did not understand the problem they confronted; they and their staff had a clearer perception on the characteristics of the Cape society than did the settlers themselves. They failed because the characteristics of British society and the magnitude of the problem made success impossible.[66]

Galbraith therefore argues that, although British statesmen *thought* they determined policy, in fact British policy—to 'achieve order'—was doomed to failure because of the sheer complexity and intractability of the South African situation.[67] He concludes his introduction to *Reluctant Empire*:

> A succession of ever more expensive Kaffir wars seemed to demonstrate that humanitarianism, instead of transforming the savages of southern Africa into orderly inoffensive Christians, made them more formidable ... The conclusion seemed inescapable that intervention benefited neither the tribesmen, who demonstrated their hostility in a most emphatic manner, nor the settlers, who lost their self-reliance and became ungrateful mendicants.[68]

If this really was the conclusion of the Colonial Office and its officials and politicians in the 1850s, then one can only say that their perception of 'the characteristics of Cape society' was jaundiced and not entirely well-informed; if on the other hand this is Galbraith's conclusion, then it is a somewhat limited view, for there are many other factors which need to be taken into account. Even by the 1850s Africans in the Cape and Natal *were* having their lives 'transformed': some had in fact become 'inoffensive Christians'[69]—and the phrase is indeed revealing as to what the Colonial Office considered the function of missionaries; many more were being influenced by an alien ideology and a new technology, even though the results of this were only to be seen clearly a decade later. If at this stage imperial intervention did little to benefit the African, it did a great deal to benefit the settlers, both Afrikaner and British, even though they did not appreciate the function that the British administration and troops were performing at the time. Settlers, whether in Cape Town or on the 'frontier' never had been 'self-reliant'.[70] Both were dependent on the metropolitan market; they had always, given the opportunity, tended to live off the imperial authorities, and, in common with most other sorts and conditions of mankind, were not particularly grateful for what was being done on their behalf—and indeed they generally asked for more.

Galbraith's characterization of British expansion in South Africa as 'reluctant' to some extent further blurs the issue, as does the usual concentration on imperial withdrawal of formal control from the interior in 1852–4. True, Britain was always anxious to minimize costs—and therefore the less of an administrative and military infrastructure she was liable to maintain the better: always provided her essential interests could be as well protected by informal as by formal means. Whereas this was by no means clear in the early days of the trek, when the Voortrekkers had their eye on a seaport and threatened to negotiate with foreign powers, in Britain's golden fifties all this seemed far less of a threat. By this time it was clear that a politically independent Orange Free State was stable enough to offer sufficient economic openings for British trade to be left to its own devices,[71] while the Transvaal, totally cut off from the sea, internally divided, and dependent economically upon the Cape and even more so upon Natal banks and merchant houses,[72] could equally well be granted its 'sovereignty'.

It is not the withdrawal as such which needs scrutiny, but the conditions which made such a withdrawal possible. So long as Britain maintained its monopoly of the area—and by the mid-century there was little evidence of any other contestants—and so long as the territories remained underdeveloped and controllable by informal means, there seemed little need of formal empire.

By the 1870s, however, both the internal and external configuration of events had changed. As Robinson and Gallagher and Eric Hobsbawm acknowledge, though in different ways and with different intent, by the late nineteenth century imperialism was nothing new for Britain: Robinson and Gallagher ascribe the difference between the two periods to the difference between the mid-Victorian 'golden age' of British imperialism and the late-Victorian beginnings of contradiction and decline. 'The early Victorians had been playing from strength. The supremacy they had built in the world had been the work of confidence and faith in the future. The African empire of their successors was the produce of fear lest this great heritage should be lost in the time of troubles ahead.'[73] Hobsbawm describes the change in terms of the 'end of the virtual British monopoly in the undeveloped world and the consequent necessity to mark out regions of formal imperial influence against potential [and indeed actual] competitors, often ahead to any actual prospects of economic benefits, often, it must be admitted, with disappointing economic results.'[74]

Apart from broad economic statements of this nature, however, Robinson and Gallagher veer sharply away from any further and more precise economic analysis of the events they portray, whether in South Africa or elsewhere. For them, the partition of Africa—and they include in this category, British expansion into the interior of South Africa—was the result of local 'crises or emergencies', which impelled British policy-makers into taking involuntary, and *ad hoc* actions. It is a highly sophisticated argument, but is also, in a way, Janus-faced: 'policymaking . . . is the unified historical field in which all the conditions for expansion were brought together',[75] even though they acknowledge that the appreciation of events by policy makers—'the official mind'—was severely limited:

Because those who finally decided the issue of African empire were partly insulated from pressures at Home, and remote from reality in

Africa, their historical notions, their ideas of international legality and the codes of honour shared by the aristocratic castes of Europe had unusually wide scope in their decisions.[76]

If this were the case, then the ideologies of these castes would require a far more detailed analysis than either Robinson and Gallagher or anyone else has hitherto provided; it also however emphasizes the danger of too heavy a reliance on the official record for any analysis of either local or metropolitan situations. Nevertheless, Robinson and Gallagher insist, if the 'official mind' was conditioned by its own ideologies, its policies towards the end of the century, in particular in the partition of Africa, were largely demanded by catastrophes in that continent.[77]

These catastrophes, 'emergencies', 'crises on the periphery of empire', are remarkably like Professor Galbraith's 'turbulent frontier' in the earlier nineteenth century. Yet both these 'explanations' leave unexplored, except in very general terms, the questions—why these constant recurring crises on the frontiers of empire and why the British response to them at these particular moments in time. As Eric Stokes has pointedly stressed, it is insufficient to point to the coincidence of these crises without probing further: the breakdown in order on the 'frontier', the eruption of crises in the areas of informal empire are closely related to the break-down of indigenous authorities under the weight of the demands of an increasingly industrialized Britain.[78] In the earlier nineteenth century, it was the African societies of the eastern Cape which bore the brunt of the demands, from missionaries, traders and land-hungry settlers, the informal agents of empire; the eastern frontier was thus the main arena for crisis. In the later nineteenth century, however, with the shift in British interests and the dramatic changes wrought in the economy of South Africa as a result of the mineral discoveries in the interior, the scene of crisis also shifted to the interior. And here it was not only black societies which could not stand up to the role demanded of them and were disrupted or subject to rapid social change: in many ways this was even more true of the societies established by the Voortrekkers, particularly in the Tranvaal. And this was the case both in the 1870s and the 1890s.

For interests are not static, any more than the social and economic structure which underlies them is static—though officials and politicians may continue to think in terms of older clichés; thus Robinson and Gallagher inform us that 'supremacy in southern Africa seemed indispensable to British statesmen of the 1870s and 1880s for much the same reason as it had to Pitt ... [The] traditional strategic doctrine [of protecting the searoute to India] ... continued to inspire the pursuit of South African supremacy for the remainder of the century.'[79] Yet this emphasis on the continuity of motives for empire blurs crucial changes in the situation. On the one hand, the era of 'high imperialism' coincided not only with the emergence of new competing industrial powers, but also with a considerable shift in the nature of British interests overseas: the demand for raw cotton and a market for textiles had given way in the later nineteenth century to a new era not only of increased overseas railway building and greatly increased overseas investment, but also the creating of 'modern' infrastructures in the underdeveloped world; by the nineties the role of London in the gold-based money market of the world had also led to further changes in 'interest'. On the other hand, concomitantly, and by no means entirely accidentally,[80] the discovery of diamonds in 1868 along the Vaal-Hartz river, and then, in the 1880s, even more dramatically, the discovery of vast quantities of gold on the Witwatersrand, deep in the interior of South Africa, brought a totally changed socio-economic configuration within South Africa itself. Within thirty years, South Africa, from being the 'Cinderella' of the empire, had become the world's largest producer of gold—and this at a time when the gold standard was being applied universally[81]—and the focus for immense British investments.[82] Robinson and Gallagher's contemptuous phrase for the rest of Africa— 'scraping the bottom of the barrel'—is hardly applicable here.

Yet the **implications of these immense economic changes** both for the social structure of South Africa itself and for imperial policies towards South Africa have barely been explored, though historians generally pay some kind of lip service to the discovery of minerals. For African societies all over Southern Africa the repercussions were immeasurable, as again they felt the full thrust of the demands for labour to service the extraordinarily rapid economic revolution and the very different kinds of controls necessitated by these demands. Within a generation all the remaining African independent territories had been brought under imperial or local sub-imperial control.[83] In the new era, there was no room for independent African kingdoms; they were in Sir Bartle Frere's words an 'anachronism'. For Africans, their pro-letarianization, whether complete or incomplete ,was no less painful and considerably sharper and more brutal on the whole than the making of the British working class; for it to take place their societies had to be conquered—and this they were, by British soldiers, armed with the new and devastatingly efficient maxim gun. By the century's end Cecil Rhodes could remark with satisfaction in the Cape Legislative Assembly

> There is, I think, a general feeling that the natives are a distinct source of trouble and loss to the country. Now I take a different view. When I see the labour troubles that are occurring in the United States, and when I see the troubles that are going to occur with the English people in their own country on the social question and the labour question, I feel rather glad that the labour question here is connected with the native question, for ... we do not have here what has lately occurred in Chicago, where ... the whole of these labour quarrels have broken out, and the city has been practically wrecked. This is what is going on in the older countries on account of the masses as against the classes getting what they term their rights, or ... those who have not, trying to take from those who have ... I do not feel that the fact of our having to live with the natives in this country is a reason for serious anxiety. In fact, I think the natives should be a source of great assistance to most of us. At any rate, if the whites maintain their

position as the supreme race, the day may come when we shall all be thankful that we have the natives with us in their proper position. We shall be thankful that we have escaped those difficulties which are going on amongst all the old nations of the world.[84]

But it was not only the subjection of African societies that was necessary if they were to 'co-operate' in South Africa's industrialization. There were other 'anachronisms'.[85] With the discovery of diamonds in South Africa, and with the changing economic structure in Britain at this time, none of the white colonists societies in the 1870s—the first decade of industrialization—proved capable of successfully performing the role of collaborators, with the possible exception of the Cape Colony. Even the Cape, at that time, was, however, preoccupied with its local political problems, having just received responsible government; subject as it was to the pressures of Afrikaner and English wool farmers, it evinced little desire to expand and undertake responsibility for the whole of South Africa in the imperial interest;[86] for the Cape 'informal empire' could still serve its essentially mercantile interests. Natal was proving in the 1870s singularly inept at handling the vast African population within its frontiers, while it was clear that neither the Orange Free State nor the Transvaal were equipped to control the greatly changed situation on the diamond fields.

The result was a complex and confused situation, which has however been reduced by its most recent historian to what is perhaps the most extreme example of the kind of monocausal explanation which is the main burden of our criticism. Thus Goodfellow, who provides detailed analysis of Carnarvon's attempts to promote confederation in South Africa, concludes:

> yet the policy of 1874–8, and therefore its consequences, ... were essentially the products of the personal preoccupations of one man, Lord Carnarvon ... The conclusion is inescapable: the origins of this major episode must be sought not in terms of forces and factors, pressure-groups and interests, or influences and circumstances, except in the important but negative sense that the absence of significant pressure from such sources constituted the condition of freedom which was the necessary condition for the formation of Carnarvon's intentions. Instead, these origins are to be found in the personality of Lord Carnarvon, and by implication, if further detail is sought, in biographical and psychological researches.[87]

Goodfellow briefly considers what he calls 'certain hypotheses' to explain British imperialist activities in South Africa in the 1870s: philanthropic concern, especially towards indigenous peoples; commercial considerations of pressure groups determining imperial policy—here he cites Hobson's 'economic parasites', and Professor C. N. Parkinson's 'people who mattered' in determining policy towards Malaysia in the 1870s; and finally the 'reactive imperialism' of Robinson and Gallagher—and here again Goodfellow quotes the indomitable Professor Parkinson as providing the 'essence' of this theory: '... we know both from history and experience that no long-term imperialist plan has ever been made in Britain, not at least by those in a position to carry it out.' In reference to his specialised knowledge of the Confederation period, Goodfellow rejects all three hypotheses. Carnarvon *did* have a long-term imperialist plan, and his dream of a British Africa 'demolishes Professor Parkinson's dictum'. But this plan was not a response to philanthropic pressures, nor was it determined by 'commercial considerations'. Goodfellow likewise rejects—in one sentence— the diplomatic explanation of imperialism by Professor Mansergh (in *The Coming of the First World War*), and Schumpeter's aristocratic atavism theory. Instead, he reinforces his own conclusion with a suggestion made by Pierre Renouvin (*Les Politiques d'Expansion Imperialiste*), in writing of the 'best-known imperialists of the forty years before the First World War': 'they were all, or nearly all, driven into action by their own temperaments.'[88] Goodfellow spells out the logic of his argument thus:

> It would appear likely . . . that the material power and political systems of European countries during the nineteenth century combined to place men from time to time . . . in positions where their exercise of power was virtually untramelled. Thus on the one hand imperial policy was the produce of personal hopes and visions, and on the other the peoples of Africa and other non-European continents were at the mercy primarily not of impersonal forces, but of the irresponsible wills of individuals.[89]

The questions that these 'conclusions' beg are formidable; the knowledge about how societies work and relate to one another, which have been ignored, are immense. They fail to distinguish adequately between the local imperatives for confederation, of which Carnarvon may or may not have been fully informed and which he may have only imperfectly understood, and the personal predilections of the Secretary of State. Events between 1874 and 1878 took their contour from the interaction of Carnarvon's policies with the situation he found locally. One does not have to show that Carnarvon was either aware of or particularly interested in the economic changes taking place in South Africa to suggest that the underlying reasons for confederation then as both earlier and later had an economic base. Looked at from the South African end, rather than from London, the crucial forces pushing in this direction were socio-economic, whatever Carnarvon's notions of security and imperial defence. Given the transformation of the African populace into an 'internal' work force from an 'external enemy', the notion of security however takes on a new edge. Carnarvon's schemes achieved the impact they did precisely because the solutions he sought for possibly idiosyncratic goals coincided with the dominant trends of local developments.

Thus, there were reasons other than the temperament of Carnarvon for British South African expansion—in the name at least of imperial interests—into the interior of the sub-continent in the 1870s. Some of these are forcibly indicated in the official correspondence relating to the annexation of the Transvaal, especially in the letters of Shepstone. As early as 1875 Acting Governor Southey was complaining that the Transvaal Pass Laws, enacted in 1873 and 1874, were preventing the free flow of labour to the diamond fields of Griqualand West and to the Cape, to assist in railway construction.[90] While Carnarvon himself, the aristocrat by birth and temperament, may have been uninterested in the problems of labour supply, his famous despatch on the need for confederation in South Africa, stresses first and foremost the need for a uniform 'native policy' and the danger to the small, disunited European population of a disaffected African population.[91] There can be little doubt that one of the major reasons for African restlessness at this time arose from the increasing pressures on them to provide labour for settler societies, exerted through increased taxation and the steady encroachment on their lands. It may also have been exacerbated by their own increased and changing social stratification in response to the developing market economy in South Africa following the diamond discoveries. After the absurd annexation, Shepstone for one showed that he was only too well aware of what was at stake:

> The Makate or Basutu race, ... are not unwilling to travel hundreds of miles on foot in large parties in search of suitable employment at the diamond fields, and in the Cape and Natal Colonies, and many of them have done so in spite of the insecure condition in which they have left their families ... Measures are being taken to prepare the way [to] ... bringing all the native tribes in the Transvaal under the control of intelligent Government officers, and I have no doubt that although this will be costly at first, it will far more than repay any expenditure upon it ... I have remarked more at length on the native question, because I believe that in it is included the most valuable resource of the country.
>
> The agricultural and mineral riches of the country can best be made available by the free labour which these people are willing to give for moderate wages as soon as confidence in the stability and justice of Government is established, and the readiness with which they, so unlike the Zulus, adopt European clothing, will soon add thousands to the number of those who consume the many articles of England.[92]

Labour resources and a potential market for British goods first; the Transvaal's agricultural production and its mineral potential—gold, copper, lead, cobalt, iron and coal were all known to be present by this time[93]—clearly second. From this time on, the demand for indigenous labour—in the greatest possible numbers at the lowest possible cost[94]—was to become the predominant concern of every colonial interest—imperial officials, Cape liberals, Natal segregationists as much as Afrikaner farmers and 'cosmopolitan' capitalists and Chartered Company directors. This is so overwhelmingly witnessed in such a mass of diverse documentation as to provide *the* dominant theme of southern Africa's history.[95] The imposition of a 'market economy' in southern Africa was indeed inseparable from this demand for the assistance of the state to procure cheap, highly controlled labour, which at times was very difficult to distinguish from 'forced' labour. In this context, we find Trevor Lloyd's recent contention that the Chartered Companies were *not* primarily concerned with acquiring supplies of cheap labour disingenuous.[96] In southern Africa at least they, together with every other economic interest, were obsessively so concerned. Without this supply, there would have been little inducement for investment; their concern for 'law and order'—which Lloyd terms 'peace and quiet'—was primarily to ensure this 'free flow of labour', as Shepstone termed it in the 1870s; one of the Chamber of Mines' most bitter complaints against the Kruger régime in the 1890s was similarly its inability to ensure its labour supply, by administering effective pass and liquor laws. And they were able to swing Milner round to their point of view remarkably rapidly.[97]

If the 'free flow of labour' was crucial to the industrializing colonial economy of South Africa in 1877, as it was to be in 1899, on both occasions of British intervention, there are other signs of malfunction and crisis in Tranvaal society; indeed in part it is the failure of the Transvaal government under President Burgers in the 1870s to cope with some of these underlying tensions which appear to explain the early quiescence of the Transvalers in the British take-over, as well as the stridency of the demands from the Cape and Natal for the take-over. One aspect of this which sorely needs further examination is the role of land speculators in the Transvaal and the increasing social stratification of Afrikaner society into rich and poor, 'the gentry' and the landless.[98] According to Shepstone, immense tracts of the best lands were, by 1877, in the hands of speculators. There were 'many' who owned between two hundred thousand and three hundred thousand acres of land;[99] in general the speculators were of British or colonial, not Transvaal, origin. Much of the land was in the hands of large companies, who drew their profit here, as elsewhere in South Africa,[100] from rent paid by the African population living on these allegedly 'unoccupied' lands until their market price had risen sufficiently to make their sale more profitable than their rent. So long as the land was in the hands of absentee speculators however there would be little inducement to Africans to supply labour for white farmers and mines, especially as they were quick to take advantage of the new markets for their crops to provide both for their consumer needs and to pay the greatly increased taxation demanded by the British administration.[101]

In this and a host of other ways, the 1877 annexation, however abortive, foreshadowed the period of Milner's reconstruction of the Transvaal after the South African war. The Transvaal in the 1870s was as much an obstacle to the achievement of the kind of Southern Africa demanded by imperial interests as Cetshwayo's Zulu kingdom; and both had to be removed, their state apparatus 'modernised'. The fact that both in the 1880s, and more importantly in the first decade after the South African war, the Transvaal was able to throw up a sufficiently educated, modern élite, capable of fulfilling the required role (a fact clearly related to the stratification of Afrikaner society, their control over firearms, their roots in European society, and ability to draw on metropolitan or Cape 'advisers' and officials as well as their continued links with a 'market economy') meant that the outcome for the two groups was to be very different.

The whole question of the first British annexation of the Transvaal has been blurred by historians by a preoccupation with the withdrawal syndrome, and by the fact that after the battle of Majuba Gladstone's ministry actually *did* order a withdrawal from the territory. Thus Professor L. M. Thompson's chapter in the *Oxford History of South Africa*, maintains that this 'most dramatic interference' in the period between 1870 and 1895 was intended not as a step to suppress the liberties of the Afrikaner republics, but as a 'step towards withdrawal from responsibility for the internal affairs of South Africa'.[102] This may be true, but it was to be withdrawal only on certain terms set down by Britain—as indeed was to be the case in 1910. The fact that these conditions were not achieved when Gladstone's ministry withdrew after Majuba—and this it seems to us is perhaps the only feature of this episode which can be explained in 'personal terms'—was to lead ultimately to the South African war of 1899–1902.

Gladstone, with his philosophy of 'peace, reform and retrench- ment'[103] epitomized the older era of 'Free Trade' which was to become increasingly inapplicable as the century drew to its end; his 'scuttle' from the Transvaal without securing the necessary structural altera- tions in the state was to become even more serious for Britain. The discovery of the vast new field of gold on the Witwatersrand changed the entire economic configuration of the sub-continent, and enabled the Transvaal to play an independent role in southern Africa, in league with German and perhaps also Dutch capital (many of Kruger's Hollanders had close links with the principal Dutch banks). Alongside the shift in the economic balance of power in South Africa was the manifest inability of the Transvaal state 'to deliver the goods' in the terms demanded by many of the mining magnates.

Clearly historians have to take full account of 'personal, political [in the more narrow sense of party political?] and psychological factors'[104] in their analyses of any historical event, and much depends on the level of interpretation being attempted. Nevertheless in their eagerness to confute Hobson (and mistakenly thinking they are also confuting Lenin),[105] they have tended to throw the baby out with the bath water, and have emphasized the precipitating causes of conflict, those features which have given conflict its precision and shape, at the expense of analysing the underlying structure of the societies which predisposed conflict. This has been particularly marked in historians' attempts to grapple with the complex issue of the South African war.

The argument of Robinson and Gallagher (in the last major chapter of their work, entitled 'South Africa: Another Canada or United States?') is immensely subtle, but they hardly do merit to the logic of their analysis in reaching their conclusions. 'Drastic imperial action,' they write, 'took place at a time when British enterprise had at last achieved high profit and great success in developing South African resources,' and they acknowledge that 'it was commercial success which raised up republicanism and undermined British influence'.[106] But it was also economic 'success', and the local response to it, that made it imperative to reassert imperial control over the area. More recent assessments of the situation reveal that the success (if such it were) was narrowly based and superficial—literally so, because the high profits came from the companies engaged in low-grade outcropping gold mining operations. Robinson and Gallagher further argue that the British ministers 'could find no way of keeping South Africa permanently within the empire but to follow where the Rhodesians and *Uitlanders* led them',[107] but Rhodes and his associates, and the mine magnates, the leading figures of the *uitlander* community, many of whom were the associates of Rhodes, led precisely to a greater measure of British control over the heights of the South African economy. In their comparison of the 'golden age' of mid-Victorian strength, optimism and informal empire, with the hectic imperialism of the end of the century, the *leitmotiv* as it were of the whole work, Robinson and Gallagher conclude that the 'empire went to war in 1899 for a concept [the restoration of supremacy] that was finished, for a cause that was lost, for a grand illusion'.[108] We would argue rather that at least one important reason why Britain went to war was to establish a modern polity in South Africa, one which would provide the necessary infrastructure for the maintenance and development of crucial British economic interests. The international economic situation in the 1890s and the early 1900s was radically different from that of the 1850s (although the one had obviously developed from the other); the power that industrializing nations could wield had been greatly enhanced, was more dangerous and more brutal; but protecting this power was anything but a 'grand illusion', although the terms by which the situation was assessed might have been anachronistic and therefore illusory.

Gann and Duignan suggest a dichotomy between politics and economics, often in absolute terms, when in reality none such exists. 'The British,' they write, 'would not give way, because they saw the Cape and its vast hinterland as an indispensable link in a great imperial chain' and continue to negate a number of the factors which must be considered positively in analysing the conflict situation:

> Compared with these great political issues, the economic questions were of only secondary importance. The British did not fight to make their mining concerns on the Witwatersrand safe against the exactions of unenlightened pastoralism. The Transvaal government, though inefficient, did not threaten British gold investments on the Witwatersrand; nor did the mining companies have sufficient cause to stir up hostilities because of the financial burdens laid upon them by Boer corruption and red tape. The Transvaal administration could usually be 'squared'; ... the majority of Boers had no wish to set the economic clock back. ... [They] had no intention of destroying the gold industry. The great mining ventures provided them with a steady revenue and a growing market for their farm produce. The Boers therefore had no wish to drive out the uitlanders. What they desired was political supremacy.[109]

But political supremacy is the obverse face of economic hegemony: it is a total situation that needs to be analysed.

Professor Thompson seems to explain the war in terms of the pressure that the South African League (founded in 1896, after the 'humiliation' of the Jameson Raid), with its 'jingo rhetoric', was able to exert upon the British government of Lord Salisbury, and also in terms of the personal decisions of Milner and of Chamberlain—the first especially suspectible to the League's 'partisan interpretation of the issues':

> Milner had a stronger will than Chamberlain. Consequently, the Colonial Secretary and the High Commissioners jointly carried Britain into a war with the Afrikaner republics. Milner inflated the jingo forces and blocked the moderating forces inside South Africa and presented Chamberlain with arguments for intervention; and Chamberlain . . . allowed diplomatic pressures to pass from brinkmanship to military commitment and then persuaded the British cabinet that war was necessary.[110]

This emphasis on the personality of the High Commissioner is also stressed by Professor Le May,[111] in his analysis of the 'causes' of the war, who entitles his chapter, revealingly, 'Sir Alfred Milner's War'. For him this major conflict was simply the product of Milner's calculations, of his determination to put his 'grand design' into practice. 'Neither side,' writes Le May, 'blundered blindly into war'—notice the personalizing of the 'protagonists' (itself another individualizing term); and Le May immediately moves to the star performers' wills and actions:

> Kruger sent his ultimatum because he believed that he had no choice between fighting and surrendering the independence of his country. Milner had at last convinced Chamberlain and Chamberlain had convinced the British Government, that British supremacy in South Africa would be jeopardised unless the power of the Transvaal were broken. Each of the protagonists adopted the logic of the ultimate consequence, the argument of the irreconcilable alternative.[112]

Milner's 'grand design' is shown by Le May to be the meeting point of a complex of political and economic frustrations and requirements, but Le May dismisses various economic and political interpretations— what he terms capitalists' and Pan-Afrikaner 'conspiracies'—in the course of what is undoubtedly a sophisticated argument; there may have been no united and concerted' 'capitalist conspiracy' (although confronted with the Jameson Raid, it is hardly surprising that Hobson should have thought there was) but simply to dismiss the economic factor is to eliminate what could be at least the starting point of integrating a body of theory which might provide not only insights into the nature of the Anglo-Boer war but also into the course of the history of imperialism in South Africa before and after this war. Here, however, the argument simply reduces this interpretative material to the personal factor: 'Chamberlain and Milner, when they pushed Kruger to war, were thinking not of goldfields but of the political supremacy of Britain in South Africa.'[113] This level of historical argument is both too specific, and too rarefied. The Krugers and Milners and Chamberlains though important did not *really* 'push' each other's countries around; their activities, when isolated from all the diverse and multifarious strands that make up the past of 1899, were divorced from a great deal of reality. The presuppositions in this personality argument remain implicit, and history becomes crudely deterministic: Carnarvon was 'responsible' for a lot of hostility, which was the main ingredient of early Afrikaner nationalism, and Milner was 'responsible' for the war—not, as it happened, the war he wanted, but the war he actually got, and its aftermath. This kind of determinism explains nothing. There is a machine—or a number of machines—which are manipulated by Great Men; we are told how the manipulations were carried out, but nothing, or next to nothing, about the workings of the machines. Obviously, machines have to be driven or steered; the problem for the historian is to examine their interaction and the constraints imposed by both the nature of the machine and the temperament of the driver.

Historians with the advantage of hindsight do not have to argue in terms of conspiracies to analyse the implications of the gold discoveries of the Witwatersrand. And contemporary politicians had no need to be reminded in cold print—or in hot debate—of the importance of the South African gold mines, a problem for future historians duly recognised by Robinson and Gallagher: 'there are many things too well understood between colleagues to be written down.' Nonetheless, the professors stick to their guns, that 'official calculations ... offer a unique method for making a first approximation to the relative strength of the different drives [towards expansion]'.[114] But this seems to us to confuse one set of sources—albeit important—with the methodology of historical analysis. Let us, by way of conclusion, examine some of the 'hidden factors'.

In 1890 Baring Brothers, the most powerful institute in British finance after the Bank of England, collapsed, after a long period of financial instability: the immediate cause for the collapse was the rumour of an impending default in Argentina—Baring's assets actually exceeded its liabilities by £3m, but could not be liquidated in time.[115] The collapse of Barings brought financial panic. The main problem was the huge discrepancy between the liabilities and the assets of banks and other financial institutions which had developed over the previous few decades—a dilemma that did not actually affect Barings. The underpinning of this chronic instability was supposed to be the gold standard, which had been adopted by Britain after the Napoleonic wars, and by most of the capitalist countries between 1870 and 1900.[116] Goschen, the Chancellor of the Exchequer, who had an extremely perceptive understanding of the crisis, admitted that, 'for good or evil, the immense liabilities of this country would have to be discharged, if need there were, in gold ... any large amount, withdrawn from such a comparatively narrow base for the weight of so enormous a pyramid, will have an effect quite disproportionate to the extent to which gold is withdrawn or the reserve diminished.' Goschen proposed a much increased amount of gold reserve, or, even better, the formulation of a second reserve of gold. But at the time when there was an unprecedented demand for gold, from capitalist countries, as the very basis of their economies, in the period from the 1870s, there was a marked decline in the world production of gold;[117] this did not pick up until 1892–3, when Witwatersrand gold had at last made up the shortage from other areas; by the end of 1898 the Witwatersrand had become the world's leading gold producer—more than one quarter of the total world output—over £15m out of £59m.[118]

Several recent articles have demolished the notion that the Rand mine owners were indifferent to the nature of the political rule over them: certain of the mine-owners *were* opposed to the Kruger régime, because of its inefficiency and avarice, its inability to give them the kind of political and financial security they required to carry on their protracted and expensive mining operations, and—most importantly, they were fed up with Kruger's inability or unwillingness to provide them with a controlled cheap labour force.[119] By 1899—after a recovery from the Baring crisis—the reserves of the Bank of England were again falling rapidly. In January 1899 the *Bankers' Magazine*[120] asked 'Can it be prudent or safe that the Bank of England—the central point of the financial system which is the clearing house of the world—should not maintain a sufficient reserve of specie to meet its own requirements'. Throughout the spring and summer of 1899 British financiers clamoured for an increase in the gold reserve—this was the theme of the Chancellor of the Exchequer, Hicks Beech, in his speech at the Lord Mayor's banquet in June.[121] By October Britain was at war with the South African Republic.

This is of course *not* to say that the gold and monetary crisis 'caused' the Anglo-Boer war. It is very difficult, if not impossible, to use monetary or any other economic information as hard evidence in an academic exercise. All that can be done is to present the material, to analyse it, to extract interpretations from it, and to suggest that these interpretations might form one of the factors leading to such a critical event as the outbreak of a war. But to ignore this factor is to impose unnecessary limits upon the view of a complex area of history. If there is a single theme running through our observations, it is that during the nineteenth century Britain attempted to fashion its colonies and dependencies in South Africa according to its own requirements, and to some extent according to its own image: these attempts make up the developing process of metropolitan-colonial relationships. And to an extent not fully realised by most observers at the time, and by historians subsequently, Britain was not unsuccessful in these attempts. In spite of the animosities engendered, the confusions compounded and the latent conflicts involved, the outcome say in 1910, was satisfactory rather than injurious to British imperial requirements. In this respect we disagree with Professor Thompson, who, writing in the *Oxford History* on Union, concludes that an imperial power must be judged by the kind of society it leaves behind upon withdrawal; this, in the case of South Africa, Thompson thinks was a decidedly illiberal society, in terms of such concepts as freedom and justice.[122] Thompson, we suggest, is mistaking rhetoric for reality: Britain's interests in South Africa rarely had very much to do with freedom and justice particularly for the black man, though it always made useful propaganda. An imperial power should be considered successful if it has created a colonial society that generally well serves its—the imperial power's— interests; there is little doubt that at least until 1948 and probably even after that (notwithstanding the flutter in Whitehall because of the Nationalist victory in that year's election) Britain has found in South Africa's white governments entirely satisfactory collaborators in safe- guarding imperial interests, whether one regards these as strategic or economic.

NOTES

1. 'The Imperialism of Free Trade', *Economic History Review*, 2nd Ser. Vol. IV, no. 1, 1953, reprinted in A. L. Shaw, (ed), *Great Britain and the Colonies*, (London, 1970), 142–63. The quotation is in Shaw, 142. For ease of citation, future references to this article in Shaw as well as others will be given the page reference in Shaw.

2. See L. M. Thompson, 'Afrikaner Nationalist Historiography and the Policy of Apartheid', *J[ournal] of A[frican] H[istory]*, III (1962), and 'South Africa' in R. Winks, *The Historiography of the British Empire-Commonwealth* (North Carolina, 1966); S. Marks, 'African and Afrikaner', *JAH*, XI, 3 (1970); A. Atmore and N. Westlake, 'A Liberal Dilemma: A Critique of the Oxford History of South Africa', *Race*, XIV, 2 (1972).

3. In *Comparative Studies in Society and History*, II (1959–60), 150–68.

4. Robinson and Gallagher, 'Imperialism of Free Trade' in Shaw, 145; see also J. S. Galbraith, 'Myths of the "Little England" Era', *American Historical Review*, LXVII (1961), in Shaw, op. cit., 27–45. For an attempt to defend mid-Victorian anti-imperialism, based on Cobden's speeches, see O. MacDonaugh, 'The Anti-Imperialism of Free Trade', *Economic History Review*, 2nd Ser. XIV (1962), in Shaw, op. cit., 162–83; for a reply to this, pointing out the exaggeration of this 'anti-imperialism' at the level of practical politics, R. J. Moore, 'Imperialism and Free Trade in India, 1853–4', also in Shaw, op. cit., 184–96.

5. J. A. Hobson, *Imperialism: A Study* (London, 1902), and *The War in South Africa* (London, 1900).

6. R. Koebner and H. Dan Schmidt, *Imperialism, the Story and Signifi- cance of a Political Word* (Cambridge, 1964).

7. J. S. Marais, *The Fall of Kruger's Republic* (Oxford, 1961); R. Robinson and J. Gallagher with A. Denny, *Africa and the Victorians, The Official Mind of Imperialism* (London, 1965); G. H. L. Le May, *British Supremacy in South Africa, 1899–1907* (Oxford, 1965); Leonard Thompson, 'Great Britain and the Afrikaner Republics' in M. Wilson and L. Thompson (eds.), *The Oxford History of South Africa*, II (Oxford, 1971); L. Gann and P. Duignan, *Burden of Empire: An Appraisal of Western Colonialism in Africa South of the Sahara* (London, 1968).

8. By African history we mean the history of all the societies of Africa, whether black or white, based on the study of local evidence and from the vantage point of the local inhabitants, rather than that of the metropolitan centre.

9. W. M. Macmillan, *Bantu, Boer and Briton: The Making of the South*

African Native Problem (Oxford, 1963); *Cape Colour Question* (London 1927); *Complex South Africa* (London, 1937); C. W. de Kiewiet, *A History of South Africa, Social and Economic* (London, 1941), *British Colonial Policy and the South African Republics, 1848-1872* (London, 1929), *The Imperial Factor in South Africa: A Study in Politics and Economics* (Cambridge, 1937); see also their respective chapters in the *Cambridge History of the British Empire*, VIII, ed. E. A. Walker (Cambridge, 1936).

10. For the most recent versions of this, see for example, F. A. van Jaarsveld, *The Awakening of Afrikaner Nationalism* (Cape Town, 1961), and the latest 'composite' history, C. F. J. Muller, (ed.), *Five Hundred Years, A History of South Africa* (Cape Town and Pretoria, 1969), passim.

11. One might note here the contradiction between van Jaarsveld, op. cit., who argues that Afrikaner nationalism was very largely a response to imperial intervention in South African affairs, and Robinson and Gallagher, who maintain that it is the growth of pan-Afrikaner unity which prompts British intervention. Clearly one cannot have it both ways. D. M. Schreuder, *Gladstone and Kruger, Liberal Government and Colonial 'Home Rule', 1880-1885,* (London, 1969) maintains that it is largely the spectre of Afrikaner nationalism which provoked British action over Bechuanaland in 1884-5. For most of the nineteenth century, pan-Afrikaner unity had more reality in the minds of colonial office officials than on the ground, though the 'whig' interpreters of South African history like to trace its aetiology back to the beginning of the seventeenth century when the first white settler said 'I am an Afrikaner', in the confrontation between the free burghers and the Governor, Willem Adriaan van der Stel.

12. J. S. Galbraith, *Reluctant Empire: British Policy on the South African Frontier, 1834-1854* (California, 1963), 259, 271-4.

13. Gann and Duignan, op. cit., 178, 190.

14. The phrase is Galbraith's in 'Myths of the "Little England" Era' in Shaw, op. cit., 44. He also shows the 'great diversity of interests' that this garb covered—see especially 43-5.

15. Edited by M. Wilson and Leonard Thompson, 2 vols. (Oxford, 1969 and 1971). For a variety of criticisms from very different points of view, but all making this point, see Atmore and Westlake, op. cit.; M. Legassick, 'The Dynamics of Modernization in South Africa', JAH, XIII, 1 (1972); S. Trapido, 'South Africa and the Historians', *African Affairs*, Vol. 71, No. 285, (Oct. 1972); S. Marks, 'Liberalism, Social Realities and South African History', *Journal of Commonwealth Political Studies*, X, 3 (Nov. 1972); and Richard Gray, 'The Oxford History of South Africa Volume I', *Race*, XI, 1, July (1969), and Volume II, *Race*, XIV, 1, (July 1972).

16. R. Robinson, 'Collaboration in the Politics of the Colonies', unpublished paper given to the Seminar on the Recent History of the Commonwealth (Institute of Commonwealth Studies, London, 1969).

17. Probably the most outstanding examples of these were the Griqua polities along the Orange River and the Mfengu in the eastern Cape. In neither case did the collaboration last very long.

18. S. Marks and A. Atmore, 'Firearms in Southern Africa, A Survey', *JAH*, XII, 4 (1971), 519.

19. W. Freund, 'The Eastern Frontier of the Cape Colony during the Batavian Period, 1803-6', *JAH*, XIII, 3 (1972), 631.

20. C. W. de Kiewiet, *Imperial Factor*, op. cit., 5.

21. Gann and Duignan, op. cit., 178.

22. For an account of this process, see M. Newitt, *The Zambesi Prazos* (London, 1973).

23. This is one of the dominant themes of John Barrow's *An Account of Travels in the Interior of Southern Africa*, 2 vols. (London, 1801), but see also a much less hostile witness, H. Lichtenstein, *Travels in Southern Africa in the years 1803-6*, transl. A. Plumptre, 2 vols. (Van Riebeeck Society, Cape Town, 1928-30), for a description of the large patriarchal, self-sufficient pastoral households of the Boers, passim, but esp. Vol. I, 57.

24. See M. Legassick, 'The Frontier Tradition in South African Historiography', in *Collected Seminar Papers on the Societies of Southern Africa in the 19th and 20th centuries*, Vol. 2 (Institute of Commonwealth Studies, London, No. 12, (1970–1), 1–34; R. Ross, 'Speculations on the Origins of South African Society', unpublished seminar paper, St. John's (Cambridge, 1972); J. A. Heese, *Die Herkoms van die Afrikaner* (Cape Town, 1971). We are grateful to Mr. Ross for this last reference.

25. Freund, 'The Eastern Frontier'.

26. S. D. Neumark, *Economic Influences on the South African Frontier, 1652–1836* (Stanford, 1957).

27. J. Barrow, op. cit.

28. K. M. Jeffreys (ed.), *The Memorandum of Commissary J. A. de Mist .. 1802*, (Van Riebeeck Society, Cape Town, 1920), 192.

29. Freund, op. cit., 633–5, 645.

30. H. A. Reyburn, 'Studies in Cape Frontier History', *The Critic*, Vol. 3 (1934–5); see also C. R. Kotzé, 'A New Regime' in Muller, (ed.), *500 Years*, 104.

31. This arose in 1814 when a certain Frederick Bezuidenhout ignored repeated summons to appear in court to answer allegations of ill-treatment of his Khoi servant; when he resisted the Khoi troops sent to arrest him, he was shot dead. His brother then raised a small rebellion amongst the frontier farmers to avenge his brother's death. This was easily subdued, and six of the ringleaders were sentenced to death, while some of the remaining rebels were deported. The episode became part of the Afrikaner allegation that the British favoured black over white, and plays an important part in Afrikaner nationalist mythology.

32. See Tony Kirk, 'Some Notes on the Financial State of the Eastern Cape, 1840–50 and the Fate of the Kat River Settlement' in *Collected Seminar Papers on the Societies of Southern Africa in the 19th and 20th centuries*, Vol. 3 (Institute of Commonwealth Studies, London, No. 16, 1971–2).

33. Freund, op. cit., 633.

34. See I. Edwards, *The 1820 Settlers in South Africa* (London, 1924); H. E. Hockley, *The Story of the British Settlers of 1820 in South Africa* (2nd edition, Cape Town, 1957); Arthur Keppel-Jones, (ed.), *Philipps, 1820 Settler* (Pietermaritzburg, 1960).

35. In 1800 Sir George Yonge wrote to Henry Dundas that 'the importance of the Cape grows in Its every Hour. It is and will become the Centre of Commerce with India, America and Europe'—Yonge to Dundas, 29 March 1800, private and confidential in G. M. Theal, *Records of Cape Colony* (36 volumes; Cape Town, 1899–1907) III, 94, cited in Galbraith, *Reluctant Empire*, 35. See also J. Barrow, op. cit., passim, and R. Percival, *An Account of the Cape of Good Hope* (London, 1804). Although many of these expectations proved illusory, this did not become clear until later on. On the 1820 settlement, see particularly H. J. M. Johnston, *British Emigration Policy, 1815–1830* (Oxford, 1972), who argues that 'fear of working-class disturbances' prompted the British parliament to vote £50,000 for the emigration scheme to the Cape in 1819. He cites the determination of Lord Sidmouth, the Home Secretary, to 'suppress the traitorous designs of those who would "subvert our happy constitution, under the pretence of Reform" ' (32, 36). Johnston subtitles his book 'Shovelling out Paupers', a quotation from M.P., Charles Buller, in 1843.

36. Graham to Alexander, 21 May 1813; Graham to Bathurst, 21 Nov. 1814, in G. M. Theal, *Records of the Cape Colony*, Vol. IX, 182–6; Vol. X, 206–8. 1813 and 1814 were the years when the great 'clearance' of Sutherland got under way. The motives of the land-owners were admirably stated by Patrick Sellar, one of their most 'enthusiastic' factors: 'the people should be employed in securing the natural riches of the sea-coast, [while] the mildew of the interior should be allowed to fall upon grass and not upon corn, and ... the several hundred miles of alpine plants flourishing in these regions in curious succession at all seasons, should be converted into wool and mutton

for the English manufacture' (our italics) quoted in John Prebble, *The Highland Clearances* (Penguin, 1969), 63.

37. R. N. Ghosh, 'The Colonization Controversy: R. J. Wilmot Horton and the Classical Economists' in *Economica*, XXXI (1964), also in Shaw, op. cit., 110–31. For this issue, see p. 111.

38. A. K. Millar, *Plantagenet in South Africa: Lord Charles Somerset* (Cape Town, 1965), 51.

39. Nourse to Lord Sidmouth, 12 Jan. 1818, in G. M. Theal, *Records of the Cape Colony*, Vol. XI, 445–8. We cannot attempt even a brief sortie into the vast and controversial literature on the condition of England at this time; we will merely cite in addition Henry Brougham's statement in the Commons that the post-war depression had 'exposed certain parts of the population' to the pressure of hunger in 1817. *Hansard*, XXXV, 653–4.

40. Colonial Office circular letter embodying the regulations, 1817, in Theal, *Records of the Cape Colony*, Vol. XI, 388–9.

41. See footnote 34 above.

42. (London, 1968).

43. *Africa and the Victorians*, 21.

44. This has been gleaned from a number of sources, but cf. V. G. Kiernan, *The Lords of Human Kind* (London, 1972); Christine Bolt, *Victorian Attitudes to Race* (London, 1971); Prebble, *Highland Clearances*, op. cit.; Ronald Pearsall, *The Worm in the Bud* (London, 1971); Thomas Pakenham, *The Year of Liberty* (London, 1969); J. C. Beckett, *The Making of Modern Ireland* (London, 1966); Liam de Paor, *Divided Ulster* (London, 1970). We would like to thank our colleague, Dr. Richard Rathbone for first drawing our attention to this aspect of the social consciousness of the British ruling élite.

45. See for example, Tony Kirk, 'Progress and Decline in the Kat River Settlement, 1829–1854', *JAH*, XIV, 3, 1973, 411–28.

46. R. Johnson, 'Educational Policy and Social Control in Early Victorian England', *Past and Present*, 49 (Nov. 1970), 101.

47. Cf. V. G. Kiernan, op. cit.; Philip Mason, *Patterns of Dominance* (London, 1970); Christine Bolt, op. cit.; H. A. C. Cairns, *Prelude to Imperialism: British Reactions to Central African Society, 1840–1890* (London, 1965).

48. (London, 1923) 15.

49. Ibid., 17.

50. For this concept see L. Hartz, *The Founding of New Societies* (New York, 1964).

51. See, for example, A. F. Hattersley, *Portrait of a Colony: The Story of Natal* (Cambridge, 1940) and *The British Settlement of Natal: A Study in Imperial Migration* (Cambridge, 1950).

52. For an interesting re-interpretation of Wakefield's political philosophy, see H. O. Pappé, 'Wakefield and Marx', *Economic History Review*, 2nd Series, IV (1951) in Shaw, op. cit., 197–213.

53. W. M. Macmillan, *The Cape Colour Question*, op. cit. deals extensively with this issue. See also R. Davenport, 'The Consolidation of a New Society' in *Oxford History of South Africa*, Vol. I, 293, 301.

54. Ibid., 304.

55. S. Van der Horst, *Native Labour in South Africa* (Cass reprint, 1971), 34–8.

56. Cf. Macmillan, *Bantu, Boer and Briton*, 21, 333–5. See also footnote 69 below.

57. *The Making of the English Working Class*, 918.

58. 'Myths of the "Little England" Era', 40.

59. Johnson, 'Educational Policy', 105, 101.

60. 'The Growth of Peasant Communities', in *The Oxford History of South Africa*, Vol. II, 49–50.

61. See S. Trapido, 'Cape Liberalism Revisited' in *Collected Seminar Papers on the Societies of Southern Africa in the 19th and 20th centuries*, Vol. 4 (Institute of Commonwealth Studies, London, 1972–3), No. 17.

62. M. Wilson, op. cit., passim; C. Bundy, 'The Emergence and Decline of a South African peasantry', *African Affairs*, vol. 71, no. 285, October, 1972, 369–88; R. Ross, 'Griqua Power and Wealth: An Analysis of the Paradoxes of their Interrelationship', *Collected Seminar Papers*, Vol. 4 (Institute of Commonwealth Studies, London, 1972–3, No. 17; H. Slater, 'Economic Relationships in Rural Natal, 1845–1913', *Collected Seminar Papers*, Vol. 3 (I.C.S. London, 1971–2, No. 16).

63. Cited in A. J. Dachs, 'Missionary Imperialism: the Case of Bechuanaland', *Journal of African History*, XIII, 4 (1972), 657.

64. See footnote 12 above.

65. In *Bantu, Boer and Briton*, which is based on the Philip papers, Macmillan gives pride of place to Dr. John Philip's personal influence on the imperial government, and especially on Lord Glenelg, the Secretary of State for the Colonies, in achieving the emancipation of the 'Hottentots', and the more 'liberal' approach to the problems of the Cape eastern frontier.

66. *Reluctant Empire*, 9.

67. Ibid., 30, 276.

68. Ibid., 9.

69. Cf. the views of Sir Charles Somerset: 'His Excellency does not hesitate in saying that his greatest hope in permitting a missionary establishment to pass into Caffraria, contrary to the policy antecedently adopted, has been with the view of ensuring its co-operation in putting a stop to the system of plunder which has kept the frontier so long in a state of ferment'—CO4838, J. Bird, Sec. to Gov. to J. Read, 22.8.1816, cited in Millar, op. cit. There is an increasing literature on the role of missionaries in South Africa, not all of it as favourable as Macmillan, *Bantu, Boer and Briton*, or Monica Wilson in the Oxford History, vols. I and II. See for example: D. Williams, *When Races Meet: The Life and Times of William Ritchie Thomson, 1796–1891* (Johannesburg, 1967); A. Sillery, *John Mackenzie of Bechuanaland, A Study in Humanitarian Imperialism, 1835–1899* (Cape Town, 1970); B. Hutchinson, 'Some Social Consequences of Missionary Activity among the South African Bantu', *Africa*, Vol. XXVII, 2, 1957, 160–75; Dachs, 'Missionary Imperialism', op. cit. M. Legassick, 'The Griqua, the Tswana and the Missionaries, 1780–1840: The Politics of a Frontier Zone' (unpubl. Ph.D. U.C.L.A., 1969); N. Etherington, 'The Amakholwa of South East Africa' (unpubl. Ph.D., Yale, 1972); M. Dinnerstein, 'The American Board Mission to the Zulu, 1835–1900, A Study in Sociology' (unpubl. Ph.D., Columbia, 1971); L. Switzer, 'The Problem of an African Mission in a White Dominated Multi-Racial Society', (unpubl. Ph.D., Natal, 1971); Q. N. Parsons, 'Khama III, the Bamamangwato, and the British, with special reference to 1895–1923' (unpubl. Ph.D., Edinburgh, 1973); R. Moyer, 'A History of the Mfengu of the Eastern Cape, 1820–60' (Ph.D. London, in progress). For the black anti-missionary view, see N. Majeke, *The Role of the Missionaries in Conquest* (n.d., c. 1950, Cape Town) and 'Mnguni', *Three Hundred Years* (Cape Town, 1952).

70. See above, pp. 109–111.

71. Cf. Anthony Trollope's description of the Orange Free State in the late 1870s: 'A very large proportion of the wealth of the country is in English hands. The large shopkeepers are generally English; and the Banks are supported by English ... or Colonial capital'—*South Africa* (London, 1878) II, 243. That this was true in the 1850s is shown by Galbraith, *Reluctant Empire*, 271, and C. W. de Kiewiet, *British Colonial Policy and the South African Republics, 1848–77*.

72. C. W. de Kiewiet, *The Imperial Factor in South Africa*, 97; E. H. D. Arndt, *Banking and Currency Development in South Africa, 1652–1927*, (Cape Town, 1928), 340 ff.

73. *Africa and the Victorians*, 472.

74. *Industry and Empire* (Penguin, 1968) 131. See also D. Landes, *The Unbound Prometheus* (Cambridge, 1970), 239–41.

75. *Africa and the Victorians*, 19.

76. Ibid., 21.

77. Cf. their scenario: 'While in some countries, British agencies helped to create vortices of disorder and nationalist reaction, in others they helped local communities to grow until they became expansive in their own right. In these ways the process of expansion was soon receding out of metropolitan control. Some satellites tended to break up; others were beginning to throw off galaxies [sic] of their own. It is not unlikely that both these tendencies helped to drag British ministries into the African empire' (*African and the Victorians*, 18.) But why, to ask even on a superficial level, was it considered necessary that the processes of expansion should remain under metropolitan control?

78. 'Late Nineteenth Century Colonial Expansion and the Attack on the Theory of Economic Imperialism: A Case of Mistaken Identity', *The Historical Journal*, XII, 2 (1969), 293-4.

79. *Africa and the Victorians*, 89.

80. For the 'non-accidental' nature of mineral discoveries, see G. Blainey, 'A Theory of Mineral Discovery: Australia in the Nineteenth Century'. *Economic History Review*, 2nd Series, XXIII, no. 2 (Aug. 1970), 298–313.

81. Cf. Gann and Duignan, *Burden of Empire*, op. cit. 202–3.

82. Cf. the figures in A. K. Cairncross, *Home and Foreign Investment, 1870–1913* (Cambridge, 1953), Table 42, p. 185: Investment in South Africa rose from £34m in 1884 to £351m in 1911—the swiftest rise anywhere, though not the largest sum invested. (Cf. Canada—the largest colonial borrower in these years: the investment rose from £112m to £373m).

83. See the table in Wilson and Thompson, *Oxford History*, Vol. II, 285–6.

84. On moving the second reading of the Glen Grey Act, 30 July 1894, in 'Vindex', *Cecil Rhodes, His Political Life and Speeches, 1881–1900* (London, 1900), 371–2. It is interesting, and perhaps significant, that A. P. Newton, *Select Documents relating to the Unification of South Africa* (London, 1924) I, 124, citing the same speech omits all reference to the labour troubles in the 'older countries'. By 1924 it was no longer politic to be quite so blunt about having the working class 'in its proper position'.

85. The phrase was used perhaps more frequently than any other about Kruger's republic; one still hears echoes of this in the contemporary references to Afrikaners who are allegedly still living in the eighteenth century.

86. Robinson and Gallagher, *Africa and the Victorians*, 57.

87. C. F. Goodfellow, *Great Britain and South African Confederation, 1870–1881* (Cape Town, 1966), 216; see also 210–11.

88. Ibid., 217–8.

89. Ibid., 219.

90. C1748, *Correspondence re War between the Transvaal Republic and Neighbouring Tribes*, April, 1877, 1–2, Lieut. Governor, Southey Kimberley, to Sir Henry Barkly, 16 January 1875, Encl. 1 in no. 1, Barkly to Sec. St., 25 January 1875.

See also, J. D. Barry, Acting Admin. Griqualand West to High Commissioner, 19 May 1877: 'It has long been the object of Major Lanyon's Administration [in the newly annexed Transvaal] to secure a constant supply of cheap labour to satisfy the large wants of the Diamond Fields Labour Market' (C2220, 61); the Memo on several reports sent by A. C. Bailie on his 'Mission to the native tribes to secure an adequate supply of labour for the Diamond Fields', Ibid., 41–52; Q. N. Parsons, 'Khama III . . .', op. cit., 45, 'The prime motive of British official interest in the Road to the North was . . . the securing of labour supplies for the diamond industry'.

91. C1244 no. 1, Carnarvon to Barkly, 4.5.1875: 'Recent occurrences in Natal have brought the question of the condition and treatment of the native population throughout South Africa into the foremost rank of those questions which especially demand uniformity of treatment. . . . As long as natives . . . perceive that the comparatively small European population of South Africa is divided under a number of European government/which/ . . . are . . . estranged, they must continue restless and unsettled . . . The result is . . .

a distinct danger of widely extended disaffection. . . . It is then with regard to the native question that I conceive it to be most urgent at the present moment that there should be a free and friendly interchange of opinion among the neighbouring Governments in South Africa . . .'

92. C1961, Shepstone to Carnarvon, No. 27, 11 August 1877.

93. C1399, J. A. Froude to Carnarvon, No. 50, 10 January 1876.

94. As van der Horst has pointed out, the constant complaint of labour shortage simply implies that at the prevailing rate of wages it would pay employers to employ more labourers (*Native Labour in South Africa*, 167–2, 289), which has given rise to the aphorism, . . . 'If the cost of labour would have been nothing, the demand would have been infinite; as it was next to nothing, the demand was almost infinite.' Van der Horst delineates the 'non-market restraints' which made African labour so cheap in some detail.

95. It is almost impossible to do justice to this in a footnote, but see footnote 90 above; Austen to Burnet, 21 March 1868, *Basutoland Records*, ed. G. M. Theal, IV, 39–56; the entire run of Cape *Blue Books* starting in the early 1870s, but especially 1875; 'Vindex', *Cecil Rhodes*, op. cit., 158, 371–5; Van der Horst, *Native Labour*, op. cit., 61 ff.

96. T. Lloyd, 'Africa and Hobson's Imperialism', *Past and Present*, 55, May, 1972, 130–53. We wholly agree however with Lloyd's principle conclusion—the disruptive effect of the imposition of 'law and order' on African societies. Whether or not the process amounts to exploitation rather depends on one's definition of 'exploitation'. If, however, one accepts David Landes's definition ('Some Thoughts on the Nature of Economic Imperialism', *Journal of Economic History*, 12, 1961, 496–512, 499) 'imperialist exploitation consists in the employment of labor at wages lower than would obtain in a free market. Imperialist exploitation, in other words, implies non market constraint', it is hard to escape the conclusion that the imposition of taxation, pass laws, the monopsonistic recruiting policies of the Chamber of Mines, etc. were 'exploitative'. See S. Trapido, 'South Africa in a Comparative Study of Industrialization', *Journal of Development Studies*, VII, 3, April, 1971, 309–20, and generally T. Kemp, *Theories of Imperialism* (London, 1967).

97. See for example J. P. Fitzpatrick, *The Transvaal from Within* (London, 1899), 105 ff.

98. For a preliminary attempt to delineate this, see S. Trapido, 'The South African Republic: Class Formation and the State, 1850–1900', *Collected Seminar Papers*, Vol. 3 (I.C.S., London, 1971–2, No. 16); also his review article of the *Oxford History*, II, 'South Africa and the Historians,' *African Affairs*, op. cit., 447.

99. C1961, Shepstone to Carnarvon, 11 August 1877, 71.

100. For the situation in Natal, see H. Slater, 'Economic Relations in Rural Natal', op. cit., and 'The Natal Land Colonisation Company, 1860–1948', *Collected Seminar Papers*, Vol. 4 (I.C.S. London, 1972–3, No. 17).

101. It may not be that the actual taxes themselves were stepped up by the British so much as that they were more efficient in collecting them; this seems to have been true in both 1877–81 and 1902–7. For the increased African participation in the market economy through cash crop production, see Bundy, 'Emergence and Decline', op. cit.; *Blue Books on Native Affairs*, Cape Colony, 1870–1880, especially reports on Basutoland.

102. II, 289.

103. Hobsbawm, *Industry and Empire*, 108.

104. Thompson, loc. cit.

105. Stokes, 'Late Nineteenth Century Colonial Expansion', op. cit.; Lloyd, 'Africa and Hobson's Imperialism'. Stokes argues convincingly that Lenin was not a Hobsonian, and Lloyd equally explicitly that Hobson was not a Marxist. Implicit in the latter's argument is that anti-Hobsonian historians have greatly confused the problem of the partition of Africa by assuming that the theory applied to tropical Africa, whereas its main relevance and resonance is for South Africa.

106. *Africa and the Victorians*, 461.

107. Ibid., 460; also 427, 459.

108. Loc. cit.

109. Gann and Duignan, *Burden of Empire*, 36–7.

110. *Oxford History*, II, 322.

111. *British Supremacy in South Africa, 1899–1907* (Oxford, 1965), 1–37.

112. Ibid., 26.

113. Ibid., 30.

114. *Africa and the Victorians*, 20.

115. *Bankers' Magazine*, L, no. 561, Dec. 1890. Leading article, 1399. We are grateful to Mr. Paul Trewelha for directing our attention to this valuable source, and for general information on the period.

116. Gann and Duignan, *Burden of Empire*, 202–3, point out the critical importance of gold at this time—and then remark perversely that 'Rhodes did not think mainly in economic terms'.

117. Speech at Leeds, 28 January 1891, also cited in the *Bankers' Magazine* LI, No. 564, 429–30.

118. C. B. Jeppe, *Gold Mining on the Witwatersand* (2 vols. Johannesburg, 1946), I, 25, Table II.

119. In an important recent article R. V. Kubicek ('The Randlords in 1895: A Reassessment', *Journal of British Studies*, XI, 2, 1972, 84–103) has shown that, contrary to the views of G. Blainey ('Lost Causes of the Jameson Raid', *Economic History Review*, 2nd Series, XVIII, 1965, 350–66), there was no 'common concern about capital wants and anticipated returns which distinguish randlords who participated in the attempt to overthrow Kruger's republic in 1895 from those who did not', and that the financial vulnerability of mining magnates was not solely related to whether their interests were in deep level or outcrop mines. Equally, A. Mawby has demonstrated ('Capital, Government and Politics in the Transvaal, 1900–6: A Revision and a Reversion', *Historical Journal*, XVII, 2, 1974, 387–415) that Denoon's political application of Blainey's theory (see D. Denoon, *A Grand Illusion*, London, 1973) that there was a basic division between deep level and outcrop mining interests in the period after the South African war retains no validity for it 'is based on invalid evidence and also [is] dependent on certain logical links which are thus invalid' (p. 415). This does not alter our view that the mining magnates, and perhaps in particular those with deep level interests, had very specific demands on the state, most crucially in relation to the control of labour, and that certain mining capitalists played an important role in the political events of the time—although as Mawby points out, this was in ways more subtle than Blainey or Denoon suggest. Blainey's work has nevertheless had its value in stirring scholars like Kubicek and Mawby to take up some of the financial and other issues involved, even if, as yet, this has meant the demolition of existing theories rather than the substitution of any new, coherent perspectives on this vital period in South African history.

120. LXVII, no. 658, 'The Progress of Banking in Great Britain and Ireland during 1898', 28.

121. *Bankers' Magazine*, LXVII, no. 665, leading article 'The Gold Reserves of the Bank', August 1899, 370.

122. *Oxford History*, II, 364.

Vigné d'Octon and Anti-Colonialism under the Third Republic

by

Henri Brunschwig*

M. Jean Suret-Canale, speaking on Radio Guinea, characterised Paul Vigné d'Octon, deputy for Hérault from 1893 to 1906, as 'the most courageous and determined spokesman for anti-colonialism in the French Chamber'. After summarising his biography and assessing his character he concludes:

> A good child readily responsive to friendship, Vigné d'Octon was later to show himself tolerant towards parliamentary irregularities. (The Colonial Party accused him of fraudulent electoral practices.) But there is no doubt about his personal integrity. His whole career bears witness to it, and the conspiracy of silence of which he was a victim represents the sanctions imposed out of revenge by the Colonial Party on an unyielding and incorruptible opponent.[1]

This judgment is repeated in the two volumes of *Afrique noire*, in which M. Suret-Canale quotes freely from the writings of Vigné, who appeared to him to be a radical, a *franc-tireur* 'starting from a purely sentimental reflex and falling short of a fundamental analysis of the colonial system'.[2] Knowing M. Suret-Canale's keenness and good faith, and wishing to make a more thorough study of the history of anti-colonialism, which has often been sketched by French and British historians, we have re-opened the dossier and, without completing it, we have enlarged it sufficiently to clarify these works and qualify some of their judgments, which, though in general correct, are a little too categorical. We shall attempt, then, in what follows, to explain first who Vigné d'Octon was, next the place he occupies among those who may be designated anti-colonialists, and finally, what was the precise meaning of the term in the age of imperialist expansion.

I

It is difficult to reconstruct an accurate account of the life of Paul Vigné. On many details, such as precise dates, places of residence and itineraries, the few witnesses whose accounts are available to us diverge.

* Director of Studies at the École Pratique des Hautes Études, and Professor at the Institute d'Études Politiques.

However, the documents that we shall use will enable us to extract the essential points. The first of them is the booklet published after his death by his second wife, Hélia Clément-Béridon.[3] But this hagiographic text is full of errors and of borrowings from obviously improbable stories published by Vigné. It may be critically examined with the help of autobiographical details scattered over his literary work, documents in the archives, and the contemporary press.

Vigné's journalistic activity was considerable. A list giving dates of all his articles would almost enable us to follow his activities and to trace the evolution of his thought from day to day. But this long task of scholarship has not been undertaken and we do not believe that the game is worth the candle. His personal dossier for the period 1880–9, deposited in the *Marine*, is not accessible. Mr Audouy, the Keeper of the Archives, has willingly made extracts from his service records which enabled us to rectify certain chronological errors and to appraise certain ramblings of Hélia Béridon. The dossier is sparse and contains nothing on some alleged adventures of which some traces would have been conserved if they had been true. *Les Annales de la Chambre des Deputés* facilitate research on his parliamentary activity. Fortunately, some documents in the Archives clarify critical points and explain the 'conspiracy of silence' to which M. Suret-Canale refers: we shall analyse them later. The very numerous works of Vigné himself are not to be neglected. But the bibliography of forty-four titles, compiled by his wife, can no longer be regarded as very reliable. The dates which it gives of the publications do not always correspond to those of the books preserved in the Bibliotheque Nationale. Certain novels are not found in that library; others, which appeared as serials, have not been published since; still others have been published without dates. It is impossible to specify precisely the circulation of the numerous books which have gone through several editions.

Born on 7th November, 1859, at Montpellier, Paul Vigné was the second son of the baker 'A l'épi d'or', himself descended from peasants of the market town of Octon. His elder brother made his career in the postal service, his younger as a doctor in Le Havre. His father, a republican under the Empire, died in 1871. His mother, a fervent Catholic, sent Paul to a little seminary from which he passed into the lycée in 1876. Anaemic, 'withering' on the benches of the school, he made a number of sojourns in the Causses du Larzac, where an old sacristan of a parish priest who had taken an oath to the civil constitution of the clergy under the Revolution, had taught him Latin. Shepherd and pedlar, this cantagrel awakened in the child a love of rural life which turned him into the regional novelist and the individualist of anarchist leanings whom we shall find later.[4]

Taking his baccalauréat in 1876, he was drawn towards medicine, apparently by a sense of vocation; his father wished him to be a lawyer, and his mother a farmer. The interest in medicine which he showed throughout his life justified his choice. On 6 April 1880, he was accepted by the Naval School of Medicine at Toulon, and then embarked on his military service commissioned as *aide-médecin auxiliaire* by ministerial resolution dated 17 March 1881, then *aide-médicin titulaire*, 16 November, and *aide-médecin*, 29 July 1882. From 25 April 1881 to 1 February 1883 he lived in Guadeloupe (in the service of troops of the second rank, Camp Jacob Hospital of Point à Pitre and of the Désirade). After returning to France, he performed various garrison services. He was designated *médecin de 2ᵉ classe* on 3 November 1884, and on the 24th was awarded his *doctorate en médecine* at the Faculty of Montpellier.

In these periods of service there is no trace of the fanciful love story related by Mme. Clément-Béridon to the effect that while he was in detention on his ship he received his mistress disguised as a sailor. Taken by surprise, she jumped from the porthole, threw herself into the sea, and broke her neck on the side of the vessel. Her lover, ill with a fever, after passing through a grave crisis, sent in his resignation. The whole story is taken from a volume of imaginary tales by Vigné.[5]

However, Vigné did think of leaving the navy and establishing himself as a doctor. But he was then assigned to Senegal, where an epidemic of yellow fever had broken out. To refuse to go would have been cowardly.[6] On the other hand, he was in love with Madeleine d'Octon, a young girl who was married to a lawyer of her own world. After the death of the lawyer, she became Vigné's wife in October 1888, which explains the doctor's resignation from the navy at that time.

He reached Saint-Louis on 15 December. Although the disappointed lover was unhappy and diffident, 'distraught by shyness',[7] the liveliness and the picturesque scenes of Saint-Louis were to furnish him later with the materials of various tales and scenes in his novels. Then, in March 1885, he was assigned to the expedition to the Rio Nunez.

In 1867 France had occupied the three posts of Boké (Rio Nunez), Boffa (Rio Pongo), and Benty (Mellacorée) in the Rivers of the South. She had negotiated with the local chiefs but they had never hesitated to negotiate simultaneously with the Portuguese and the English. The whole of this coastal area, in which plantation coffee was a possibility, seemed to promise a great commercial future. Caravans coming from Fouta-Djalon had their terminus there, and communication with the Sudan, by the Fouta and the valley of the Tinkisso, a tributary of the Niger, seemed comparatively easy. The rivalry between France and Britain had ended in 1881 in a compromise which fixed boundaries between the Sierra Leone and the Mellacorée. But the posts occupied were too weak to impose French authority on the chiefs in the hinterland, who challenged it continually. Nor had any agreement been reached with the Portuguese in the north.

As soon as the conflict with Britain had been settled, a decree of 12 November 1882 had established under the Governor of Senegal a post of Lieutenant-Governor, the holder of which was to give particular attention to the Rivers of the South. Dr Bayol was appointed to the post in October 1883. He carried out various missions along the coast between December 1883 and February 1884, again in July 1884, and then in 1885. The region was unstable in spite of the Franco-British accord. Nachtigal was the cause of the first alarm. Charged by Bismarck in April 1884 to place under the protectorate of the Reich the German factories installed on the coast and still vacant in the Gulf of Guinea, by an error he hoisted the German flag at Dubreka, where France was dominant. The affair had no sequel; and Bayol, in the course of his mission in July, was able to record that all was in order again. He was then, on 4 July, 'held in readiness to leave in order to supply the information that he would be able to furnish to the Conference of Berlin on the situation on the Rivers of the South'; and on 25 October 1885, was further instructed 'to hold himself in readiness to leave in order to assist the French Plenipotentiary charged to carry on the negotiations relating to the delimitation of the Franco-Portuguese frontier on the west coast of Africa'.[8]

The negotiations with Portugal required that the rights of France should not be left in doubt. Now, though the country was peaceful in Mellacorée and Dubreka, there were serious disturbances in the Rio Nunez area, owing to rivalries among the native peoples. Two chiefs of the Nalous laid before the French protectorate claims to be the legitimate successor to the deceased Youra Towel. They were Dinah Salifou, chief of Sogobouli, and Bokary, chief of Katinou. Each had his partisans and the war was endemic. On several occasions the Government had tried to collect adequate information to evaluate their claims. At the time when serious negotiations with Portugal were to begin, a decision was imperative. In Paris it was decided in principle to intervene, and the Government of Senegal, on 20 March 1885, despatched Lieutenant Aubert, commanding the *Ardent*. His mission was to visit the Casamance, the rivers Nunez, Pongo, and Mellacorée, and to collect political and hydrographic information. In particular he was to meet Maillat, the French trader at Boké. Actually, on 25 March, he obtained information from another trader, Guichard, at Bel Air, at the mouth of the estuary; then, at Boké the next day, he listened to Maillat and the *commandant*, Paul de Beeckmann.

The latter was born in Brussels in 1846 and took French nationality following his participation in the war of 1870. An impecunious cavalry officer seeking a livelihood, he had entered the colonial administration in 1881. Throughout his career he had a dubious reputation.[9] He made a bad impression on Vigné when the latter saw him parading up and down on the bridge of the *Ardent*.

However, Aubert,[10] in the light of the information he had obtained, decided 'to modify his instructions considerably', to cancel the plan to visit the rivers Cassini and Pongo, and to return earlier to Dakar and propose appropriate measures to restore order. He was to get under way on the morning of the 28th. But on the evening of the 27th, Bayol arrived in the *Héron*, with a detachment of fifty marine infantry. He had been given a mission to intervene, but was charged to take very seriously the information given by the principal French merchants in the neighbourhood before undertaking military action.

Aubert and Beeckmann asserted that they had come from there, and that the merchants were unanimously of the opinion that the situation was untenable, that it was essential to remove either Dinah or Bokary and to establish the other firmly as chief of la Rivière. 'At the meeting which was held,' stated Aubert in his report, 'because I was the senior of the captains of the two sloops, M. Bayol requested me officially and in writing to destroy the villages of Catinou, Koutchoukou and Victoria, which supported Bokar Catinou, and to eliminate the principal chiefs with the villages over which they ruled.'

This account differs from the evidence of Vigné, which in *Journal d'un Marin* reveals the two officers as hesitating for several days between the rival claimants, who both made several visits to them, offering presents and hoisting the French flag. Finally, the balance was tipped towards Dinah, under the influence of the civil administrator of the area, 'a dissolute man about town" whom a friend had rescued and dispatched to the African coast. His clothes were extravagantly ornate and decorated. As forbidding in appearance as he was small, talking only of grapeshot, vengeance, exemplary punishment . . . wearing a prefect's peaked cap, he proudly displayed the superb military jacket of a General, and trailed a cavalry sabre. Unimpressed by his doings, some of the officers thought his bearing was undignified, and were heard to murmur "his embroidery and his crosses and his orders of the day".'[11]

That it would have sufficed to exile the undesirable chiefs and to distribute some presents to the others seems obvious. But the really responsible person, whose presence is not even mentioned by Vigné, was Bayol, this 'dear Bayol', to whom Vigné dedicated his *Terre de Mort* in 1892; this 'friend Jean Bayol, with whom,' he writes in *Le Gaulois* of 12 April 1892, 'I have served during four years on the coast of Africa, under whom I have many times been in action.'

It seems that Vigné was right and that the massacres of Katinou should have been avoided. But why did he exonerate the person truly responsible, the Lieutenant-Governor who gave a free hand to the military?

The sequel to Aubert's report reveals the war plan which was deliberately organised. The villages of Katinou and of Koutchoukou were surprised by night and burned. Bokary was killed. The native allies who had lent a strong hand—Dinah Salifou and Toquebah, chiefs of Sogobouli and of Caniope—threw off all restraint after the withdrawal of the infantry. They tortured and finished off the wounded and shared the prisoners, who were reduced to slavery. The details of this story may be found in the reports of the chiefs of detachments which were added to that of Aubert. Our knowledge is not confined to these reports. Dr Augier, the medical officer of the *Héron*, did not make any report. Vigné, an ordinary passenger of the *Ardent*, took the place of the doctor, Huas, who was ill. He submitted a brief report on the treatment given to the only wounded Frenchman and to some of the African allies. His infirmary was situated in the rear and he regained the ship with the soldiers of the detachment. What exactly did he see of the combat, and above all, of the abominable settlement of accounts between the natives which followed it? And what did he hear on the ship in the course of the voyage to the post of Benty in Mellacorée where, later, he was left? Why, when he recalled this carnage in the Chamber of Deputies in 1894, did he attribute his account to an army doctor named Delbenne, whose name appears neither on the ship's complement nor in any of the official reports?

However that may be—and we shall return to the subject later—the affair of Katinou, hardly a glorious page in the history of French expansion, deeply affected the young doctor. He often recalled it, never forgot it, and conceived a lasting animosity towards the military, their punitive expeditions, their columns of troops, their striving for insignia and decorations.[12]

He lived in Benty between April 1885 and June 1886, passing his leisure time in studying the manners and customs of the African population,[13] fretting impatiently, feeling towards the indigenous peoples a sympathy mingled with repugnance which we shall analyse later. In March 1886, tired and disheartened, he sent in a request to be placed on leave without pay for three years to serve in the capacity of doctor in the Compagnie du Chemin de Fer de Dakar-Saint Louis. Placed on the 'specially employed' list, he served with the company until 9 April, when he was laid off for health reasons. Repatriated on 24 May, he was reinstated in the general service of the officers of the Service Santé de la Marine by a ministerial resolution of 27 July. When on leave in Paris, he sent in his resignation on 7 February 1889, and his name was removed from the list.[14]

He was bored to death in the service of the railway company. Later, in *Journal d'un Marin*, he described the melancholy landscapes through which the railway line passed, and returned to the same theme in *Au pays des fétiches*. He noted the corruption in the company, the unashamed exploitation of its personnel. His Senegal is no more attractive than that of Pierre Loti's *Roman d'un Spahi* (1881).

He had used his leisure to write three 'scientific' articles. The first two were published by the Bulletin de la Société de Géographie Commerciale de Bordeaux, during Vigné's stay in Senegal. They were aimed at justifying the construction of the railway from Dakar to Saint-Louis and from the port of Dakar.

The railway would transform Senegal from a military to a civil colony. 'Gradually, railway stations and warehouses will take the place of costly military garrisons.' A patriotic task would be accomplished by supplying information and accurate documents to politicans and scholars. France had a strong interest in promoting 'the development of Senegal and in hastening the introduction of civilisation and commercial life into the Sudan'. The Compagnie des Batignolles, which obtained the concession in 1882, limited its losses by repatriating its European personnel during the unhealthy winter season. The author forsees the future resources of the regions through which the line runs and concludes by estimating 'the total value of the immense colony (Sudan) which it lies with us to conquer, and which, if we forsake this glorious enterprise, others will soon know how to appropriate for themselves'.

The second article, in the same strain, is on the port of Dakar and its future as an outlet for the French Sudan, and the vocation of Dakar in the role of chief town of the French West African possessions.

None of this is inconsistent with the anger that Vigné felt at Katinou. Against bellicose colonialisation by the military he set peaceful civilisation carried to the indigenous peoples. He was a supporter of the 'Colonisation chez les peuples modernes' extolled by Paul Leroy Beaulieu from 1874. He returned to the ideas expressed by Aimé Olivier de Sanderval in his book, *De l'Atlantique au Fleuve Niger*, in 1882. He adhered to the doctrine of the Geographical Societies, particularly that of the commercial geographers of Bordeaux.

The third article, published by the *Revue scientifique* in October 1888, after his re-entry into the navy, is more polemical. He criticised the academic ethnographers who based laws on 'facts' reported by ill-informed travellers. He studied the Guinean populations pressed back towards the coast by the Mandingues and the Foulah. Taking issue with Hecquard, Elysée Reclus and Bérenger-Féraud, he called attention to their errors of interpretation. He noted in passing that the Nalous 'made brave and disciplined soldiers'. He recommended the recruitment of native soldiers. He deplored the ignorance of the dialects and of the habits and customs of the native people among the administrators, which created an underlying hostility to French influence, sometimes culminating in bloody revolts. 'Finally,' he wrote, 'we reach a conclusion which no doubt falls a little short of a scientific approach. We think that science is not prejudiced by seeking to draw practical results from it. Above all, this obligation is binding on us when the results are of interest from the triple point of view of colonisation, of administration and of the assimilation to our country of the rich territory of the Rivers of the South.'[16]

This again conforms to the doctrine of the Geographical Societies. The least that one can say is that, in spite of this experience, Dr. Vigné, in 1888, was not anti-colonialist. His resignation was caused, not by a profound disagreement with the railway company, nor certainly by the reasons of health given. It is to be found elsewhere. Madeleine, the woman he loved, who had escaped him, and who had married a lawyer of her own circle, had become a widow. Paul, back in Paris, was no longer the needy student who had to fulfil his military service far away. He was a doctor of medicine, a naval officer and still in love. He was married at Octon on 24th October 1888. He sent in his resignation on 7 February 1889, and established himself in medical practice at the Chateau d'Octon in 1890.

II

Back in his native country, rediscovering memories of his childhood at each step, and readily recalling also his long exile far from that which he loved, he had to care conscientiously for his patients. But did he have many of them?

His period of service in the navy had been too short to entitle him to a pension. Already, before his marriage, he was anxious to find means of support, and in 1888, in *Figaro littéraire*, in the *Revue bleue*, some articles of his, of which we do not have a list, were published under various pseudonyms, one of which was Gaétan Kérouel. The pseudonyms did not protect him from a reprimand for not having requested authorisation in the prescribed manner, and, according to Mme Hélia Clément-Béridon, this explains his taking a few months of leave before his resignation. It was Alfred Perivier, the Director of *Figaro*, who advised him to add 'd'Octon' to 'Vigné' in his first novel *Chair noire*, published by Lemerre in 1890.[17]

Chair noire relates the history of a naval doctor of the second class, Franz, at a time when he was about to resign to marry his fiancée, who awaited him in Languedoc. Before reaching his post in Benty, he took part in a punitive expedition. Moved with pity, he bought a little girl who was being led away by 'our native allies' in a column of miserable slaves. Aïssata followed him and amused him; then she became adolescent and very pretty. After having for a long time resisted the temptation, he seduced her and fell madly in love. She experienced nothing; her sensual feelings had not yet awakened; nor were they to be, until she was drawn outside the post by the native festival of the moon, brilliantly described at great length in 'The Festival of Sensual Love'. The women circulated in the village.

> Every one's eyes burned with desire. Those who that evening were exposed to the influence of the Moon displayed it to their companions in immodest terms. They spoke of their future pregnancies and the importunate desires awakened in them by this secret work of nature, and they evoked, in crude terms, fetishes to the monstrous phallus.

Then the dance swept everybody along with it,

> ... the villages and the huts were carried along in a swirl of dances, aggressively obscene and erotic to the point of bestiality, at the end of which the hardly conscious negress embraced her male deliriously.

Aïssata was attracted by the shepherd Malik Si, whom Franz, from motives of jealousy, had expelled from the post.

> He had not dreamed when he had felt her cold and indifferent to his passionate kisses that on the day when her passions awakened, palpitating in waves of desire, she would seek satisfaction in the arms of a man of her own race, whose skin would be of the same colour as hers, who would speak her language; that when that day came, she would throw herself unconsciously into the arms of the male designed for her by nature! And he had not realised that the unspeakable repugnance which she had always shown for him in moments of intimate caresses was merely the instinctive reaction of her race, obedient to the invincible law of conservation!

He had not grasped this earlier—he, a doctor, an enthusiastic admirer and convinced partisan of Darwin.[18]

The long preface "to the reader"[19] expounded the thesis,

Between a member of the white race and one of the black race (the latter living in his original environment), love in the psychological sense of the word cannot exist. In the relations with the black woman which the climate, the isolation and the abnormal life impose on the European living on the west coast of Africa, there are and can only be one sided matings.

In this inexplicable sexual attraction of the demoralised European to the black woman, it is only the male whose senses are actively at work, and he is usually the victim of a morbid sensibility, the negress herself playing an absolutely passive role in every sense of the term.

To put it more simply, the black woman feels an instinctive loathing for the white man.

The other ordinary relations of life are almost always those of master to slave . . .

In representing the black female differently, in endowing her with qualities, in attributing to her sensibilities . . . , in representing her as capable of sentiments which only a female of the Caucasian race can feel or experience, it is possible, through the magic of words, to create the most poetic and attractive fictions, but they are far removed from the realism towards which, with renewed energy, modern novelists seem to be directing their efforts.

The 'modern novel' in his eyes was naturalism. He explained this in the same year in the preface to *Fauves Amours*, dedicated to Emile Zola, whom, sixteen years later, he characterised as the 'illustrious and venerated master' after he had consulted him on the possibilities of a novel devoted to parliamentary life.[20] In *Fauves Amours* we see a peasant who is a pervert but who, because he is a victim of the laws of heredity, cannot be held responsible, creating a panic in a Languedoc village, where castrations and suicide in a melodramatic setting were to constitute part of 'a series of psycho-physiological studies'. It constitutes a sequel to *Chair noire*

which analysed a primitive soul in her medium of origin, in which neither cross-breeding nor civilisation could have altered the type. I set out to record carefully the awakening of her instincts, her sensibilities and her sentiments. I tried to unravel and set in perspective her personality, physical and psychic, possessed by the need to love.

. . . This book . . . though a simple monograph on the mind of a negress, raises, among other ethnic problems, that of the impossibility of union between the human races, and brings some unexpected arguments before the advocates of polygenism.

The black woman has neither the qualities nor the sensibilities nor the feelings of the woman of Caucasian race. Love in the psychological sense of the word cannot exist between her and the white man. Such, in fact, was my conclusion, which caused François Coppée and others to say 'It is very sad, but it is true.'

In accordance with the habits of mind acquired in the course of my medical and biological studies, I proceeded from the simple to the compound, as the evolutionary approach demands.

Then, after my discussion of the simple soul of the negrito race, I took up the study of beings immediately above them in the ethnological scale, who, though they belonged to a superior type, had remained primitive and had been only lightly touched by the civilisation of their race. Thus my attention was drawn to the peasant...

Having, in the first two essays, dwelt on the need to love which possesses every creature like a reagent with the help of which it seems to me easier to analyse the composite elements in a personality, I applied it in *L'Eternelle Blessée* to some superior individuals, who, however, were of average cerebral development.

The next study in the series, *Le Roman d'un Timide*, will describe how the intellectuals whose high culture has placed them among the élite of humanity react to the pains of love which torment everyone.

Le Roman d'un Sculpteur, which follows, will recount the loves of individuals of still more powerful intellect...

This cycle, which I propose to enlarge later, will thus be completed. To the study of this microcosm of morals and passions which passes from the negro to the artist by way of the peasant, the middle class and the scholar, I shall apply, as in the past, the method which I believe to be correct, because it emanates from scientific positivism and makes no attempt to break the indissoluble duality of life.[21]

This taste for the cycle, after the manner of *La Comédie Humaine* and *Rougons Macquart*, recurs to the last days of Vigné d'Octon's life, when he outlined a series of studies on psycho-analysis. He planned to group together *L'Amour et la Mort*, a frankly pornographic novel published in 1895, *La Vie et l'Amour*, an enquiry into psycho-analysis which appeared in 1934, and *Psycho-analyse de ma vie d'enfant*, which did not appear.[22]

Of the eleven books published before 1894, four are concerned with Africa (*Chair noire, Au pays des fétiches, Fauves Amours, Terre de Mort*), four are peasant idylls in regional settings (*Le Pont d'Amour, Les Petites Dames, Les Amours de Nine, Les Angoisses de Docteur Combalas*); two are medico-psychological cases (*L'Eternelle Blessée, Le Roman d'un Timide*); one has not been available to us (*La Dot de Mlle Coupiac*). All of them are more or less erotic.

Vigné d'Octon, the writer, made a living mainly from his books. His patients in the region of Octon were of no great account. Some of his books went through several editions, but we do not know the extent of their circulation. However, *Comment on étouffe un livre*, published in 1905, contains some detailed information. The publisher, Taillandier, with whom Vigné d'Octon had made a contract for his novel on parliamentary practices, had anticipated a circulation 'divided into as many editions as he would consider necessary'. The sale price was to be 3 fr. 50, and the author was to be entitled to 0.60 fr. per copy on the first 3,000, 0.70 fr. for the next 2,000, and 0.80 fr. thereafter. The author renounced all rights to publication by installments or as a serial in a periodical. He considered this a draconian clause, for

> 'the published novel does not usually bring a substantial remuneration to the author ... 2,000 copies of a novel of average quality, by an already known author, are printed and sold, yielding at the end of the year a meagre sum of 1,000 francs to its author. On the contrary, publication as a serial in a daily paper or a magazine of middle or top rank, brings in a substantial sum at once. Such a novel, embodying two years of labour may, so far as the book trade is concerned, bring a return of only five to six hundred francs to its author, while preliminary publication in a newspaper or a magazine brings him two or three thousand francs.

To this may be added the rights of reproduction recognised by the Society of the Men of Letters.[23]

If, for each of the eleven volumes which appeared between 1889 and 1893, we assume an average circulation of 3,000 copies, this comes to 19,800 francs, plus 2,000 francs for the serial *Coupiac*, which adds up to 21,800 francs in five years. If the average circulation we assume appears high, the amount may be made up by the rights of the Society of the Men of Letters, the extracts published in the form of serials, and the numerous articles given to various journals. Vigné, therefore, earned more than 4,000 francs per annum, which exceeds the pay of a European colonial administrator of the first class.[24] In 1887 the starting salary of the fourth class was 2,500 francs. This was not a gold mine, but it was more than adequate for a beginner. In this way the fecundity of the author may be explained as well as the procedures which he followed later, when his reputation was at its height, of reincorporating in his new books extensive passages taken from his older works. Thus in the *Journal d'un Marin* (1897), he incorporated more than eighty pages of *Au pays des fétiches* (1890), which had already been reproduced in *Terre de Mort*. In 1898 *Siestes d'Afrique* borrowed from *Terre de Mort* the sixty-seven pages of the history of Djilai etc. ...

III

Up to 1893 Dr. Vigné did not appear to be much interested in domestic politics. However, he could not ignore the events which led to the

election of a solid bloc of some fifty new deputies, mostly belonging to
the left. The socialists represented this 'fourth estate' whose entry on
the political scene had been announced by Clemenceau in a famous
speech in the Chamber, following the workers' demonstration on 1 May
1891, which had been clumsily suppressed at Fourmies. The strike at
Carmaux in 1892 had assured the success of Jaurès at the by-election
in January 1893. In 1892 the Panama scandal had cast a shadow over
many deputies, even among republicans. The first bombs thrown by
anarchists had exploded in Paris in 1892 and the Ravachol trial at the
end of April had contributed to the growth of hostility towards the
parliamentary system.

In the small towns of the Midi passions ran high at a time when
the winegrowers were beginning to worry over the slump in the wine
trade. In the arrondissement of Lodève, as in the rest of the Department of l'Hérault, the Republican party had carried the day in the
elections of 1885. Ménard Dorian, who was the representative in 1889,
had signed the declaration of principles in common with republican
representatives of the Department. But this time it had been a fierce
struggle against the catholics and conservatives of the Department,
who had rallied round Pierre Leroy-Beaulieu, a great landowner, who
had called attention to several irregularities in the conduct of the
election. The disputed election was annulled by the Assembly when it
came up for verification. Ménard Dorian himself wished to seek re-
election. The long debates in the Chamber at the time of the annulment
of the election in January, and in March 1890, and then after the re-
election of Ménard Dorian in July, aroused local passions. Leroy-
Beaulieu, in order to be in a position to demonstrate that some of the
voting papers had been falsified or substituted for the cancelled papers,
had 'organised a system of surveillance of the bureaux, and the men
assigned to this task had as their mission, by some means to photo-
graph each voting paper which had been annulled'.

Some of the mayors had knowingly cheated. The state of excitement among the voters was revealed, for example, by an incident mentioned in the Chamber by the deputy, Le Provost de Launay: 'A young
royalist girl had danced at a ball with a young republican; ever since
that time this young girl has been pointed at.'

Ménard Dorian had won the day, but after being admitted in
April 1890, he was placed on leave at the end of the year, and up to
the close of the session never again intervened in it.[25] When the election
campaign opened in 1893 he does not seem to have been a candidate.
Dr. Vigné, who had attracted public notice during the cholera epidemic,
was sought after. He presented himself as an 'advanced' Republican
opposed to the opportunists of the government majority. His statement of policy, favouring a 'revision of the constitution in a more
democratic direction, made a very vague allusion to Panama:

> I shall set myself against the imprudent handling of the finances of
> the country which was habitual in our last assemblies. I shall raise
> my voice against those hasty discussions of the budget which pain-

fully surprised the country and compromised the Republic at the present time and for the future. I shall vote for the abolition of tolls.'

One paragraph, which did not re-appear in later electoral campaigns, condemned colonial expansion.

I shall be an uncompromising opponent, to the bitter end, of the colonial expansion which, for several years, has impelled our governments towards the most hazardous and ill-considered expeditions. The seven years of my life passed in these distant countries as a doctor in the Navy, and the studies to which I have devoted myself, enable me to speak with knowledge on these questions and I shall be only too happy if, by opening the eyes of my colleagues in this way, I contribute towards putting an end to the squandering of our financial resources, and towards saving the lives of our gallant little marine infantry whose blood continues to water sterile and blighted lands.

Next the candidate promised to defend the winegrowers, 'to struggle with all my might against the deputies from the North, whose interests are so divergent and who have only one aim—the economic suppression of the Midi.' Finally, he attempted to win the support of the workers and various other discontented local groups: '... sons of the workers, sprung from the people, I shall never lose sight of what I owe to the worker, of what I owe to the people'. He promised 'laws on trade unions, more democratic laws on hunting, which would permit men of small incomes to obtain from the tobacconist a permit for a day's hunting, enabling them to take a day off for recreation ... Laws on the Retirement Funds for old people, on mutual assurance, on trade union federations, on the miners' delegates, on hygiene in the factory and the workshop . . .'[26]

He was elected on the second ballot and was admitted to the Chamber when credentials of members were verified on 16 November 1893.

He occupied his seat regularly and appeared to take an interest in his mandate during the course of the first of the three legislatures in which he sat. Out of fifteen appearances in the records over twelve years, of which five are limited to matters concerning the orders of the day or to waivers of the right to speak, ten actually took place between January 1894 and May 1898. This undoubtedly explains his re-election on the first ballot, without any statement of policy, in 1898.[27]

Out of these ten interventions, three which were concerned with the order of the day, were negligible. One of them—the first—dealt with the banning of Gerhardt Hauptmann's Ames Solitaires, which had already been shown at the Odeon to a select audience just before the Première. This followed the throwing of a bomb into the half circle of the Chamber by the anarchist Vaillant. Another intervention expounded a project on the constitution of the universities. Another was concerned with the rich coal deposits of Aveyron and Hérault, the exploitation of which two other deputies also called for, and with the strike of workers in the basin of Graissessac (7 July 1894). The remaining four, more fully developed, concerned the credits requested for the Madagascar expedition (22 November 1895), and the scandals concerning the railway between Senegal and the Niger (10 February 1896). This last intervention took place in the course of the debates on the Budget. In this connexion Vigné also concerned himself with the clothing of reservists and territorials, with the Chancellery taxes, and with the subventions to the departmental societies for the promotion of agriculture.

Colonial policy, then, carried the day, especially since the interpellations of Vigné on the subject had not been long and passionate. Can it be said that, in the Chamber, where there were moderates like Le Myre de Villers, Le Hérissé, d'Estournelles de Constant, de Lanessan, radicals like Camille Pelletan, socialists like Rouanet, Vigné set out to make himself a reputation as a sound, well-informed specialist? Actually, in the course of the next two legislatures he intervened only twice on the colonies, speaking at length on 23 and 30 November and 7 December 1898, on the Voulet-Chanoine affair, and briefly on 11 July 1905, on the mining administration of Madagascar. He appeared neither in the discussions on the concessionaire companies, nor in connection with Fashoda in the same year, nor in the course of the interpellations on the scandals in the Congo in 1906, nor, above all, during the annual discussions on the budget of the colonies, where all the overseas problems were regularly raised.

This abstention, moreover, was more general. At the time of the great debates from October to December 1901 on the crisis in the wine industry, he intervened only to request a subsidy of ten million francs for the communes affected, and the bill he proposes, the seventh of the thirteen filed on 6 December, is strikingly meagre. When the majority of the others proposed precise measures—revisions of the plan of the commune, an increased price for sugar, the use of which increased the prices of wines, etc.—he contented himself with '. . . inviting the Government to take all the necessary measures'.[29]

In reality politics do not appear to have interested him greatly. We do not find him intervening either in regard to the Criminal Law of 1894, or in the Dreyfus affair, or in the discussion of the law of 1901 on associations, or in favour of the separation of the Church from the State. It is impossible to prove that he was in the Chamber. But it can be established that the periods in which his name does not appear grow longer and longer. There is nothing in the official Journal of the debates in the Chamber of Deputies from 23 April 1896 to 19 October 1897; nothing, after his re-election, from June 1898 to November 1900; nothing from 8 January to 29 November 1901. From 14 January 1902 to 13 July 1905, he intervened, after the elections, only to signify to the Ministry of Justice, 3 July 1903, 'the situation in which the judges of Lodève were placed by illness of the President of the Tribunal';[30] then to request, in April, 1905, the addition of an interpellation on 'the abuses of colonial politics in Madagascar' to those anticipated in the Congo.[31] On 13 July, before an empty Chamber, he refrained from developing his arguments on the organisation of mining in Madagascar, and did not intervene again between October 1905 and May 1906.

His re-election in 1902 seems to have been due to local political passions. He was the candidate of the Radical and Socialist Union of the left-wing bloc, opposed by the right-wing led by Pierre Leroy-Beaulieu. Vigné's statement of policy was a personal attack on this candidate of 'the nationalist coalition'. An appeal is made in it to the winegrowers and the workers. There is no further question of colonies, unless it is in Vigné's mention that 'in 1896 I secured the participation of our factories in the adjudications for the furniture of the ministries of the colonies, of Finance and of Agriculture . . . in 1899, I obtained their participation under the most advantageous conditions in the adjudications of posts and telegraphy . . . some time afterwards I obtained, after exceptional efforts, the extension of the war markets for four years . . .'

But in 1906 he found himself facing a competitor of the left, M. Pelisse, a landowning wine-grower, pharmacist of the first class, licentiate in law, supporter of a policy of union with the Radicals and Socialists, hostile to the addition of sugar to the grape juice before fermentation, a practice which led to overproduction. The candidate emphasised the necessity of an *avant-garde* social policy. 'I am not a republican who marks time . . . I am a republican in all the fibres of my being, in all the lobes of my brain. I belong to no one. I am not subject to the authority of anyone. My wish is to belong wholly to the Republicans, to all the Republicans, but only to the Republicans . the true Republic, the democratic and social Republic.'[33]

The pharmacist defeated Dr. Vigné, while at Montpellier 'Pierre Leroy-Beaulieu, former student in the Polytechnic School, landowning wine-grower' was elected by the Right, being opposed to the Left blocks, to the separation of church and State and to the squandering of public funds.

Vigné's modest political activity is undoubtedly sufficient to explain his defeat. Lodève voted red. When it was more red than he was, Vigné was unable to put up a struggle. He was not, like the pharmacist, always on hand. He was no longer closely in touch with the world immediately around him as he had been in the times when he practised medicine at Octon. But it is somewhat misleading to say that politics did not interest him. Everything interested him. It is nearer the truth to say that he felt himself to be better endowed for writing than for speech, and that he preferred polemics to working committees. All his interpellations have been published on his initiative, in his books, in the brochure on *Les Universités nouvelles*, or in *La gloire du sabre*. During his time as a deputy he continued to produce one or two novels each year, and innumerable articles in journals and reviews.

We shall now try to determine whether Vigné d'Octon really was the victim of a conspiracy of silence, sanctions and revenge organised by the Colonial Party against an uncompromising and incorruptible opponent. In considering as a whole the positions which he took up to

1914 we are impressed by the relative moderation of his conclusions and by the fact that in the chamber he was approved of, supported or surpassed by some of the moderates included in the colonial group. The latter, Alype, Le Hérissé, Le Myre de Villers, d'Estournelles de Constant, de Lannesan etc., were, no more than he, no more than the radical Camille Pelletan, or the socialist, Rouanet, anticolonialists, in other words, adversaries of the principle of colonisation. None of them had ever envisaged the evacuation of the colonies, even of those which, like Madagascar, had been acquired against their wishes and their votes in the Assembly. The term 'anticolonialism' is inappropriate; 'anti-militarism' would be more appropriate at a time when the Dreyfus affair traced the line of separation between the left and the right. This anti-militarism signified the condemnation of bellicose expansion overseas, not a calling in question of the rationale of colonies from the standpoint of their benefit to the metropolis. The socialists themselves, in France as a foreign countries, approved that colonisation which assured employment to the workers. On this subject Mme. Rébériouse and M. Haupt have carried out a study which leaves no room for doubt.[34]

Dr. Vigné was a sentimentalist. He was profoundly shaken and stirred to passionate indignation by the abuses which he had known and which he had spoken about on the rostrum. But he usually stopped there, and only on rare occasions did he raise the discussion to the level of principles, to which these abuses led the more brilliant of the questioners of the 'colonial group'. It is for this reason that historians concerned to elucidate general ideas have not preserved his name. He aligned himself with the opponents of a certain kind of colonisation, but was not their leader. A brief analysis of his interventions in the Chamber demonstrates this.

In the course of his first interpellation, on the 22 November, 1894, on the credit of 65 millions requested by the Government for the expedition to Madagascar, he recalled the solemn engagement taken two years before by the Under-Secretary of the State for the Colonies Emile Jamais:

> Speaking for the Government, I declare to the Chamber that the era of colonial conflicts is at last ended, and that all our efforts, all our vital energies, are going to be devoted to organising the development of our conquered possessions.

He deplored the costly operations which were still being carried on in Dahomey and in the Sudan, referring to Colonel Frey's book *Campagne dans le Haut Sénégal et dans le Haut Niger* (1885–6)[35] in regard to the 'traffic in black flesh', and recalling at length his own African experience. But it was not his own recollections which aroused the deputies. Why, speaking of Katinou, did he cite a book by Dr. Delbenne, a naval doctor, instead of his own?

The evidence of this colleague was devastating.

'The village was taken and the chief killed, the white troops returned to the sloops, and only our native auxiliaries remained on the debris. Oh, the lamentable, the macabre, the appalling acts which these people committed—with signs of pleasure in their faces. One of them, laughing and jeering, disembowelled a dying woman and amused himself by breaking her teeth under his feet... (On several benches: 'Enough! Enough!' On other benches, 'Read on', Read On!')...

Vigné did 'read on', reciting further atrocities before describing the flat.

Another took pleasure in castrating a sort of Hercules who was still breathing in gasps and whose charred arms were raised to implore mercy; a third moved to and fro, trampling on all the bodies in an indescribable frenzy, plunging the end of his assegai into all eyes which showed the last signs of agony. He wound bleeding intestines around the barrel of his gun, and his neighbour, with the jagged edge of his sword, cut off the breasts of an old woman whose lean body still quivered. I saw a little girl of six or seven years old whose body had been cut into two equal parts; by the side of the remains lay a little child, no doubt the brother, his little neck flattened like a cheese, and I perceived, stretching towards them, the arms of a woman lying stiff and contracted, her stomach laid open, in a mess of visceral organs.

I recoiled in horror, and as I was regaining the side of the ship I met a troop of prisoners conducted by our auxiliaries. It was a horrible procession of adults with scarred chests and skulls covered with gashes, whose limbs were riddled with sabre blows and whose backs had been grazed by rifle bullets. The hands of many of them were charred, their noses cut, and three-quarters of their ears torn off. The faces of some of them were covered with wounds and, their eyes destroyed by the flames, they stumbled along, supported by their neighbours. However, a selection had been made and the iron collar put only on those who were saleable and whose wounds would be cured before the caravans passed. The rest had met a frightful end.

There were more women than men. They had suffered less and, although the pupils of their eyes were still enlarged as a result of what they had gone through, they followed their new masters with a resignation and indifference that was revolting. The children hobbled along behind, their little feet crippled, torn and burned.

Next he described the flat and scorching coastlands where the French posts were supposed to be protecting a sparse trade. His conclusions were in line with those of several speakers who preceded and followed him at the rostrum. Paschal Grousset, Pierre Alype, Gaston Doumergue, René Le Hérissé. On the 24 November he supported the protests against the fictitious concessions of the Comte de Vogüé, who wished to see genuine colonists attached to the expeditionary corps. Investigations have been made about this Dr. Delbenne. He was actually on service in the maritime hospital in Cherbourg at the beginning of 1894. But on 30 September he embarked on *Le Furieux* on a commercial mission of long duration in China. No one could then have reached him at the end of November, at the time of Vignés inter-pellation. But, what is still more conclusive, Dr. Delbenne, who was born on 17 November 1853, had never set foot on the Atlantic Coast of Africa. His military service was done in Réunion and at Nossy-Bé between 1876 and 1879. He embarked on *L'Alouette* for Indo-China as an auxiliary doctor of the second class. He remained there until the end of 1885.

Repatriated from Saigon for reasons of health on 2 September 1885, he could not, then, have witnessed the massacres at Katinou in March. All his career was spent in the Far East and in France, where he died on 29 January 1903.

There is no book by Delbenne in the *Bibliothèque Nationale*. Moreover, no one doubted at the time that Vigné was the author of the text read to the Chamber. In the preface to the *Journal d'un marin* (1897), where the text in the *Journel Official* is reproduced without allu-sion to Delbenne, Cammille Pelletan praises 'the unforgettable speech' of Vigné, and similarly the three principal Paris dailies give an account of it without mentioning Delbenne. All show themselves firmly on the side of the Government and little impressed by the revelations of the speaker. *Le Petit Parisien* and *Le Petit Journal* make fun of the declamatory style of the speaker (23 November). *Le Matin* at more length gives him a paragraph with the subtitle 'A Serial Novel'.

> We cannot describe in any other way the effusion of M. Vigné (d'Octon). This writer of serial novels has the voice and eloquence of a street orator. He has been a colonial doctor, an extreme colonial. At any rate he is now no longer colonial.
>
> His voice vibrates when speeking of 'human flesh' and 'ebony wood'. In the style of Ponson du Terrail, he recalls his personal recollections of the horrors of colonial war, of famine, of thirst, of fever ... He speaks of women disembowelled, of a Hercules castrated, of breasts sawn off, of dead bodies violated, of eyes gouged out. Excite-ment reaches its highest pitch. It is like a novel of Gustave Aymard. The conclusion is beyond doubt. Embellishing the facts which in part he had witnessed, the novelist Paul Vigné carefully prepared the text which he read to the Chamber and then published in the *Journal d'un marin*. Dr. Delbenne saw nothing of this affair. Why did not Vigné at once acknowledge the paternity of his work? Why did he dare to implicate an absent colleague? These are perhaps questions for psychoanalysis.[36]

In the following year, on 27 November 1895, Vigné was among the interpellators on the organisation of the sanitary services of the Madagascar expedition. But there again the abuses were condemned by deputies representative of all viewpoints.

In the intervening period, on 'the 26 June 1895, he joined Le Hérissé in an interpellation on "the colonial policy of the Government in West Africa, particularly in Sudan and the Ivory Coast'. The two deputies, the radical and the moderate—who was a member of the colonial group reinforced each other in criticising the military detach-ments and in bringing abuses and useless cruelties to light. At the time of the vote on the request for supplementary credits for the Sudan, six orders of the day were proposed. The deputy Lagnel wanted the Chamber to refuse to vote the credits without knowing who had the responsibility for military operations in the Ivory Coast and in the Sudan, and to invite the Government without delay to make known to it who are the responsible persons.' Le Hérissé wished the Chamber to adjoin the vote on the supplementary credits and to set up a commission of enquiry. This commission having been rejected by a separate vote, Le Hérissé proposed a motion of adjournment.

Vigné himself proposed.

> The Chamber, recognising that the time has come to renounce in West Africa the policy of conquest and of military penetration, which is burdensome to our finances and murderous for our soldiers, and to replace it by a policy of rational colonisation of those territories which have some value, decides to adjourn.

Could this be called anticolonialism?[37]

The motion from the right (Maurice Faure-Habert) approving the Government was passed.

At the time of the discussions on the Budget of 1898, Vigné intervened on 10 February in opposition to the credits requested for the railway from Senegal to the Niger. According to him the best route to penetrate the Sudan was that which started from the coast of Guinea. He requested a subvention for the construction of a route Conakry-Niger.[38] The longest and most spectacular of his interpellations was made on 23 November 1900, a short time after the publication of *La gloire du sabre*, in regard to the affaire Voulet-Chanoine. He stood up courageously on behalf of justice 'in the name of the unfortunate natives who are being sold, who are being pillaged who are being massacred'. He regretted that the Minister for the Colonies, Decrais, had not taken action after the publication of his book, and maintained that he was moved by no other sentiment than that of 'justice and humanity'.

> I am not, [he continued], an enemy of the Army.... Certainly, Messieurs, we all love this army with a profound love, because it is made up of that which is best in France, of those we hold most dear, of our brothers, of our children (applause from the left and the extreme left) and because, in the hour of danger, its flag symbolises the very soul of the fatherland.
> As for the colonial army ... how could I forget that I have passed a long period of my life in it? How could I not love those of whom I have been a comrade in arms, with whom I have shared hardship and dangers? And it is because we love it that we proceed against those who bring dishonour on it and on its flag.

He then returned to his book and enlarged on the misdeeds of the Voulet-Chanoine detachment, whose movements he had followed. He described their exactions and their senseless cruelties, up to the assassination of Lieutenant Colonel Klobb, an envoy on a tour of inspection. After an interruption by the nationalist, Paul de Cassagnac, he concluded,

To put an end to these deplorable acts, which may seriously compromise the future of our colonies, is a matter of urgency.

He then passed on to the abuses of the system of forced labour
in Madagascar, basing his case on a report of Le Myre de Vilers. A
second speaker. Lasies, who took up the defence of Voulet and pointed
out numerous errors in *La gloire du sabre*, nevertheless agreed with him
in deploring the resort to auxiliaries, whose brutality and cruelty could
not be imputed to the French Officers, who tried to restrain them. The
Minister for the Colonies, Decrais, replied on 30 November, defining
the policy of the Government 'to introduce more justice and humanity
into the relations of France with the native peoples; to make France
loved as well as feared and respected'.

Mr. Paul Vigné: 'That is very well spoken!' It was necessary to
find 'a solution on which our whole colonial future depends, to carry
out research into the most appropriate methods and systems for im-
proving the material and moral conditions of the native peoples'.

Decrais, in his turn underlined the errors and exaggerations in
Vigné's revelations on Madagascar. Then Le Myre de Vilers raised
the level of the debate. He condemned the method of sending military
detachments.

A great nation has no right to deprive another people of its independence in order to subject it to tyranny and to exploit it with in-
human severity. It owes its new subjects security, a proper system of
justice, and improvement of their moral and material conditions ('Very
good, very good'). It ought to enable them to share in the benefits of
a superior civilisation. . . .

As you see, I am completely in accord with M. Vigné in principle, but we differ absolutely on where the responsibilities lie. Our
honourable colleague places them on the executive agents. For myself,
I accuse the Governments. They cannot be ignorant that, in sending
troops several thousands of kilometres from their base of operations
without means of transport, without provisions, without merchandise
to exchange, these troops will be obliged to live off the land, to
requisition innumerable porters whose bodies will be strewn along the
tracks.

Addressing the Minister of War, he added:

These detachments are no longer regular troops, they are bands of
partisans.

The Governments send real expeditions without consulting their
respective Parliaments, without requesting the resources that are indispensable . . . these Governments cannot be unaware that, when they
invest these officials with excessive powers, giving them neither
instructions nor directions, imposing no control over them, even permitting them to subsidise metropolitan newspapers to sing their glory
in France, these officials, these agents, end by losing their sense of
proportion, believing that they are called to the highest destiny,

sacrificing everything to their own interests, having no other guide
than their own convenience.[40]

Thus, once more, the moderate overshadowed the radical.

The debate ended on the 7th December. Vigné then renewed his
charges—contested by Lasies and by the Minister—and Count
d'Agoult requested information about a mission which the Minister
had entrusted to Vigné. Pelletan, who followed, dealt with the opposition between civilians and the military in the colonies, and the military
censorship over the information transmitted to Paris. The commission
of Enquiry demanded by Vigné was rejected by 409 votes to 116 and
the vote to adjourn was carried by 441 to 1.[41]

Vigné's last brief intervention, nearly five years later, was again
concerned with policy in Madagascar. He had to speak after several
of his colleagues—Rouanet, Le Hérissé, Ursleur and Ballande,
whose names were down for questions on colonial officials or on the
Congo. Responding to the President's appeal on 11 July 1905, before
an almost empty Chamber, the interested parties agreed to postpone
the debate until they returned. However, Vigné, who, on 11 April, had
requested that his interpellation should be included with those relating
to the colonies, wished to state his viewpoint on the mines.

> The question, [he said] is whether, in the new regime of Madagascar,
> at this stage of our enquiry, to reserve the inalienable rights of the
> State, and to find out practical means of benefiting, so far as we
> consider appropriate, the soldiers who have fought in the conquest of
> the Great Island, the families of those who have died, and the fund
> for retired workers.[42]

He was given reassurances, and Rouanet denounced this 'piece of bluff
about gold mines' in which many people believed. No one had the
absurd idea that perhaps the product of these mines belonged first to
the natives.

Why did not Vigné intervene, as had been forecast, in the great
debate on the Congo from 19 to 21 February 1906? In a small fort-
nightly publication, *Le feuille coloniale et diplomatique*, which he
started in 1906, he announced in an editorial in the second number his
intention to take part in it. 'To my dossier on Madagascar I will add
that on the Congo. The one is not less voluminous than the other and
both make the same painful impression'. It appears that only a few
numbers of the *Feuille* appeared. Judging by the praise bestowed in
this same number on the Minister Clémentel and his policy of
association, it was not systematically in opposition.[43]

An exhaustive study of Vigné's articles in the press would confirm
the conclusions drawn from his parliamentary activity. Vigné would
often be seen to defend the expansionist thesis. In the *Dépêche
Coloniale* of 8 October 1898, he expressed indignation that there were
some who wished to exchange 'the unquestionable rights to Fashoda
that we have today' for British Gambia. It was essential on the contrary, that in the name of the rights, henceforward indefeasible at

Fashoda ... the settlement of the question of Egypt always evaded by England, may be again brought before Europe ...'[44]

From this it can be seen that he was interested in everything that had to do with the colonies, and that he always took up a position vigorously, but without ever giving any indication that what he said was based on a profound study of the problems.

Was he anti-colonial? It would be difficult to say so of one who did not hesitate, with the inconscience and bonbomie which made him so attractive, to solicit missions to the colonies from ministers whom he was ready to interpellate.

IV

The elections of 1906 carried his old friends the radicals and socialists into power. Vigné, with free time, and perhaps a little embarrassed by the cessation of his parliamentary allowance, again took up his projects for study missions and turned towards a new career as explorer and ethnographer. He made use of his friends, particularly Stephen Pichon, who was Minister of Foreign Affairs in the Clémenceau and Briand Cabinets, from October 1906 to March 1911, and Doumergue, Minister of Public Instruction from October 1906 to July 1909, to whom he dedicated his *Visions Sahariennes*, published without date, but certainly after these ministers had given him missions in North Africa.

His first attempt in this direction had not succeeded.

The question raised by the Deputy d'Agoult on 7 December 1900 has led us to investigate the series *Missions* in the Archives d'Outre-Mer ... We have found traces of three requests from Vigné. The first was concerned with 'a study on the methods of colonisation in the Far East'. On the basis of an analogous request, Foreign Affairs had promised 2,000 francs. The Minister for the Colonies offered the same amount, together with a free passage, first class, from Marseille to Saigon. On the eve of the interpellation, however, the sum does not seem to have been disbursed. Vigné then notified the Minister, Decrais, that at the opening of the session he would put a question to him on this study voyage. 'In case you do not believe that you can accept this question, I have the honour to inform you that I shall ask to speak on a personal matter.' Decrais replied: 'It is not possible for me to accept this question'; and Vigné kept quiet. But the relations between the interpellator and the Minister were known, and d'Agoult, after Decrais had inpugned part of the evidence produced by Vigné, disclosed them.

> M. le Comte d'Agoult: 'M. Vigné published in the month of September a letter in which he said that you had entrusted him with a mission. The mission is confidential. I beg you to disclose to us whether you had really entrusted a mission to M. Vigné, and whether you have promised him funds for his mission ... and whether you intend to support him in it.'
>
> The Minister for the Colonies: 'I have not given a mission to M. Vigné. M. Vigné has made known to me his desire to undertake

a voyage of study and exploration (Exclamations from the centre and the right), particularly in foreign colonial possessions, and he has asked me, I believe, as well as my colleague, M. Delcassé, whether I would place at his disposal a certain sum that would facilitate his study. I, like my colleague in Foreign Affairs, have replied to him that if he gave effect to his project, I would willingly remit to him a sum of 2000 francs. These are the facts.'

M. le Comte d'Agoult: 'After having declared that the sources on which M. Vigné has drawn were suspect, do you now support his mission?'

The Minister did not reply and there the matter rested.[45] After his setback in the election of 1906, Vigné made a lengthy application to the Minister for the Colonies. Milliès-Lacroix for a subsidy which would be added to the 4,000 francs promised by Foreign Affairs for a mission of scientific and literary studies in West Africa. The programme was vague, referring to past publications and to periods of residence as deputy in Algeria and Tunisia. Milliès warned Etienne, who supported this approach, that the credits for 'missions' were exhausted (24 July). Vigné then addressed himself to Public Instruction. A report of 22 March 1910, indicates that:

In the course of 1908 and 1909 M. Paul Vigné, a former deputy, was entrusted by the Ministers of Foreign Affairs and of Public Instruction with a mission having as its aim an anthropological, ethnographic and literary study of the Musulman tribes in North Africa.... Under the date 20th December last. M. Vigné informed the Department that these studies were terminated and that he wished to extend them to the A.O.F., particularly in Guinea and Senegal. In this connection he has requested that a mission in these possessions should be entrusted to him ...

Trouillot, the Minister for the Colonies, after consulting the Governor of the A.O.F., Merleau-Ponty, on 1 April 1910, granted him subsidy of 3,000 francs towards his expenses, particularly the cost of the return fare between Paris and Dakar. On 13 December he requested a report from him. Vigné rejoined that for health reasons he had not been able to leave but was about to embark. When he was asked either to give the precise date for his departure or to refund the 3,000 francs to the Treasury (30 March 1911) he did not reply. On 26 September, Lebrun, the Minister, decided to annul the mission and to direct the legal agent of the Treasury to recover the sum; on which Vigné, who was already travelling, directed a lawyer at the Council of State to appeal in his name against the revocation of his mission.[46]

This deterioration in the relations between Vigné and his former colleagues is undoubtedly explained by the publication of *La Sueur du burnous*. In fact it would require a high degree of insensitivity and naïveté to think that the revelations or denunciations piled up in this work would not antagonise those who, in renewing over three years the subventions requested, had shown confidence in the author. The dedication must have seemed to them more impudent than clever;

To the Ministers

> Honourable Ministers of the third republic: During three consecu-
> tive years you have been very willing to entrust me with missions of
> study in our possessions in North Africa, and in this way to facilitate
> a minute and thorough inquiry into their present situation to which,
> on leaving Parliament, I had decided to devote myself. My books, my
> interventions at the tribune during three consecutive legislatures, my
> campaigns in *l'Aurore* against the crimes of military Colonisation,
> under the direction of Clemenceau, have enabled you to judge me.

Having made it clear that he would not be a toady he announced, under
the general title of 'Official brigandage in North Africa (Tunisia,
Algeria, Marocco)' a series of three works, *La Sueur du burnous*, *Terre
à galons*, *Biribi et la légion étrangère*.

After denouncing the abuses practised by the ruling native and
European groups and condemning the French bourgeoisie ('shame and
malediction on the bourgeois republic in the name of which raids,
pillage, rape and murders of tattered wretches take place') he referred
to the 'French sharks', former ministers or deputies who speculated in
land—Bouchez, Cochery, Chaumié, Hanotaux, Mougeot, Chailley-Bert.
He assailed 'the Etienne and Thomson gang', drew up a list of the
former rapporteurs of the Tunisian budget who had become great land-
owners (Bouchez, Mougeot, Cochery, Hanotaux, Chaumié, Krantz,
Pedebidou, Chailley-Bert). He attacked Stephen Pinchon in connection
with the loan of 75 million, and analysed the business affairs of the
railway and of the Compagnie de Gafsa.

All this was too polemical to be quite convincing and the work
did not create a scandal. But was it astonishing that the bourgeois of
the Third Republic would refrain from acting when the hand of this
paragon of political virtue was in the state purse?

A foreclosure was attempted by the Ministry of Finance with the
agreement of the Ministry for the Colonies. Vigné opposed the proceedings and summoned the two ministries before the tribunal of the
Seine (7 December 1911) arguing that he had already spent more than
3,000 francs when the death of his mother obliged him to return and
that, moreover, no fixed time had been given for the execution of his
mission. The tribunal declared itself incompetent to deal with the
matter, which was then taken to the Council of State, while on 27
December the bailiff sent to Vigné's house to seize the furniture, the
sale of which had been announced for 9 September, came up against
the opposition of Madame Vigné, who owned the greater part of it.

However, Vigné, who declared that he was always ready to leave,
furnished documents accounting for more than 3,000 francs. Fourteen
of them were examined by Bertin, legal agent of the Treasury. Some
of them seemed to be concerned with household expenses, others with
fare between Paris and Algiers and hotel expenses in Algeria. None of
them concerned the A.O.F. Nevertheless Bertin was inclined to accept
these papers, and Lebrun, in July 1912, proposed to the financial

authorities that they should give clearance to Vigné, who similarly refrained from pursuing his case before the Council of State.

But Lebrun's successor at the Ministry for the Colonies, Morel took up the matter again in the next year. He would not admit that the voyage to Algeria had been the 'beginning of the execution of the mission'. On 12 June 1913, the Ministry's legal counsel wrote to Duchêne, the Director and chief of the Secretariat:

> M. Vigné d'Octon, although the allocation for his mission was in forfeit to the amount of 3,000 francs, presents a note of his expenses, particularly of a voyage in Algeria as far as Colomb Bechar from where he expected to make a journey of 10,000 km on the back of a camel. This is in the style of Tartarin, but since the plea must be taken seriously it is necessary to enlighten the judges. Now, he had to reach Senegal by sea; the ministerial dispatch confiding the mission to him took care to stipulate that the expenses of transport to Dakar would remain in his charge. To prevent Mr. Vigné from posing as a victim and from claiming, as he has done, that this allocation (which he had solicited) was ridiculously inadequate, I would very much wish to know the first-class fare to Dakar.

The *Messageries Maritimes* informed him that the fare was 700 francs return between Bordeaux and Dakar, with a reduction of 25% to 30% for persons charged with official missions.

The war interrupted the proceedings. It was not until 1927 that the minister, L. Perrier, ended them by sending to the President of the Council, the Minister of Finance, Poincaré, who was a man of stubborn temper, a long reply to his request for information on the measures taken in regard to M. Vigné d'Octon, in debt to the Treasury. Perrier concluded:

> Taking into account finally the silence maintained by the parties to the case for almost thirteen years, I consider that it is quite useless to resume these lawsuits, so costly to the Treasury (the honorarium of the Council and of the solicitor of the Ministry have already risen to 2,200 francs). In these circumstances I consider the affair to be definitely terminated.

Vigné was certainly not alone in collecting subsidies in a somewhat illegitimate manner. The credits for missions given by various Ministries were not closely controlled, and many other politicians, writers, and artists, sent on distant travels, neglected to keep accounts and send in statements justifying their expenditures.

In his book in 1928, *Les grands et les petits mystères du Palais-Burbon*, the former deputy recalled the atmosphere of cameraderie which prevailed among the parliamentarians outside the meetings, and it is understandable that he did not feel that he had committed a dishonest action in drawing on the 3,000 francs from the Ministry of the Colonies in the same way as he had drawn on various subsidies from the Ministries of Public Instruction and Foreign Affairs, without troubling to render accounts of his expenditures on his various journeys.